Colonial Development and Population in Taiwan

UNDER THE EDITORIAL SPONSORSHIP
OF THE OFFICE OF POPULATION RESEARCH
PRINCETON UNIVERSITY

COLONIAL DEVELOPMENT AND POPULATION IN TAIWAN

BY GEORGE W. BARCLAY

PRINCETON, NEW JERSEY
PRINCETON UNIVERSITY PRESS
1954

London: Geoffrey Cumberlege, Oxford University Press
L.C. Card 52-13153

Printed in the United States of America
by Princeton University Press, Princeton, New Jersey

Preface

To those outside the field of population studies a book on Taiwan's demographic development must seem an example of academic escapism. When even the general reader is becoming aware of the difficult population problems facing Asia's mainland, why should the Office of Population Research devote personnel and resources to the careful study of a few million people on a rather small island in the Far East?

The question is reasonable, but the answers are compelling. Taiwan is the only place where it is possible to study the processes of change of a Chinese population over a substantial period of time on the basis of excellent data. Any information that can be gained about the growth characteristics of one of the world's largest ethnic groups is well worth obtaining. Under Japanese rule an unusually accurate statistical record was maintained in Taiwan from 1905 to 1943, providing an unbroken series of data that is longer, and in some respects richer, than that for Japan proper.

Indeed, the Taiwanese material provides much more than a unique demographic record of Chinese people. It is, if not the only case, then certainly one of the very few cases in the world in which the trends in fertility and mortality can be traced with precision from the initial stages of modernization. In virtually every other case the statistical record begins long after death rates have begun to decline. In Taiwan, the vital record can be traced over almost the whole of the period during which the island was being transformed from one of the least healthy to one of the most healthy places in the Far East.

At a time when much attention is being given to problems of economic development and to discussion of its interrelations with population growth, the Japanese experience in Taiwan is especially appropriate. The Japanese wanted a source of food and a market for the home industries, and their program for the island was directed toward achieving these ends. Here, then, is an opportunity to study the impact of an aggressive program of agricultural development on population growth, and the limitations imposed by the nature of such a program on subsequent economic development when the objectives changed, as they did under the strain of war preparation.

PREFACE

Mr. Barclay's book is not intended to be another regional study. It is designed to trace the demographic record in relation to the record of social and economic change. It is the fourth volume sponsored by the Office which deals with problems of non-industrial regions. The others are: Kingsley Davis, *The Population of India and Pakistan* (Princeton, 1951); T. E. Smith, *Population Growth in Malaya* (Chatham House, 1952); and Paul K. Hatt, *Backgrounds of Human Fertility in Puerto Rico* (Princeton, 1952). A fifth volume by Harvey Leibenstein, *Theory of Economic-Demographic Development*, is being issued by Princeton University Press at about the same time as the present book.

Mr. Barclay's work was made possible by the generous support which the Office receives from the Milbank Memorial Fund and The Rockefeller Foundation, neither of which, however, has the slightest responsibility for the conclusions reached or, indeed, for the specific topic selected for study. For this opportunity to work in complete freedom, my colleagues and I wish to express our gratitude.

Frank W. Notestein
Director
Office of Population Research

November 1953

Introduction

TAIWAN, or "Formosa," as the island is still widely known to Westerners, has been the scene of international contention as long as it has had a recorded history. From its discovery by curious Chinese and Japanese before 1600 down to the present time, the island has repeatedly been visited, occupied and fought over. No one can claim that Taiwan has failed to receive its full share of attention by the outside world. The people of the island would be the last to make this complaint, for, while opinions may differ as to whether the intrusions have been beneficial to the population, it is certain that they have not been welcome.

But for people who have long felt the disadvantages of being small and weak with large and powerful neighbors, the inhabitants of Taiwan have in some respects fared remarkably well. They avoided, through hardly more than chance, the domination by Western nations that has called forth great bitterness and aroused quixotic nationalism in many parts of Asia. They fell under the control of Japan at a time when that country was willing to invest strong efforts in developing Taiwan's productive resources. So far they have emerged from the war that destroyed the Japanese Empire without suffering the mass bloodshed or wide devastation that followed the regular military operations elsewhere in the Far East. And, ironically, during the fifty years of "exploitation" and "oppression" by Japan, they enjoyed more peace and prosperity than their former countrymen on the mainland of China.

As the aftermath of these events Taiwan has acquired a status that is uneasy and insecure, poised again as a prize desired by rival powers. It is not the purpose of this book to trace the sequence of steps leading up to this situation, or to speculate about the future international status of the island. Because prominence has not come to them of their own seeking, the Taiwanese have usually played a passive part in shaping their position in world affairs. Knowledge of the island's external relations therefore does not offer much in understanding the social order of its people, and information about the internal structure of the society fails to contribute anything of great value in appreciating its present international position.

For similar reasons, this book will not be concerned with the prospects for the island under the present Chinese Nationalist government, since they are likewise closely allied to international developments that have not yet taken place.[1] This present era of Taiwan's history has just begun; discussion of its future in these terms necessarily rests on conjecture and may have little to do with the facts that are known about the population. The half-century of colonial rule, on the other hand, is over, and most of the facts are in. Hence this is the phase that can be investigated to the best purpose, for it can serve as an instructive example of its type in other places.

It is a well-documented case. There is no lack of thoughtful research on the island during this period. While under Japanese rule Taiwan probably had the distinction of being the most thoroughly inventoried colonial area in the world. Huge compilations of statistics and numerous special surveys were made from year to year. The economy, the terrain, the aboriginal tribes, the mineral wealth, the agricultural output, the industrial production and the foreign trade have all been studied and restudied until there is little to be added to this knowledge unless new evidence is uncovered that is not now available.[2]

Strangely enough, with all this interest in finding out about the island, there were very few attempts to study the social institutions and cultural patterns of the people, and the attention devoted to these matters has been scanty and perfunctory. Yet the numerical data relating to the population are the best of all, since their collection was most directly linked to the very effective system of control imposed by the Japanese. The largest task required of this investigation has been to test and evaluate these unknown source materials, and to introduce them into the Western literature. They comprise one of the most ample and creditable records for a population of this size that has ever been at the disposal of demographers, and the only systematic set of data for a portion of the Chinese population.

This is not to say that the subject of Taiwan's population has been entirely neglected. Nearly every published work about Taiwan, especially since 1945, has included a section on the people of the island.

1 There is growing literature on Taiwan dealing with its political status. See, for example, Riggs, F. W. (1952), Ravenholt, A. (1952), Bate, H. M. (1952).

2 Some of this material has already appeared in the form of special studies. See Yanaihara, Tadao (1929), Grajdanzev, A. J. (1942), Ch'en Cheng-hsiang (1950), Taiwan Keizai Nempo (1941). For a study of the characteristics of Taiwan's population, see Ch'en Cheng-hsiang and Tuan Chi-hsien (1951). The most useful single compilation of statistics is the *Statistical Summary of Taiwan for the Past 51 Years* (Taipei, 1946), which will be referred to hereafter simply as *Statistical Summary*.

Such discussion is often confined, however, to establishing *how many* of them there are, and frequently begins and ends with the premise that there are "too many." This issue lies afield from the topics that we propose to consider—a population could not attain its present size, flourish or decline, or even remain in existence were it not for the complex societal arrangements that have made these things possible. Population thus could not become a "problem" by itself, but is a fruitful way of viewing problems in these other spheres. These, along with trends in the numbers of people, are the subject matter of this study, and the succeeding pages are an endeavor to discover what Taiwan's demographic data can be made to reveal about the nature of the society.

The following plan of procedure has been adopted. We shall first describe how Taiwan came to be settled, and take note of the growth of its population, for these are features which mark it off at the outset as a special type of case and furnish clues as to what else one should expect to find. We shall then turn to examine the aims and policies of Japanese colonial development and their consequences for the population. It is not proposed to dwell on what is commonly treated as the "economic" side of this colonial program, such as the spread of the Japanese banking system, the corporate structure of their industry, the expansion of output, construction of factories, or contribution to the "welfare" of the population. A catalog of these direct achievements gives but a very superficial idea of their most interesting aspect—the form in which these innovations were communicated to the Taiwanese.

It will appear that participation in this program on the part of Taiwanese was impeded by barriers at nearly every point, and that they felt its effect on their livelihood and their customs only by indirection. Some of the reasons for the cleavage between these two groups are to be found in the restrictive measures of the Japanese, and some in the stability of Taiwanese social institutions. Evidence of this stability will be shown in the economic activities of the people, their immobility, the persistence of certain mortality patterns, and the organization of marriage and family affairs. These various aspects of Taiwanese life will also be drawn upon to see how and where minor social changes tended to be fitted into this agrarian system. Finally, we shall assess one overshadowing result of this social stability, the steady high fertility of the Taiwanese.

Throughout, of course, much of the interest in the Taiwanese as a people stems from the fact that almost all of these are of Chinese origin, and that their behavior under Japanese colonial adminstration may be said to represent the reaction of Chinese cultural norms to selective innovations which fail to attain the dimensions of sweeping societal changes. But this is a pattern of change that has not been uncommon elsewhere in the world. Additional significance can be attached to those findings in Taiwan which have counterparts in other agrarian countries, and the following chapters have been organized with considerable care to emphasize these matters of more general interest.

G.W.B.

September 1952

ACKNOWLEDGMENTS

FOR a long and patient investment in the work involved in this study, full recognition and thanks are to be given to the Office of Population Research, Princeton University. Invaluable counsel was received from individual members of this office, in particular from Irene B. Taeuber, Frank W. Notestein, and Wilbert E. Moore, which should be recorded here for want of a more adequate form of acknowledgment. Special thanks are due to Daphne Notestein, for distinctive execution of the maps and diagrams, and to Erna Härm, foremost among several, for her care in the statistical computations on which the study is based. Finally, for contributions of assistance and encouragement at every stage, a debt of a broader kind is owed to Audrey N. Barclay. Of course, responsibility for all statements and conclusions in the book rests with the author.

Contents

Tables

Figures

Colonial Development and Population in Taiwan

CHAPTER I

The Growth of Population

IN the last century and again in modern times, Taiwan has repeatedly become the object of rivalries among some of the most powerful nations of the world. Though its history has been a succession of disruptive incidents resulting from such contacts, by its size alone the island scarcely seems to merit the covetous attention that outsiders have given to it. It is not large—only 250 miles from north to south, and about 90 miles across at the widest point. The area that it covers is only 14,000 square miles, or slightly less than that of the Netherlands. There is little in the way of precious minerals that would arouse the desire of industrial countries. It offers no great area into which other peoples can expand. It has only its significant location in the path of transportation routes off the coast of China, and a territory potentially rich in agricultural output. While the former of these has had the greater attraction to foreign nations, it is the latter that actually yielded—perhaps exceeded—the full measure of wealth that was expected.

The topography and climate of Taiwan in the past have combined to make the island inhospitable to settlement. Being at the fringe of the tropics, the climate is hot and rainy, with marked changes of season and variations from one section to another. The greater part of its surface is not readily put to human use. Over half of this area consists of rugged mountains, rising steeply from a plain along the western coast and extending to the Pacific Ocean in the east. Heavy rainfall therefore runs off very quickly, creating torrential floods and occasional droughts in between. Large parts of the island are frequently swept by typhoons and shaken by earthquakes.

Within the span of recorded history, the difficulties presented by the physical environment never succeeded in discouraging human habitation. There were vague reports of residents there before A.D. 1000. When Taiwan first came officially to the attention of China, during the Ming dynasty, some tribes of primitives were known to be living near the western coast. Since the 16th century people swarmed to Taiwan from the relatively crowded parts of South China, and prospered there as agriculturists. The Japanese, who ruled the island from 1895 to 1945 and exploited its possibilities more thoroughly, developed it into a highly profitable colonial enterprise.

There was some solution to each of its principal deterrents to settlement; but the deliberative and organized approach that many of these solutions required was adopted only by the Japanese. Under them production expanded and population increased at a rate that was prodigious, until the very success of these solutions created its own uncertainty—how and when the increase of people would cease.

Early Settlement in Taiwan

Piecing together the history of Taiwan's population before 1895 is a difficult task. It cannot be pursued very far, since relevant information is lacking. There is no reliable record to show even the number of people on the island before the 20th century. The dimensions of population growth, and its nature, must therefore be surmised from the reports of travelers, tradesmen and Western missionaries.

Prior to 1600 Taiwan was sparsely occupied by a few tribes of "savages," of origins that are unknown. The island at this time had attracted very few people from China, though its mountains were actually visible from the mainland, and its coast less than a full day's sail with the tide. Some Chinese and Japanese used it as a base for commerce and piracy against other shipping along the coast. The early tribes of non-Chinese ranged over most of the inhabited area, sometimes repelling visits by curious foreigners, sometimes warring among themselves. These were forebears of the present aborigines of the interior, the "real" Taiwanese.

At about this time the Dutch entered regular and quasi-legitimate trade in the Far East, and became interested in Taiwan as a base for this purpose. In 1622 they established a few fortified outposts on the island, commenced trading across the straits, and formed a limited government to minister to what they took to be the civil and religious needs of the native population. Their rule left nothing of lasting importance in Taiwan except the early chronicles that they faithfully kept of their experiences, which form the safest repository of information about contemporary events.

From such sources we are informed of a growing influx of migrants from the mainland. These were a special category of Chinese, the so-called Hakka people from Kwangtung Province. They were an ethnic minority in China, and as such they occasionally were targets of organized abuse. Following an outbreak of such disturbance in Kwangtung a considerable number went to Taiwan for refuge, where they were not easily persuaded to respect Dutch rule, and hence were not eagerly received. But even while Taiwan was nominally in the hands of a Western power, these migrants represented a substantial Chinese settlement there.

The Dutch were not able to remain very long in Taiwan. As an aftermath of a change of dynasties in China, the slow stream of Hakka people became engulfed in an organized movement of a defeated faction from South China. Led by the celebrated personage Cheng Ch'eng-kung, the newcomers drove out all Westerners from Taiwan in 1662, only to succumb after some years to control by the new Manchu regime in China. These events were followed by continuous migration of Chinese. Most of this flow started from Fukien Province, the new base for administration of Taiwan.

These new migrants soon outnumbered by far the previous settlers. Thereafter, the Chinese coming into Taiwan gradually spread out over the flat area most suitable to intensive farming. Little by little they displaced aborigines from the lowlands, and pushed them back into the mountains. Steady movement from the mainland raised the population of Taiwan from a few thousand in 1600 to more than two million by 1895.

The occupied area was enlarged during this period from a few scattered points along the western coast to the entire level portion of the island.[1] More important, in the process of this settlement Taiwan was changed into a land that was thoroughly Chinese, imprinted permanently with the characteristics of Chinese culture. The aboriginal people of Taiwan became a small minority, and remained apart in the interior where they could better hold off further incursions on their territory.[2] Hence the "Taiwanese" that one can speak of at any later date consisted almost entirely of these early migrants from China and their descendants.

By the time Taiwan was ceded to Japan, this population had made it culturally an extension of China. From the sphere of politics and economic activities, as we shall see in later chapters, to matters of

1 See Ch'en Cheng-hsiang, *Atlas* (1950), Fig. 15.

2 They made good use of the advantages of rough terrain in protecting themselves. In spite of the fact that the tribes quarreled among themselves and failed to present a united front against conquest, it later took the Japanese over thirty years to subdue this interior part of the island, in a campaign with modern weapons, airplanes, and reportedly even poison gas.

village life and family relationships, the people of Taiwan retained the heritage of tradition and custom that they had brought from the mainland. These cultural institutions did not succeed so well in maintaining order in Taiwan as in China, for there were new situations to be met and resolved. Chief among these, for example, was the constant arrival of new persons for whom the obligations of a particular locality might not be binding. But once established in Taiwan, there is no evidence that these institutions underwent any major change throughout the 200 years while Manchu authorities ruled the island.

Historical accounts of this period are little but repetitions of the same events. They show a sequence of misrule, intrigue by privileged groups or classes, frequent bloody insurrections, and strife with the aborigines. The island gained a continual atmosphere of violence and unrest. By one important circumstance the disorders were prevented from being an invitation to social change—they were not revolutions, but rebellions. They arose from dissatisfaction with particular persons in the social order—landlords, officials, or members of rival clans or villages—rather than dissatisfaction with the social order itself.[3] As a result, the disorders often served in the end to establish tradition more firmly.

Taiwan under the Japanese

The most decisive event in the history of Taiwan after being opened to Chinese immigration was its annexation into the Japanese Empire. Japan in the 1890's was newly arrived as a nation to compete in Far Eastern political rivalries, and many of its leaders were eager to find areas for its expansion as a respectable colonial power. They magnified a relatively minor incident in Taiwan, together with other grievances, into a pretext for provoking war with China in 1894.[4] It was a brief war of several quick military victories for the Japanese. When peace was negotiated in 1895, they insisted that Taiwan be ceded to them, and in the same year they took possession of

[3] Rebellions were ultimately settled by reasserting the established order, though often not without the use of force in the form of troops. Many of them, however, were actually organized within its framework from the beginning. Much of the disturbance was apparently created by the type of large clan organization found in South China, and by secret societies that were able to develop rivalries on a large scale between formidable groups.

[4] Japanese forces had as early as 1874 made an exploratory expedition to Taiwan, under a similar pretext, that formed the basis for expansionist designs on the island and provided valuable information about its terrain.

the island and set out to discover the responsibilities and rewards of colonial administration.

Japan embarked on this first colonial venture without having at the outset any very clear idea of what use to make of it. The first few years were taken up in consolidating their control over the population and in deciding what to do with the island. As their experiment progressed, the Japanese began to introduce some profound and subtle changes. Their objectives became clarified, and their policies toward Taiwanese more firm. Gradually they evolved a system of managing affairs in Taiwan that developed into one of the most successful colonial programs in the world. As long as they remained, Taiwan repaid them handsomely for their initial investment of care and expense.

Some of the more important aspects of this program will be discussed in subsequent chapters. Here it is appropriate to establish what were broadly the consequences in terms of population trends, and to discover what sorts of information about Taiwan's people can be gained from the records of this administration. The Japanese rationalized certain parts of Taiwan's agriculture, so that the island produced a substantial surplus of farm commodities each year. They established a strong and efficient government, the first that the island ever had. With a shrewd combination of police force and political guile, they imposed strict public order and penetrated every town and village with a structure of organized control.

They constructed excellent facilities for transportation and communication where there had been none before, founded modern business institutions and commercial centers, promoted some industrial processing of the island's products, rebuilt the major cities, and stamped out the principal epidemic diseases. In short, they transformed Taiwan from a "backward" and neglected land into a thriving region that could regularly export a large share of its agricultural produce. This was a success that would satisfy most of the countries striving for modernization today.

All these material accomplishments of the Japanese in Taiwan are well known. With some justifiable pride, they publicized this side of their rule and compiled an imposing set of statistics to document it. What we propose here is to examine the human side of these developments and to appraise some of its consequences in the

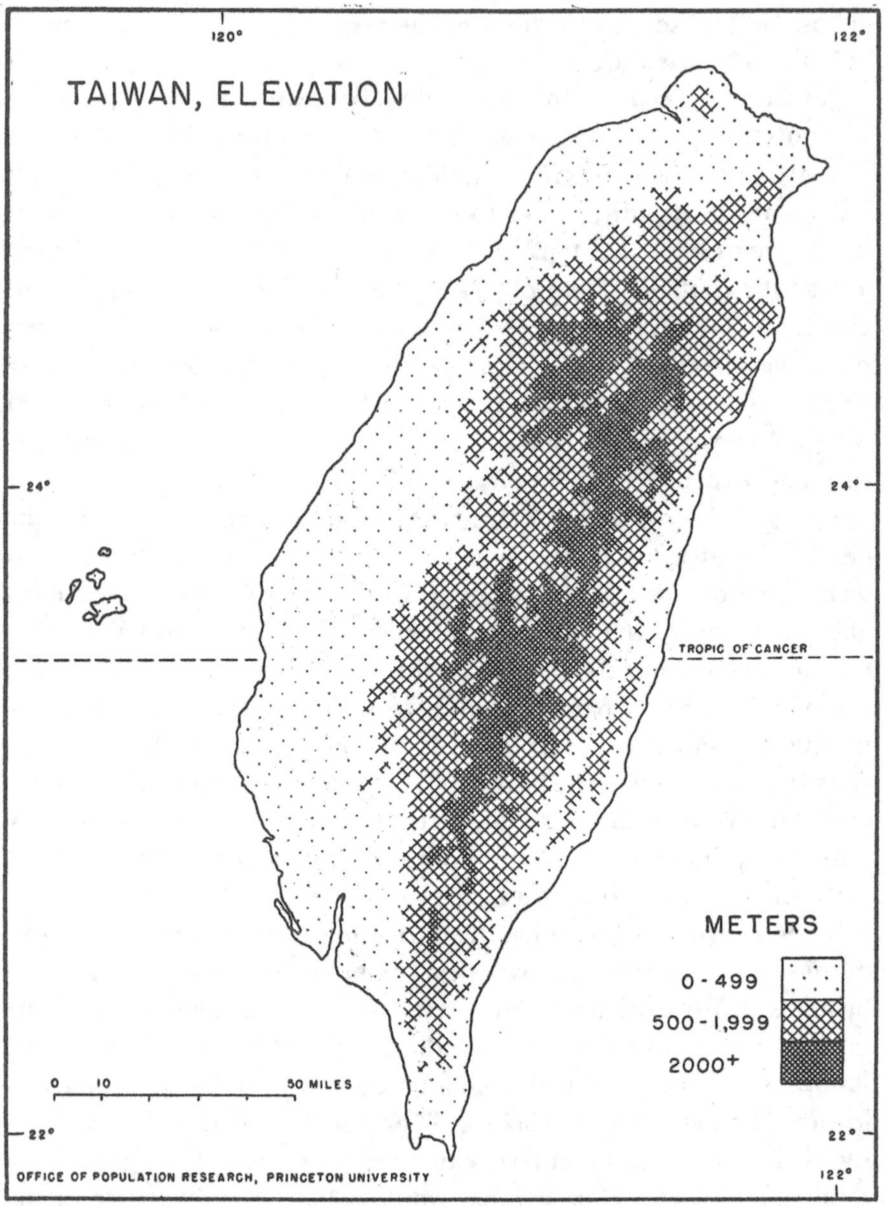

Fig. 1. Topography of Taiwan. (Adapted from Taiwan Provincial Government, Department of Communications, *A Map of the Main Roads of Taiwan*, February, 1950.)

lives of the population. This aspect of Taiwan's history, and of "economic development" in general, receives a surprisingly small share of attention as compared with questions of technological advance.

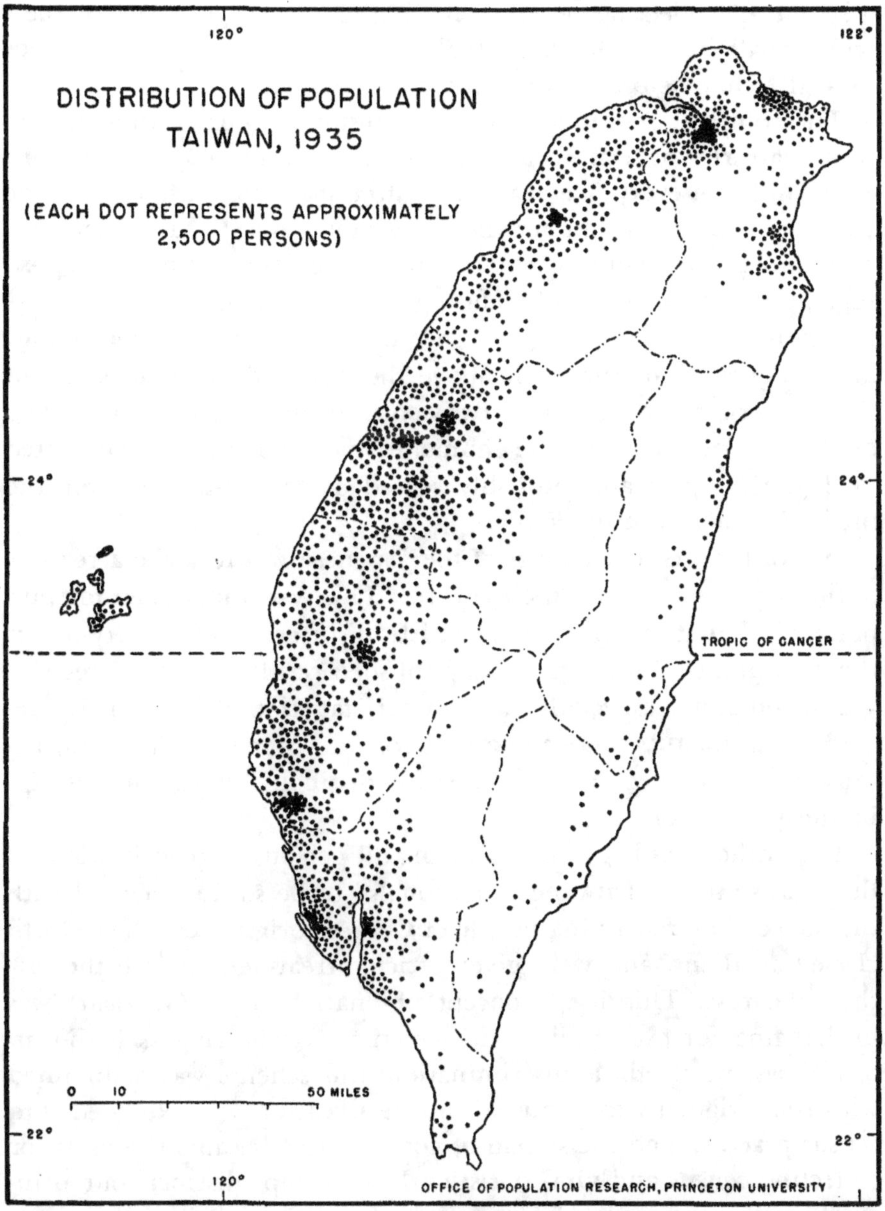

Fig. 2. Distribution of Population in Taiwan, 1935. All nationality groups.

The Japanese and Statistics of the Population

The only trustworthy information that we have about the numbers and kinds of people in Taiwan at any time is the evidence of the censuses taken by the Japanese. They conceived and established a system of collecting population data, as an integral part of their wider goals in the island. Factual materials of this order have not existed either before or since their occupation.

The complete monument to their enumerative capacities in Taiwan is a series of seven censuses, the first one in 1905, the next in 1915, and one every five years thereafter stopping with 1940. Some were more detailed and are therefore more useful than others. All maintained uniformly high standards in the completeness of reporting, in the consistency of defining ethnic classes, and in the accuracy of information such as age reporting. In these respects they often ranked in quality well above the more advanced censuses of the Western world. The first two censuses, in 1905 and 1915, were carried out before a genuine enumerative census was ever conducted in Japan Proper[5] and probably served as testing-grounds for the initial Japanese census of 1920.

One of the first official acts of the Japanese was to make a register of the population under their control. This was undertaken for purposes of regulation, and not to satisfy disinterested curiosity about the inhabitants. To judge by its published results, the early registry was incomplete, especially in its vital statistics. But the rules regarding nationality were important for later demographic data, because they provided the first basis for distinguishing ethnic groups in the population.

The authorities began by requiring all persons who acknowledged the legal status of Taiwanese "nationals" to be so documented with the police. The remaining people of Chinese origin were thenceforth classed as aliens, and were given stricter treatment before the law than the rest. This legal concept of "nationality" (*Minseki*) was unchanging for each individual over time.[6] Reflecting as it did an official system of ethnic discrimination, this scheme was maintained with some rigor by the police. The classification was extended into census practice, and the system of control later became the basis for collecting census and vital statistics data. It kept distinct four principal groups of people—"Taiwanese" (or "Islanders," as they were called until 1939 in the statistics), Japanese, Koreans, and Mainland Chinese.

[5] The Russo-Japanese War intervened in 1905, the World War in 1915. See Taeuber, Irene B., and Beal, Edwin G., Jr. (October, 1946), p. 9.

[6] The privilege of adopting Japanese nationality was extended to natives of Taiwan only in later years, and was not widely used.

By these actions the Japanese set apart from all others those who were descended from the original residents of Taiwan. This segregation in the statistics extended from the most obvious differentiation—that of Japanese nationals—down to fine distinctions within the Taiwanese population itself.[7] It was consistent in both the population censuses and vital statistics, making it possible to amalgamate the two systems of record-keeping continuously as long as they were maintained.

TABLE 1

TAIWANESE BORN OUTSIDE OF TAIWAN, 1920 AND 1930

Proportion of All Persons Who Have Been Born "Abroad," by Age and Sex

	Census of 1920		*Census of 1930*	
	Male	*Female*	*Male*	*Female*
All ages	0.2	0.1	0.1	0.0
0-9	0.0	0.0	0.0	0.0
10-19	0.0	0.0	0.0	0.0
20-29	0.1	0.0	0.0	0.0
30-39	0.1	0.0	0.0	0.0
40-49	0.5	0.1	0.1	0.1
50-59	1.3	0.2	0.3	0.1
60-69	1.9	0.3	0.8	0.1
70 and above	2.6	0.7	1.0	0.3

Sources: *Census of 1920, Descriptive Report with Appendix*, Table 79.
Census of 1930, Statistical Tables, Table 55.

Regulating the conduct of "alien" Chinese nationals in Taiwan was not the sole purpose in establishing the legal status of residents. The authorities also set out to halt the further migration of people from the mainland. In this they were apparently successful. Taiwanese were required to verify their nationality by certain proofs, chief of which was evidence of having been born in Taiwan. Taking this as a criterion, there seems to have been little admixture from the mainland to the category of "Taiwanese." For example, tables showing Taiwanese who were born "abroad" were published with the censuses of 1920 and 1930. If the information was accurate, practically the entire population of Taiwanese born after 1895 was ac-

[7] This fine detail was confined to a slightly different classification, based on "race." It provided categories within the group with Taiwanese nationality—aborigines, Taiwanese of Fukien origin, and Taiwanese of Kwangtung origin. The two classifications were not precisely the same, the one based on "nationality" being the more consistent at different times.

tually born in Taiwan (see Table 1). Almost none under 25 years of age in 1920, or under 35 in 1930, were recorded as having been born outside. Some who were older at these two dates had been born in China, but they were very few and were probably living in Taiwan at the time of annexation. These figures imply that migration after 1895 was probably confined to people who were appropriately registered by nationality, and counted as *aliens* in census enumerations.[8]

Hence the census category of "Taiwanese" was defined so as to exclude migrants to and from the island. This is significant to know, for it means that Taiwanese counted in any census after 1905 were exactly the survivors of those who had been counted before (plus those who had been born in the meantime). It also means that the population of Taiwanese was for statistical purposes a "closed" population—one which neither gained nor lost people by migration. All change in the size of the Taiwanese population was therefore due to "natural increase," or the balance between births and deaths. One can thus speak precisely of population "growth" in Taiwan, without reference to migration as a complicating factor.

Half a Century of Rapid Growth

The total population, and the sub-total of Taiwanese, are shown in Table 2 as counted on October 1 of each census year, along with the annual geometric rates of growth that are implied at each intercensal stage. Every year showed an increase. The only setbacks were between 1915 and 1920, when the island suffered three near-epidemic attacks of disease. Even over this relatively poor span the average yearly rate of increase was close to one per cent. The original population of 1895 was more than doubled by 1945; when the vital statistics were discontinued in 1943, there were nearly six million Taiwanese.

[8] By evasion of the law some Chinese might conceivably have slipped into Taiwan and passed themselves off as Taiwanese. A further acquaintance with the regulatory system in later chapters, however, will make this appear most unlikely.

There is evidence of another sort that the Taiwanese were not diminished by removals to the mainland. Briefly, detailed testing of the validity of birth and death statistics has shown that practically all persons born in Taiwan were later accounted for in a census enumeration, or as registered deaths if they failed to survive. Practically all who were enumerated in one census were similarly accounted for at later dates. During the 1930's, Japanese permitted small numbers of Taiwanese to leave the island for special purposes. The effect of these departures was very small, and raises no difficulty in dealing with the data of earlier years. Thus, if there was emigration, it too was clandestine and very small.

TABLE 2

GROWTH OF POPULATION IN TAIWAN

Total Population and Taiwanese Enumerated at Successive Census Dates and Average Rates of Growth for Taiwanese

Year	*Total Population (All Groups)*	*Taiwanese Population*	*Per Cent Annual (Geometric) Rate of Growth*
1905	3,039,751	2,973,280	
			1.12
1915	3,479,922	3,325,755	
			0.83
1920	3,655,308	3,466,507	
			1.71
1925	3,993,408	3,775,288	
			2.22
1930†		4,218,663	
1930‡	4,592,537	4,313,681	
			2.48
1935	5,212,426	4,882,945	
			2.42
1940	5,872,084	5,510,259	
			2.42
1943		5,962,000*	

* This figure represents the Taiwanese enumerated in 1940 plus their registered natural increase from the census of 1940 to the end of 1943.

† Excluding Aborigine Territory.

‡ Including Aborigine Territory.

Sources: *Statistical Summary*, Table 57.
Census of 1930, Statistical Tables, Table 2.

These figures are significant also because of acceleration in the *rate* of growth, for it increased together with the number of people. Over the entire census period growth averaged 1.76 per cent per year. By 1940 Taiwanese were increasing at close to the rate of 2.5 per cent per annum. Compounded continuously, this latter rate would have enabled Taiwanese to increase twofold every 28 years, and twelve times in a full century.

Natural increase of such dimensions is exceptional. Such growth in itself implies that some change has taken place in the organization of human activities. It necessarily reflects a situation that could not have continued long, and that cannot persist forever. In the world at large, for example, the increase of people that has populated most of the earth's surface has progressed steadily only in a few centuries of sweeping changes. It has maintained an average yearly rate of half of one per cent, only one-fifth that of the Taiwanese. At their more recent rate of increase, they could supply the entire world's present population in less than 250 years.

Growth at this pace, for all its associated virtues in the saving of life and postponement of death, can be a costly way of expanding the membership of a society. It imposes on the adults the burden of supporting more dependent children than would otherwise be required. Consequently, at any particular time growing populations contain large proportions of young children and infants.

The increase of Taiwanese left this kind of mark on their age composition. By 1940, they had passed through 50 years of growth almost unbroken by periods of high mortality. The age structure, both of males and of females, was one that expanded steadily at each lower age to a broad base of infants at the bottom (see Fig. 3). The progression was almost smooth, with few irregularities in between.

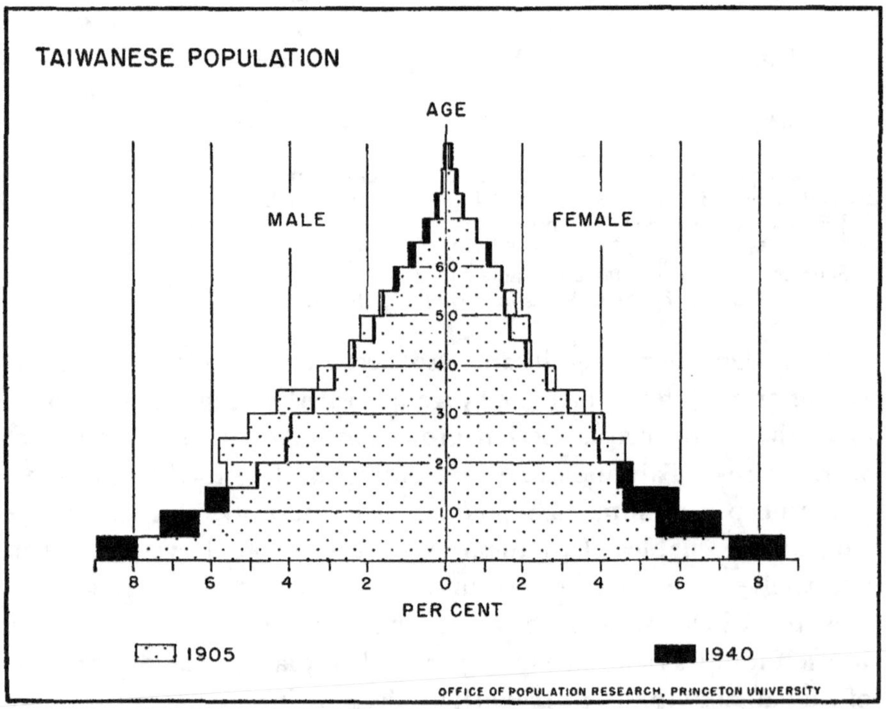

Fig. 3. Age Composition of the Taiwanese Population, 1905 and 1940.

In 1905 there were only a little more than half as many Taiwanese as in 1940. Their distribution in different ages presumably had not been subject to this past influence of steady growth. It nevertheless had many of the indications of potential expansion. Births were at high levels in relation to the numbers of adults. Through the effects of high and erratic mortality, many never reached maturity.

The inroads of past deaths had been far more irregular and generally more severe than in the population of 1940. As reflected in the dearth of persons from 5 to 20, for example, the turbulence that prevailed in Taiwan from 1890 to 1905 must have taken a heavy toll of infants and young children, and possibly prevented many others from being born. Even so, the population of Taiwanese in 1905 was an extremely youthful one. Provided that the supply of new infants each year would continue undiminished, it needed only an energetic set of measures for the control of mortality in order to produce the growth that ensued.

Because in most census tables "nationality" was adopted to classify the population, the Taiwanese must be considered for most purposes as a single group. It was not, however, a completely homogeneous category. It contained the remnants of the aboriginal inhabitants, and people from many different parts of China. Those of Fukien origin were predominant; their ancestors had made up the largest portion of all the migrants to Taiwan. The majority who reported ancestry in Kwangtung were descendants of the earlier Hakka migrants. These two principal classes of Chinese had begun to mix by intermarriage, which explains the lesser gain in those of Fukien origin by 1935. But during the great natural increase of Taiwanese they both grew almost evenly.[9]

The aborigines had ceased to be an important part of the population by 1905. No longer able to contest the seizure of their lands and destruction of hunting grounds, they had retreated to the mountains of Taiwan where most succeeded in avoiding Chinese influence. It took many years before they were finally subdued by the Japanese. The statistical information about the aborigines is incomplete and cannot be compared from one date to another, and we must all but ignore them in discussing the rest of the Taiwanese. Paradoxically,

[9] Already by 1905 the boundaries between these two groups were less pronounced than they once had been. Separate tables of the population in that year according to principal language spoken showed a certain amount of mixture between the two. The remarkable fact is that they remained as distinct as they did.

this small and obscure minority have been subjects for an immense amount of anthropological investigation during Japanese rule in Taiwan, while the peoples of Chinese origin (for whom accurate and precise information has been available these many years) have been almost entirely neglected. The increase of aborigines in census enumerations probably signifies nothing in the way of growth; it was not until the 1930's that they were brought fully within the scope of the census.

TABLE 3

ETHNIC COMPOSITION OF THE POPULATION OF TAIWAN

Censuses of 1905 and 1935

	1905			*1935*		
	Persons	*Per Cent of Total*	*Males per 100 Females*	*Persons*	*Per Cent of Total*	*Males per 100 Females*
Japanese	57,335	1.9	152	270,674	5.2	116
Korean*				1,479	0.0	60
Taiwanese						
Fukien Origin	2,492,784	82.0	112	3,939,966	75.6	103
Kwangtung Origin	397,195	13.1	108	735,334	14.1	103
Other Chinese Origin	506	0.0	218	265	0.0	109
Aborigines	82,795	2.7	96	207,900	4.0	101
"Others"	9,136	0.3	1,757	56,808	1.1	217

* Koreans included with "Others" in 1905.
Source: *Census of 1935, Statistical Tables,* Introduction, p. 32.

The numerical position of the Japanese community in Taiwan gives no clue to its strong influence in the course of events after 1895. Its growth was not of the same sort as that of Taiwanese. Few if any Japanese regularly lived in the island in 1895.[10] By 1905 a settlement of 57,335 was recorded for the census, increasing to 270,584 in 1935 and 312,386 in 1940, or five times its earlier size.[11] Japanese in Taiwan did not add to their numbers through natural increase alone, especially since their community was a highly masculine one (see Table 3).[12] As a matter of fact, their registered natural increase from

10 One foreign writer at the time went so far as to assert that prior to 1895 "there was not in the whole island a single Japanese resident." See Davidson, James W. (1903), p. 592.

11 The military garrison was supposed to be excluded from all of these enumerations.

12 Marriages with Taiwanese were prohibited until 1932. Offspring of such illicit mixed unions were rarely if ever counted later as Japanese, making the shortage of women a serious restriction on the per capita reproduction of Japanese.

1906 to 1940 amounted to only 146,597, and if accurate could account for only 57 per cent of the total gain. The numbers of Japanese in Taiwan therefore increased very largely by migration. As we shall see, this was a special type of migration, based on opportunities that did not prevail for others in Taiwan or for Japanese at home, and brought special kinds of migrants. By recruiting new members relatively faster than the natural increase of the Taiwanese, they also raised their proportion in the total population (see Table 3).

The only other non-Taiwanese group, excluding an insignificant number of Koreans, were the Chinese from the mainland. They are shown in Table 3 as "Aliens," mixed with a few other foreign nationalities. Numerically they were even smaller than the Japanese. Being the ones most likely to blur the ethnic boundaries, Chinese nationals were classified and marked out with great care from the rest of the population, as we have indicated. In census enumerations they would have been indistinguishable from Taiwanese, but for the necessity the Japanese felt to control their activities and forestall the development of close ties between Taiwanese and the mainland.[13]

The Taiwanese, however, were the group of major consequence for demographic study. Up to 1945 they comprised practically the whole of the population taken at large. The proportion of non-Taiwanese never reached 7 per cent. Distributed in the total, all these others were minor elements; only when special considerations are introduced do they become important. In the following pages, attention is given to the Taiwanese population almost exclusively, for their development under Japanese rule, which produced this natural increase, is the main problem to be investigated.

[13] [Taiwan.] Government of Formosa. *The Special Population Census of Formosa, 1905*. [English translation] p. 161.

CHAPTER II

"Economic Development" in Taiwan

RULING TAIWAN was a task that the Japanese approached with high hopes. Because their goals were ambitious, the problems were more formidable than they might have been with a more modest and conventional colonial program. Their officials in Taiwan were the first overseas administrators in the Empire, and felt a responsibility to make the colony appear worth while at home.[1] Whatever their wider aims, their strongest aspirations for the island expressed themselves in energetic economic policies—policies pursued with such determination that they profoundly altered many aspects of Taiwan's economic life. In the course of their administration, Japanese nationals came to look upon enhanced production with a two-fold purpose: to secure profits for certain individuals and groups, and to promote the self-sufficiency and military strength of the Empire.

Here we shall examine the techniques of their economic program, survey its operation, and endeavor to make some appraisal of the accomplishments. A closer view of its significance for the everyday affairs of the population is reserved for the next chapters.

The situation that the Japanese first encountered in Taiwan was one of long-established tradition, in which a small amount of innovation could go a long way. Agriculture was the main source of livelihood for practically all Taiwanese. The particular manner in which farming is organized in Taiwan tends, as it does in most of the Far East, to shield it from the intrusions of the modern world. Under the Manchu regime the Chinese inhabitants of Taiwan had developed farming along the familiar lines of their forebears on the China coast. Farms existed on a local village scale and were operated for local subsistence. Most of any exportable surplus of production was removed from the villages in the form of taxes or rent. What was left became absorbed in the costs of civil disturbance, misgovernment, and expansion of settlement, rather than going toward broadening commercial or other opportunities of the cultivators themselves.

Whatever may bring about such a situation, it is one that tends to

[1] Most of the later Japanese publications about Taiwan's future also stressed the island's potentialities as a base for southward expansion of the Empire. The grandeur of these proposals suggests that some of them may have been invented in search of favor for their authors more than in serious expectancy of being carried out.

discourage innovation in agricultural technique, and to keep at low levels the output per person working in agriculture. An economy in this condition requires important modifications when "economic development" is desired. Farming must be made more productive, and radical progress is necessary in other pursuits. Barring some curtailment of consumption, such a change always implies expanding production faster than what is immediately consumed.

One of the keys to the Japanese colonial program in Taiwan, and to its demographic consequences, was how they set out to induce this saving. They chose the course of concentrating the additions to income from production in a few corporate business structures, instead of relying on the savings of individuals in Taiwan. Presumably this has been a goal in the management of most colonies, since indigenous sources have rarely been relied upon for large-scale investments. Its corollary—policies to suppress gains in individual native incomes—has been the chief source of hostility against colonial powers. But while most other nations have had only moderate luck in pursuing this objective, with the Japanese it was an outstanding success.

They took care that the formation of capital proceeded rapidly and from internal savings alone. Even in Japan, which in some respects is closely comparable, the whole pattern and purpose were different. While the Japanese were leading their own economy toward self-sufficiency in manufactured commodities, economic change in Taiwan was being contrived with a still surer hand to move in an opposite direction, toward complementarity with Japan. The output of the island was gradually shaped so as to furnish a net contribution of agricultural and semi-processed food and related commodities every year to Japan. These were items which Japanese felt to be essential for their more ambitious plans at home, and which for various reasons they wished to avoid purchasing outside Japan in ordinary world markets.

All the while, they mounted an impressive program of building up physical equipment in the island itself. Thus earnings were being reinvested on a large scale at the same time that they were also being drained off at a considerable pace by exports to Japan. This feat had to be accomplished in only one way—by raising the output of the island sharply while not greatly changing the levels of consumption for the population at large.[2] In this respect the Japanese managed

[2] The alternative—of gains by depressing popular consumption—should probably be ruled out. It cannot be conclusively demonstrated either that levels of living rose or

the process of capital formation in Taiwan in basically the same way as at home, by prodding the economy at critical points with innovations and developing special social policies to divert the gains from consumption to investment. The success of domestic saving in Taiwan is simply accentuated by the steady flow of commodity shipments to Japan, whereby Taiwan as an enterprise did more than pay its own way.

This success is best summed up in the yearly figures of trade with the outside world. From 1909 on, with the sole exception of 1913, there was an export balance every year in the value of Taiwan's external trade. Most of its entire trade was carried on with Japan—over 90 per cent after 1930 if Manchuria and Korea are included.[3] Related to the total value of exports, the balance amounted to a steady share of about 30 to 40 per cent of all exports to Japan, 25 to 30 per cent of all exports to the entire world, that were not paid for in the form of imports of commodities (see Table 4). It is not proper to infer from these figures that Taiwan occupied a "favorable" position, since apparently the balance was merely carried on the books of a few companies with home offices in Japan. This being the case, such figures probably even understate the amounts taken out.[4]

The Role of Government Policy

By implication, the foregoing account reveals that colonial rule yielded quick and gratifying results in Taiwan. These were not

---

that they fell for Taiwanese. It does seem certain that on the average they must have risen somewhat, but that they did not move very far one way or the other. Undoubtedly some Taiwanese who took part in the new developments became richer, and many who did not became poorer. Agricultural output per farmer definitely increased, as the next chapter will show. There are figures (see Ch'en Cheng-hsiang, 1950, p. 151) that suggest a slight falling off of rice consumption per person, but they must be computed in a way that weakens their reliability. However, the large additions to Taiwan's economy under the Japanese were the new productive facilities, fixed equipment and market organization, which it is the purpose of this chapter to document. There is no way of showing how these improvements were shared by the Taiwanese, though we know that the Japanese took steps to keep the major shares to themselves.

[3] It is fairer to consolidate the "Yen Bloc" as a whole in computing these balances. To some extent imports from Manchuria and Korea were used to offset the account with Japan; this combined account shows a smaller balance than the account with Japan alone in most years. Separate data for Manchuria were not available in preparing Table 4. Aside from their monetary value on a balance sheet, the articles imported from Manchuria and Korea had a special importance, for they consisted mainly of fertilizers that were indispensable to Taiwanese agriculture.

[4] Grajdanzev (1942), p. 157, claims that the export balance cannot be materially reduced by taking account of hidden items; many of these, such as cash remittances to Japan, would actually increase it.

TABLE 4

VALUE OF EXPORTS FROM TAIWAN, BY PLACE OF DESTINATION, 1899 TO 1942*
(Thousands of Yen)

Years	Total Exports	Exports to Japan and Korea	Per Cent of All Exports Going to Japan and Korea	Balance of All Exports over All Imports	
				Amount	*Per Cent of Balance to Total Exports*
1899-1909	24,659	13,932	56.5	—1,574†	—6.4†
1910-1914	59,936	46,727	78.0	4,212	7.0
1915-1919	130,192	98,929	76.0	36,943	28.4
1920-1924	195,767	163,566	83.6	62,039	31.7
1925-1929	256,326	214,533	83.7	65,862	25.7
1930-1934	251,476	230,579	91.7	75,720	30.1
1935-1939	445,653	402,641	90.3	115,005	25.8
1940-1942	527,699	419,570	79.5	97,419	18.5

* Figures are yearly averages over each period.
† (—)indicates an import balance.
Source: *Statistical Summary*, Table 321.

achieved through the efforts of private individuals in a free investment market. The Government-General of Taiwan was given a free hand by Tokyo in most internal affairs, and displayed great interest and vigor in regulating all areas of business activity that it could effectively control. A large part in the formation of capital in Taiwan can be attributed to official steps deliberately adopted with this end in view.

On the one hand, these measures consisted of widespread rationalizations in agriculture and large investments providing technical economies to individual farmers; on the other, there were various devices to centralize the heavy investments in large blocs and thereby keep control over the entire venture. The former consisted mainly of improvements that could be initiated and carried out by Japanese without full participation by Taiwanese, and the latter of ways to guide the process and garner the returns. The one served to raise the average productivity of working Taiwanese without depending on them for inception; the other to avoid dissipating the earnings of the colonial enterprise as higher incomes among the Taiwanese, by confining them in the charge of a few Japanese.[5]

Although the Japanese treated their domestic agriculture in much the same way, they made use of their own farmers' earnings in furthering the growth of industry. The fiscal role of rural Taiwan corresponded to that of rural Japan, but in Japan the several lines developed together and were complementary. Fewer opportunities of this nature were exploited in Taiwan, for the complementarities were all external. This is shown in the other side of the picture of trade with Japan—that of imports and their composition. More than half of the value of imports from Japan during later years represented items that were clearly for current consumption.[6] There was surely nothing like the emphasis on heavy capital goods among the remainder that is found in the imports of Japan itself.[7]

Problems of Pacification

This study is concerned as much with broader aspects of organization in economic life as with the economic activities themselves. Thus

[5] One of the organizational devices for diverting this income away from consumption was, as in Japan, to make it flow into corporate rather than individual hands, where its disposition was more easily regulated.

[6] I.e., articles such as food, clothing, paper, beverages, textiles, manufactured consumer commodities, and the like. One suspects that a large part of these went to maintain the comforts of the Japanese living in Taiwan.

[7] For example, see Reubens, Edwin P. (1950), pp. 109-112.

it is pertinent to examine the stages by which the Japanese spread their influence over business affairs. Before the Japanese occupation, Taiwan was a busy farm area producing chiefly rice and other foodstuffs for itself and neighboring countries. It still held virgin lands that yielded well to the cultivation of Chinese farmers, and was known among Mainland Chinese as one of the few places where fortunes could be made or lost quickly. It was known elsewhere for other features not unrelated to these—foreigners established some renown for the island's production of marketable crops like tea and camphor, as well as for its beautiful scenery and adventure. Some early Taiwanese had always enjoyed years of prosperity, subject to the vicissitudes of weather,[8] warfare among powerful families or with the aborigines, and to the unpredictable greed of officials.

Although agriculture was the mainstay of livelihood, there were the subsidiary pursuits commonly found from place to place in China. Additional opportunities arose in connection with commerce, which was the most flourishing sphere of enterprise. The export trade in the few products shipped abroad was the only spot affected by foreign influence. A small number of Western traders had stayed in Taiwan, arranging for the sale and delivery of the island's produce to the outside world, but the scope of their business operations was limited to buying and shipping. Even tea-growing, which an Englishman had begun, was left entirely to the local population and Chinese middlemen, up to the stage of packing and sending the tea abroad.

The settled portion of the island, often down to the actual appearance of its villages, was a close replica of conditions on the mainland of South China, 100 miles away. The Manchu government adopted policies calculated to restrict rather than encourage any growth or diversification of economic activities. It abhorred the prospect of having the profits of any sponsored enterprise go to foreign merchants, and suffered an incapacity for such sponsorship inherent in its organization.[9] Observers of the period saw little likelihood of change.

Hence Taiwan when the Japanese acquired it was already a granary ready to function as a going concern, but with some impediments to being operated as such. In contrast to both China and Japan, it

[8] These hazards were many and frequent. Lack of systematic attention to irrigation had placed farmers at the mercy of floods, local droughts and destructive hurricanes, and severe earthquakes were common.

[9] This aspect of early political and business affairs in Taiwan is described at great length in Davidson, James W. (1903), Chs. 14, 15, and 17.

was a newly settled land whose surface still showed little strain of intensive clearing and cultivation, and whose manifest possibilities for wider exploitation in agriculture and other lines had scarcely been tapped. Merely imposing public order and effective political administration could hardly have failed to ensure general prosperity, and the Occidental community at the time contemplated the experiment with great interest.

The new authorities did not leave much room for doubt about their intentions for the economy. Even while engaged in some dissension and maneuver for power between their own civil and military officers, they quickly set about constructing railroads as a state enterprise, reinstituting an official monopoly of camphor (amounting to a world monopoly since Taiwan with Japan was the sole important world producer), nurturing one large company for practical research and experiment in sugar production, reviving the former domestic monopoly of salt, and executing a complete and accurate land survey—Taiwan's first—in order to regulate some of the discordant relations of tenancy among farmers and landlords.

Most of the administrative changes were based on a notorious need for reform of pre-existing practices. But all of these reforms were two-edged. Besides regularizing commercial practices and "correcting abuses," the official monopolies and export associations slowly made it impossible for foreign concerns to remain in operation. The revenues from key lines of business soon became centralized in either the Government-General or corporations explicitly controlled by it. Those relations began to appear between state and business that determined the future course of the fields involved. The land survey furnished a basis for levying a stiff land tax which brought forth a gratifying and dependable flow of revenue into the public treasury and helped to finance later development schemes.

If the overall design of economic expansion had been fixed in the minds of influential Japanese even before they took possession of Taiwan, and to some extent this seems likely, its timetable was not. They did not foresee, for example, that almost ten years of costly and arduous military campaign would be needed to subdue the aborigines and thousands of Taiwanese in the lowlands and foothills who had reverted to banditry. And it became apparent only after many Japanese lives had been forfeited to sickness that this "pacification" of the island had to be accompanied by full-fledged warfare against disease and a general sanitation program, in order that enough

Japanese government officers could be stationed over the island to establish political order firmly.

This delay in extending their mastery over the whole of Taiwan was a disappointment to the Japanese. It spurred them to concentrate their efforts at organization on measures other than force to bring the inhabitants under control. Once set in motion after some three years' experiment and delay, their methods brought swift results. They encircled and isolated the aboriginal tribes in the hills, and introduced a refinement of old Chinese forms of keeping local order—the so-called *pao-chia* system.[10]

Private Corporations and Japanese Investment

Other measures followed to make the Japanese rule more effective. As the exercise of authority became more a matter of routine, the policy turned more and more to exploring improvements and enlargements of production. This progress in government can be traced in the annals of specific achievements, like the drive to raise rice yields[11] and the public health program. By 1905 the Government-General felt itself well enough established to take a detailed census of the population; the descriptive report of its procedures is the best evidence of a firm degree of control and competence in performing complicated administrative tasks in Taiwan.

For the next 25 years or more, until they began to shift their energies to preparation for World War II, the Japanese proceeded to work out their policies for Taiwan (outside of the Aborigine Territory) with scarcely a serious check.[12] This long interlude between two periods of tight regulation is sometimes known as one of official "liberalism" or laissez-faire toward business affairs. It can be so designated, however, only in contrast to the strictness that preceded and followed. In steady succession the government completed several major projects. It finished the land survey of the entire island, essential to all their later engineering works as well as to the desired

[10] The *pao-chia* system was a scheme for assigning joint responsibility to village and familial groups for the conduct of their members. Its operation and the reasons for its effectiveness are taken up in the following chapter.

[11] Mendiola, N. B. (1949), p. 76 ff.

[12] The Taiwanese efforts at insurrection, as for example recounted in OPNAV, Civil Affairs Handbook (1944), pp. 173-177, tended to be exaggerated by their instigators. Due to their own clumsiness, these were quickly put down by the Japanese, though not without some local disruption. Inside the Aborigine Territory, on the other hand, the Japanese devoted many years of hard fighting and frustration to "pacification," and did not hold the entire island securely until the mid-1920's, nor peacefully until almost 1940.

supervision of agriculture. Through its own revenues the government became independent of the annual subsidy from Tokyo with which it had been launched.

By direct action and through state-owned companies, it enlarged communications facilities into a thorough public network of roads, bridges, railway lines, telegraph and telephone installations, tunnels and mountain trails; constructed harbor equipment to accommodate an ever-growing volume of shipping: expended a tremendous effort (if not large sums) on sanitation and disease control; relieved much of the uncertainty of weather for crops by an irrigation system which also reduced the destruction of floods. Finally, and in some respects the central note of the entire program, the authorities gave continual attention to ways of rationalizing agricultural production.

It must be admitted that most of their techniques of agrarian improvement were relatively well known even at the beginning. These were already part of the world accumulation of knowledge by the time the program was well under way. The Japanese did not discover new principles of agronomy in Taiwan, but drew upon this fund of information with alert but minor adaptations to fit the case at hand. The rice yields from the land, for example, were increased spectacularly through the spread of a new strain of seed, introduced in 1922 and cultivated thereafter under supervision by Japanese.[13]

Practices like breeding suitable varieties of seed, using fertilizer systematically to replace elements removed from the soil, rotating crops, and matching irrigation schedules to the growth cycles of plants have for many years been commonplace in the world. But they do not by magical properties overcome the handicaps of unenlightened farming practices. Japanese characteristically did not pin all their faith on the ability of these methods to work out improvement in yields unaided. They painstakingly supervised the application of techniques, and coordinated the use of new procedures with judicious—never extravagant—mixtures of capital.

The most crucial capital input of the Japanese in agriculture was the administrative framework through which these technical changes were introduced. It was a channel of influence that they turned to good account with a cheap outlay of resources. Japanese themselves were not cultivators. They operated experimental farms at many places to study means of improving agriculture, always from the standpoint of what was practical in a land of peasant farmers. They

[13] Mendiola (1949), p. 76 ff.

also maintained a zealous staff of workers to put new findings into effect. Taiwanese villagers were mobilized into compulsory associations to utilize the information, and the program was carried on with close cooperation by local authorities.

In addition to these measures, certain of the large Japanese expenditures on outright heavy investment helped to modify agricultural productivity of Taiwanese. The building of railroads, large-scale facilities for irrigation and flood control, and in later years factories for processing agricultural produce all worked some radical changes in the relations between the farms and the markets abroad. But these reached down only occasionally to disturb the operation of individual peasant farming. What one Japanese writer has called the process of "capitalist development in Taiwanese agriculture" was not so much a matter of developing investment in agriculture itself as of surrounding agriculture with capital improvements.[14]

Many improvements were introduced directly by the Government-General. Usually a charge was levied on their use or the expense was defrayed by heavy taxation. The government matched each of these steps of its own by prompting the large private firms to carry on parallel works inside their corporate domains. This sort of extra-curricular investment was widely undertaken by Japanese companies, and led to the growth of giant integrated concerns, some larger than their counterparts in Japan.[15]

A remarkable set of inducements existed for engaging in this sort of corporate expansion. Taiwan in the first place had the reputation of being the most profitable locale for investment in the Empire.[16] In addition to this, the Government-General frequently offered subsidies, partial subscription of funds by itself, special legal privileges, a trifling burden of taxation, and in general more cordial relations with the state than were available elsewhere. The response to these terms was apparently more enthusiastic than had been anticipated. It rose at times to feverish speculation, followed by short depressions among Japanese financial circles,[17] and led the Government-General to impose restrictive schemes for fixing prices and output.

14 Yanaihara, Tadao (1929), p. 140 ff. He points out that most Japanese held land as landlords, like the Taiwanese, not as capitalists. The exception to this rule—and it is a large exception—was the management of sugar-growing plantations by a few of the large sugar-processing companies.

15 Grajdanzev, A. J. (1942), p. 96.

16 Yanaihara (1929), p. 146.

17 Price movements of rice and sugar in Japan intensified some of these effects, especially in the late 1920's and for several years after 1930. See Grajdanzev (1942), pp. 99-101.

There was still another category, a somewhat subtler one, by which Japanese investment was injected into Taiwan's economy. This consists of what might be called organizational changes, like banking facilities and the formation of stable domestic markets for disposing of produce. Many such features had been notably absent before 1895, when most commodity markets were no more than local in scope, prices fluctuated widely, interest rates were usurious, and speculation was the principal business activity. This channel of influence was often not actually separate from others; some efficiencies of this sort appeared even as by-products of other more deliberate innovations. These advantages tended to flow from relations among the modern types of business organization. Hence such benefits went to Japanese businessmen, though they often opened up subsidiary avenues to wealth for a number of Taiwanese in commerce and in service enterprises.[18]

With no significant exceptions, the growth and spread of Japanese business activity in Taiwan served primarily to introduce capital into agriculture without greatly changing the operation of individual farms. It furnished a pattern of services between the fields and the markets in Japan through which to reap the economies of modern organization, and yet ensured that most of the proceeds were reinvested on the island in a pattern determined by official decision.

The Preparations for War

During the early or middle 1930's the Japanese Empire began to turn toward preparations for war. The colonies were called upon to increase the measure of their contribution in other lines of production besides Empire self-sufficiency in food. Taiwan was not abundantly endowed with the heavy stuff with which the war was to be made—metallic ores were lacking, and coal deposits were not plentiful—and so it was permitted to assume some of the burden of processing materials formerly supplied to Japan as agricultural and other primary produce. This decision did not issue entirely from military or strategic considerations, since in many cases it amounted to no

18 Chartered banks were an exception. They harnessed funds for industrial investment, and were all owned and operated by Japanese. ". . . modern banks in Taiwan help to collect money from the population and loan it at a relatively low rate of interest to the big Japanese firms, while the Chinese [Taiwanese] have to apply for loans to other sources where they pay two to five times as high a rate of interest as that which the Japanese firms pay." Grajdanzev (1942), p. 126.

more than following advantages which had been obscured by the official emphasis on foodstuffs.[19]

A general survey of Taiwan's part in the Japanese war program is impossible to undertake here. It is nonetheless pertinent to indicate what were some of the implications of this shift for the internal administration and economic affairs of the island. The turning point cannot be dated exactly, for the decisions behind it were probably not made at any one point of time. They rather reflected a gradual reorientation of official opinion regarding the course of development that was desirable.

From the early years of its existence, the Government-General of Taiwan had sponsored many special corporations to finance and help to organize a limited modification of agriculture. It made more intensive use of them during the 1930's to enlarge new industries that it wanted to foster. Bank credit was made available for new investments at low fixed interest rates. Subsidies were granted widely to induce old firms to enter new fields. Corporations were spared the burden of taxes, government revenue being made up through an ingenious set of other devices.[20] Under exclusive privileges, Japanese companies were attracted to exploit rapidly many of the virgin mineral and forest resources of the island owned by the government. Business activity was hedged about with countless regulations intended to invite mergers and reduce rivalries between firms.[21]

The sugar industry was the outstanding example of government indulgence toward private corporations and its effects. A few Japanese sugar companies had made an early start, before World War I. These were favored with direct subsidies, marketing advantages in Japan and imported equipment far superior to that traditionally used by Taiwanese.[22] By keeping and improving this initial advantage, Japanese producers all but drove Taiwanese competitors out of the field. Some of them grew so quickly that they were under some compulsion to branch out into providing transportation and related

[19] Special advances were made in starting hydro-electric power output and aluminum and chemical production, however, which would probably not have progressed in any such manner except by dictation from high places.

[20] For sources of government revenue, see Grajdanzev (1942), pp. 133-137, and *Statistical Summary*, Tables 335-345.

[21] Stock dividends of corporations, for example, were limited by law. Since profits were high, large sums were forced into business expansion.

[22] An even greater prop to the industry as a whole was tariff protection in the Japanese market, whereby Japanese consumers supplied the greatest subsidy of all. Here also Japanese companies were enabled to reap the major share of the benefit, for reasons given above.

services for themselves, in order to keep output in pace with their own milling capacities.[23] The industry had expanded, in fact, too rapidly for its own good. It had suffered several crises, brought on by fluctuations in the demand for sugar in Japan, where its tariff preference led it to sell.[24] To "stabilize production," the important producers organized a cartel (under the Japan Sugar Association) with government permission and guidance.

Buying of cane from farmers had from the start been controlled by agreements among processing firms; the cartel opened a concerted effort to prevent cane prices from rising. The need for this step arose from the fact that sugar cane and rice both were grown in the same soils and more or less during the same seasons. In effect, the two crops competed for land. Japanese had always complained that the Taiwanese had a perverse tendency to cultivate rice when it was more profitable. Under the cartel agreements, sugar firms avoided competitive buying by strict agreements to allocate areas of cane purchase. Owing to their size and diversity, they were able to persuade many farmers to grow sugar instead of rice by withholding irrigation water from rice fields, and by making conditional cash advances to individual families.

By such means the sugar cartel accomplished what the government could never have done unaided: it ensured a steady output of sugar at fixed prices for which it would have been irrational for individual farmers to produce cane.[25] Sugar acquired a place of high wartime priority as a source for industrial alcohol, and beginning in 1939 the Government-General assisted sugar concerns to construct distilleries and make alcohol on the island. Under these circumstances it is not surprising that the sugar processing industry tended to pass into fewer and fewer hands. After a merger in 1940 more than 95 per cent of the sugar in Taiwan was milled by five giant companies. Though more extreme, the history of the sugar industry was essentially that of all large-scale Japanese enterprise in Taiwan.

The Government-General itself began to promote industrial expansion during the 1930's by further participation in economic life.

[23] Privately owned and operated railroads attained a length of over half as great as the entire state system. Not all were built by sugar concerns; the largest belonged to lumber companies. Most were of narrower gauge than the main rail lines. See *Statistical Summary*, Tables 440-442.

[24] Costs were higher than in Java throughout the period, putting Taiwanese sugar at a serious handicap in markets outside Japan.

[25] The Government-General did its part to encourage sugar cultivation by putting rice paddies in a higher tax category than comparable sugar fields. And in 1939 it simply took over the entire cartel by issuing a set of detailed regulations to dictate its affairs.

First, it controlled certain key sources of income and authority, as before, through the legal monopolies. Net receipts from these enterprises (including salt, alcohol, camphor, tobacco and opium) made up one of the largest classes of revenue. Public railroads, irrigation and generation of electricity were also government monopolies—unofficial but nonetheless actual—which were operated more for the sake of the power that could be wielded through their services than for profit. They were developed so as to assert what amounted to administrative control over the private sphere of production.

These were really little more than refinements of earlier devices. One of the important departures from previous government policy was to partake directly in more business activity. No data were ever published to show the extent of government investment side by side with that of private firms. It was thought to be at a level nearly as great as the whole private sector, but was mixed too thoroughly to be separated in any reliable fashion from the whole.[26]

Outright government holdings in corporations went beyond scattered blocs of shares in individual companies. Many of these official firms were diversified and enlarged so as to absorb parts of related fields. For example, the larger electric power companies, owned or dominated by the Government-General, helped to build the nucleus of Taiwan's metallurgy industry. Most of the wartime aluminum production was carried out by such integrated concerns. The government itself formed the Taiwan Development Company, in 1936, as a super-corporation to promote interrelated ventures of this nature. It speedily promoted a host of subsidiaries strategic for the war program.[27] Besides all of these extraordinary activities, the regular budgetary expenditures of the Government-General leaned increasingly toward injecting new state services into the economy, and probably contributed thereby to the inflation later in the war.[28]

[26] Certain tables have been quoted many times that purport to show the amounts of these investments (see OPNAV, Civil Affairs Handbook, *Taiwan—Economic Supplement*, 1944, pp. 97-98). We shall not reproduce them here, for none of the published data on corporate investment are very trustworthy. The publications never stated what criteria were imposed in their collection, and so it is impossible to know exactly what they represent in any given instance. They conceal the weight of government as opposed to private corporate holdings, and do not differentiate between large holding companies and their subsidiaries.

[27] Incomplete data on some of the known holdings of this and other of the larger firms are given in the OPNAV Civil Affairs Handbook, *Taiwan—Economic Supplement*, Appendix, p. 86 ff. Through omissions, these figures are known to understate grossly the extent of corporate concentration.

[28] These services stretched from research grants to larger funds allocated directly for new subsidies of business. *Ibid.*, p. 59.

Industrial Growth during the War

After setting the stage for limited industrialization by their treatment of large business in Taiwan, Japanese leaders after 1940 began actively to move the players. The centralized corporate structure had been expected to be adequate preparation for most of the demands of war. The Government-General made frantic last-minute attempts to expand specific fields in which Japan itself was short, particularly aluminum and coal. But before long the subordination of Taiwan's economy to heavy industry in Japan, which had seemed so satisfactory, turned out to be a source of weakness. Naval losses started to interfere with shipping between Japan and Taiwan. Many of the small but essential items supplied from the home islands (special equipment, replacement parts, fuels, and skills) became unobtainable. Certain large imports such as fertilizer were cut off.

None of these shortages was fundamentally important for the island itself, since food was sufficient for its population and little else had previously been imported. Lack of articles of the first sort did play havoc with some of the new industrial output, and caused much of the equipment to deteriorate. Exports of aluminum and coal slowed down to a trickle by 1944, and practically all shipping to Japan—even rice and sugar—was discontinued early in 1945.[29] By the time of Japan's surrender much of the highly organized economic life had come to a stop, but Taiwan suffered no devastating damage as a result of the war. Agriculture was still conducted as usual, except that without fertilizer and other accustomed capital the yields had fallen off substantially.

Accomplishments of Japanese Colonial Policies

Having described the workings of colonial administration in Taiwan, one should have some idea of its accomplishments before going on to discuss in later chapters its consequences in the lives of the Taiwanese. For this purpose, the abundance of records kept by the Japanese is often a hindrance rather than a help. In general the economic statistics are not up to the standards of the population data. Numerical tables are plentiful, but explanations of what the numbers mean are not. They disagree from source to source, seldom with any reason given for the discrepancies. One must therefore look for summarizing measures, and not for fine detail.

[29] See Cohen, J. (1949), pp. 154-156.

The most efficient view of total changes in the island's economy is by reference to its statistics of trade. As indicated above (Table 4), Japan succeeded in securing practically all of Taiwan's external trade to itself, if exports to Korea are counted. During the 1930's even traffic with China, just across the Straits, was almost eliminated.

Compared with a wide range of other Far Eastern countries, Taiwan under the Japanese came to hold a surprisingly high rank in the value of trade per person. At its peak shortly before 1940, the total per capita value of its trade was well above even that of Japan (see Table 5). Since this rank was attained under peculiar conditions,

TABLE 5
ESTIMATED PER CAPITA VALUE OF FOREIGN TRADE OF FAR EASTERN COUNTRIES CIRCA 1939*
(Expressed in U.S. Dollar Equivalents)

Country	*Year*	*Imports*	*Exports*	*Total*
New Zealand	1939	109	127	236
British Malaya	1939	61	72	133
Australia	1938–39	67	64	131
TAIWAN	1937	16	23	39
Korea	1939	15	11	26
Japan Proper	1939	10	13	23
Philippine Islands	1939	8	10	18
Burma	1938–39	5	12	17
Netherlands East Indies	1939	4	6	10
Thailand	1938–39	4	5	9
French Indo-China	1937	3	4	7
China	1939	0.85	0.25	1

* As reproduced in OPNAV, Civil Affairs Handbook. *Taiwan—Economic Supplement* (1944), p. 73.
Source: Far Eastern Unit, Bureau of Foreign and Domestic Commerce, U.S. Department of Commerce.

however, it does not mark Taiwan as an especially "advanced" area (in the sense of supporting bountiful levels of living) except by reference to the Japanese residents in the island.

Taiwan's position in trade with the outside world was created by heavy and increasing exports of a few products, mainly crops sent abroad in only slightly processed state. Compared with what took place in Taiwan's business and financial communities, there was remarkably little shift in the composition of its agricultural output (see Fig. 4). Together sugar and rice never lost their dominant position in the value of all crops produced. Despite some greater emphasis on finished sugar as a source of alcohol, the cane harvests gained very little in value over rice, even when the expansion of manufactures after 1935 would seem to have made this likely. In these terms sweet potatoes, which were always prominent in the Taiwanese diet, kept nearly a constant share of the total.

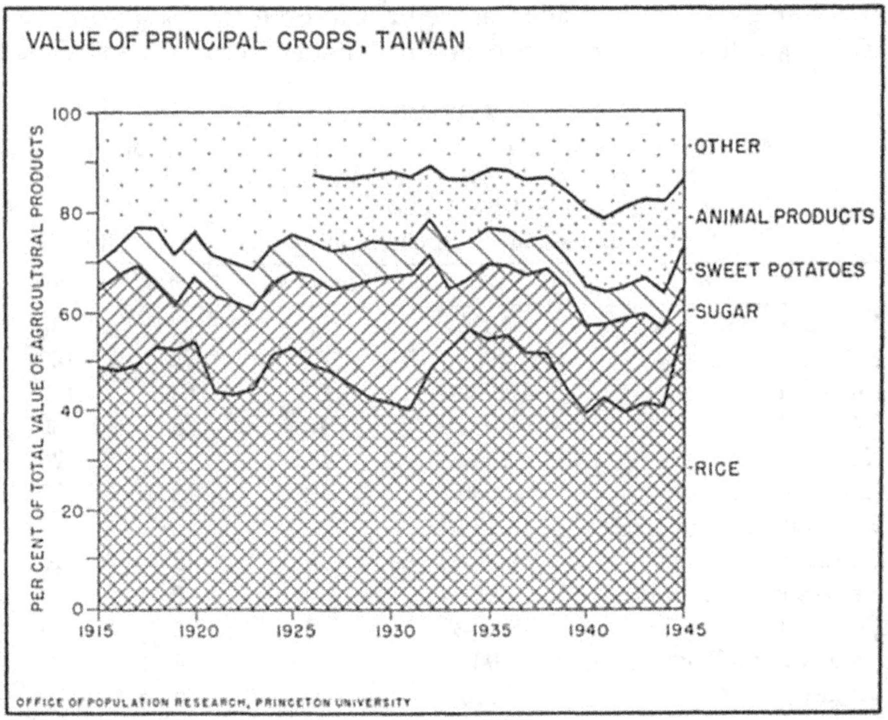

Fig. 4. Composition of the Gross Value of Total Agricultural Production, Principal Crops of Taiwan, 1915-1945.

Japanese promoted certain specialty crops, such as bananas and pineapples. These never occupied a large share in the total output of agriculture, but they more than kept pace with trends in the major crops (accounting for some of the change in the proportion of "other" products in Fig. 4). Together with tea, these crops made use of land not suitable for rice or sugar, and became important supplements to the total agricultural output. The Japanese encouraged such products by providing assured markets and technical supervision in their cultivation, and built canneries to process pineapples for export.

The various staple and other crops that made up the bulk of Taiwan's agriculture eventually became distributed in a stable spatial pattern over the island. Sugar predominated over a large area in the Southwest, where it displaced rice in most of the land within the major public irrigation system. Tea in the North, and other specialty crops in the center, occupied some of the inland and foothill sections.[80] But it is important to note that rice culture, particularly in small paddy fields, overlapped with all other crops that were raised on the broad plain of Taiwan, and the labor-intensive and traditional farming practices associated with it have continued to be spread throughout Taiwanese agriculture down to the present.[81]

The exports of staple crops would not have risen as they did unless the yields of crops did the same. Gains in rice yields from the land did not come at once. They followed almost 20 years of painstaking experiment, starting in 1906, to find a strain of seed that could thrive under conditions in Taiwan. Almost no improvement was made until the so-called *horai* variety was successfully adapted from Japan. Following its introduction the average yields per hectare for all varieties gradually rose as much as one-fourth, primarily by growth of the area devoted to *horai* rice and the special techniques used in its cultivation. Neither the *horai* nor the native strains were greatly improved in yield thereafter; in fact, it appears that *horai* declined slightly from its high performance at the start as it spread to land less favorable than the experimental farms where it was first grown (see Table 6).

Systematic irrigation was one of the measures that raised the yields of land. Between 1930 and 1936 a few projects were carried out, by the government and by private companies, to introduce controlled amounts of water into lands that previously had been cultivated as dry fields. To illustrate approximately the trend of these events, Fig. 5 shows the changes in the area of land in paddy cultivation and that in dry fields. (Paddy land does not correspond exactly with the land that is irrigated on a large scale, for there were many paddy fields not included in these projects.) Since the total area cultivated was increased over these years, it is possible that the irrigation projects brought some land into cultivation that was formerly idle. More, however, was merely converted from dry to wet cultivation (see Fig. 5).

80 See Ch'en Cheng-hsiang, *Atlas* (1950), Fig. 161.
81 *Ibid.*, Fig. 70.

TABLE 6

IMPROVEMENT IN THE YIELDS OF RICE IN TAIWAN, 1916 TO 1945

Average Yields of Different Strains in Each Year, First and Second Crops Combined (Hectoliters of Rice per Hectare)*

Years	*All Rice*	*Horai Rice*	*Other Strains*	*Per Cent of Rice Land Devoted to Horai*
1916-20	17.8	—	20.1	—
1921-25	19.3	28.5	19.3	4.6
1926-30	20.9	22.7	20.4	19.9
1931-35	23.0	27.2	21.3	33.7
1936-40	25.5	28.2	23.2	47.3
1941-45	21.6	22.7	19.7	59.8

* Crop statistics in Taiwan were not kept in metric units. Figures in the *Statistical Summary of Taiwan* were all converted before publication.

Source: *Statistical Summary*, Table 203.

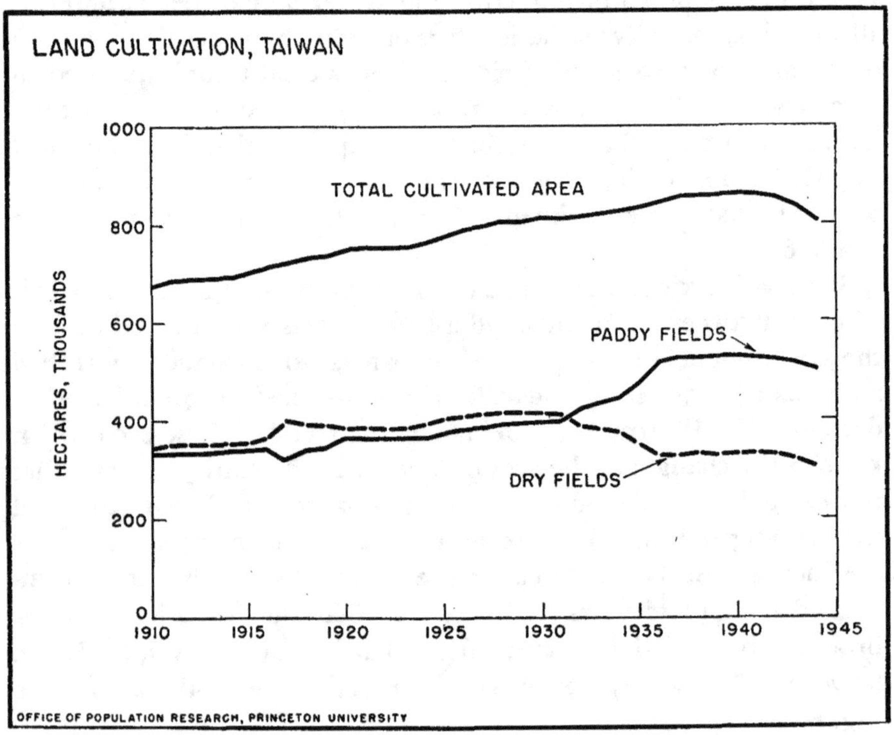

Fig. 5. Area of Cultivated Land, Taiwan, 1910-1944.

Land that was improved in this manner not only yielded more at each harvest: over a third of the paddy land yielded more than one harvest each year. Under schemes for rotation and inter-cropping devised by the Japanese, it was not unusual to take three separate harvests from many of these fields in a year.

The labor of preparing the land, of weeding, and of harvesting was not saved by these changes. They may have involved some net additions—irrigation became a more complicated process in some cases, and the aqueducts for transporting the water required special maintenance. Japanese were aware that the soil could not be farmed more intensively without losing some of its fertility, and encouraged the use of commercial fertilizers, much of which they required to be prepared on the island. The remainder comprised the largest single category of Taiwan's capital imports, greater in value than the iron and steel and machinery which are sometimes identified with the needs of agrarian countries. Importing fertilizers for sale in Taiwan proved to be a profitable line of business; it was reported to be firmly in the hands of a few large Japanese concerns, a fact which should occasion no surprise. It was shortage of fertilizers that brought on declines in average yields of crops after 1940 (see Table 6, above).

The shift in official plans for Taiwan after 1930 leads one to look for some indication of results in the composition of Taiwan's products. The search is not very rewarding. In terms of gross value of product, agriculture did not lose its place as the foremost line of production until 1940 and later. Then it exchanged ranks with "Industry"—because farm produce fell off momentarily rather than because of any sharp rise in manufacturing (see Table 7).[32] The steady but slow decline in the share of agricultural production in earlier years had indicated a tendency to submit more of the agricultural produce to processing before it left the island, and not a shift from farming to manufacturing.

It is when the category of "industrial" production is examined in detail that some of the more recent trends emerge. In Table 8, evidently industry in Taiwan had always been centered around food products. Until the mid-'thirties these had amounted to three-quarters of the value of all manufactures. Only from then on did the effects of new economic goals begin to appear. The largest advances were made in some of the fields that had been smallest, espe-

32 The sharp rise in the numbers of Table 7 was largely a matter of currency inflation.

TABLE 7

GROSS RECORDED VALUE OF ALL PRINCIPAL TYPES OF PRODUCTION, 1915-1942

(Yearly Average for Each Period)

Years	*Total*	*Agriculture*	*Mining*	*Fishing and Forestry*	*Industry*
A. Millions of Yen:					
1915-19	262.7	144.5	7.2	9.1	101.9
1920-24	411.5	207.0	12.0	23.0	169.5
1925-29	559.0	293.6	16.8	31.8	216.8
1930-34	525.5	255.8	15.5	26.5	227.7
1935-39	901.0	432.9	39.6	41.5	387.0
1940-42	1388.4	576.4	62.8	91.8	657.4
B. Percentages of Total:					
1915-19	100.0	55.0	2.8	3.4	38.8
1920-24	100.0	50.3	2.9	5.6	41.2
1925-29	100.0	52.5	3.0	5.7	38.8
1930-34	100.0	48.7	3.0	5.0	43.3
1935-39	100.0	48.0	4.4	4.6	43.0
1940-42	100.0	41.5	4.5	6.6	47.4

Source: *Statistical Summary*, Tables 225-229.

TABLE 8

GROSS VALUE OF PRODUCTION RECORDED FOR "INDUSTRY" IN TAIWAN, BY LINE OF PRODUCT, 1921-1942

(Yearly Average for Each Period)

Years	*Total*	*Textiles*	*Metal Products*	*Machinery & Equip.*	*Misc.**	*Chemical Products*	*Food Products*
A. Millions of Yen:							
1921-24	165	3	3	4	20	13	122
1925-29	217	3	4	5	32	20	153
1930-34	228	3	6	5	29	18	167
1935-39	387	6	17	12	45	38	269
1940-42	664	11	46	30	91	80	406
B. Percentages of Total:							
1921-24	100.0	1.7	1.9	2.1	11.9	7.9	74.6
1925-29	100.0	1.5	2.0	2.2	14.7	9.3	70.3
1930-34	100.0	1.1	2.5	2.3	12.9	7.8	73.3
1935-39	100.0	1.5	4.5	3.1	11.6	9.9	69.4
1940-42	100.0	1.7	7.0	4.5	13.7	12.1	61.0

* Includes Printing, Wood Products, Ceramics, and Other.

Source: *Statistical Summary*, Table 269 and Table 270.

cially in chemical and metal manufacturing; their expansion did not have an appreciable effect in the production of all the island.

In other words, in spite of its expansion, industrial production had only begun to make headway in relation to agricultural output. Before 1940, manufactured commodities were still subordinate to Taiwan's farm products (and did not amount to much beyond processed sugar). Afterwards the Japanese did not have enough time to marshal the island's resources effectively in industry. We know this was not because they failed to make an effort—it was because they started too late.

Certain types of heavy investment had received their close attention ever since earlier years. Railway construction, for example, was pushed forward with enthusiasm from the very first. The time schedule of progress in expanding the public railroads was far ahead of their actual utilization (see Fig. 6). This was an investment which

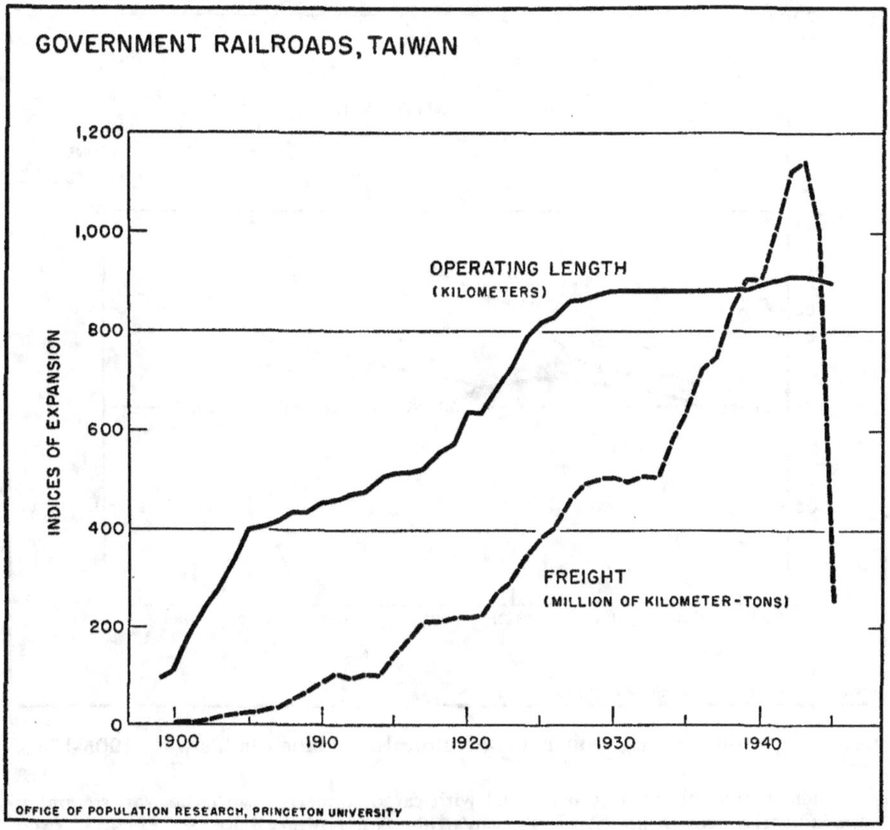

Fig. 6. Expansion and Use of Railroad Facilities in Taiwan, 1900-1945.

the Japanese undertook primarily in anticipation of long-term benefit, without being able to justify its initial cost for many years. In terms of kilometer-tons of freight carried, the railroad made only partial use of its physical facilities until late in the colony's existence.[33] This sort of schedule was also followed in establishing a system of improved roads and trails over the island. In both cases, Japanese had to bear the burden of ambitious engineering projects when they could least afford it, for basic transportation networks are more valuable as networks than they are piecemeal.

Public irrigation was a project closely tied to agriculture, and followed a different timetable (see Fig. 7). After 1895 there was no large

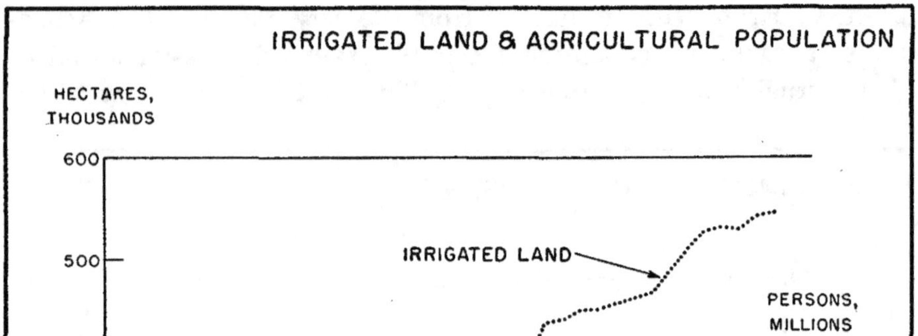

Fig. 7. Expansion of Irrigation and Agricultural Population in Taiwan, 1905-1943.

33 Then it suddenly became overtaxed with cargo connected with the war, stemming from industrial growth and from Taiwan's role as a military base. See OPNAV, Civil Affairs Handbook, *Taiwan—Economic Supplement* (1944), p. 60.

supply of unoccupied land in Taiwan that could be drawn into cultivation, and so the needs of an expanding farming population and growing export demand had to be met by other means. The Japanese turned again to large investment to improve the effectiveness of the land that there was. The manner of constructing and upkeep of irrigation canals in Taiwan depended on mass labor. They were turned into an investment of labor, employed so as to produce an important form of capital equipment. The extent of irrigation more than kept pace with rural population growth while the Japanese were in control. Water for this purpose became indispensable in maintaining the output of farms. It was a hidden element in the improvement of rice and sugar yields, for the new varieties of seed that were developed were types that needed to be carefully irrigated.

Finally, the development of electric power was so closely related to the growth of Taiwan's newer industries that it should not be passed over without mention. Generation of electricity was one of the specialized heavy investments that formed the nucleus of the "industrial" progress after 1930. This is evident in a circumstantial way from the trends of capacity in generating power and the spread of factory employment (see Fig. 8). Factories in Taiwan came to depend on the cheap electricity that was developed at state instigation from water power. Judged from the size of their employment, the most important of the mechanized factories in the island were "food" (i.e., sugar) and metallurgical plants, which were the heaviest users of electricity.

As the next chapter will indicate, the Japanese broadened their objectives in Taiwan too late to put its human resources to best use in the new effort. Drawing the developed wealth of the island together into centralized control had turned out to be singularly advantageous. It had erected an entire structure of corporate organization from specialized financial services down to the coordinating of actual physical production of commodities. The Government-General had retained a close supervision over this structure, by licensing, regulation, and participation as a shareholder. As a program it quickly marshalled the production of Taiwan's farms into a profitable colonial enterprise.

When it came to pressing this development further, however, the Japanese made no real progress, for they had frustrated these aims in advance. Under agrarian conditions, industrial skills and experience in management are slower and more difficult to accumulate

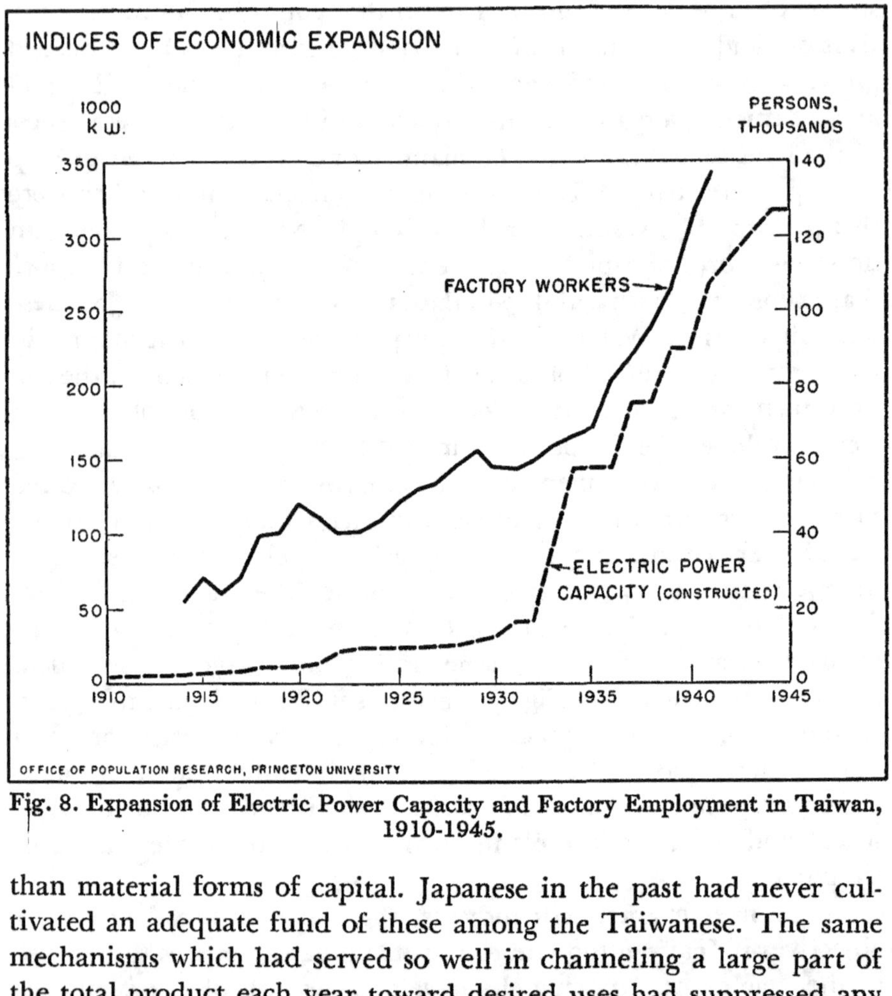

Fig. 8. Expansion of Electric Power Capacity and Factory Employment in Taiwan, 1910-1945.

than material forms of capital. Japanese in the past had never cultivated an adequate fund of these among the Taiwanese. The same mechanisms which had served so well in channeling a large part of the total product each year toward desired uses had suppressed any opportunities for industrial employment that might attract Taiwanese who had administrative skills. What the Japanese themselves referred to as the "industrialization of Taiwan" was nothing but a corporate superstructure placed on an agrarian base. This was not capable of diffusing an industrial culture thoroughly among the general population, because it had been devised to prevent this very thing.

CHAPTER III

Economic Activities and Social Change

THE activities, interests, and aspirations of the Japanese community in Taiwan were things that existed apart from the indigenous population. These elements were never effectively communicated to the Taiwanese—partly through a design to withhold them, and partly through reluctance among the people of Taiwan to accept them. Consequently the conduct of Japanese residents is not of much help in understanding the accustomed modes of life among the island's people. It is the latter problem that has the more interest for demography, and makes it essential to consider the background of social order in Taiwan and the changes under colonial rule.

The Early Agrarian Order in Taiwan

The importance of agricultural pursuits in imposing a predominantly agrarian character on a society is not a thing that can be precisely measured. Short of perfect exactitude, a great deal can be learned with lesser devices, by describing the cultural setting of agriculture in Taiwan, and pointing out how it influenced the participation by Taiwanese in the island's economy. The basis of this setting lay in the conditions that prevailed before Taiwan became a colony of Japan.

By the mid-19th century, the lowland region of Taiwan was rapidly becoming fully settled. Piracy, which had made Taiwan a scourge to sea traffic along the China coast, gradually subsided into sedentary agriculture. Most of the Chinese population was already supporting itself by farming and the marketing of farm products. Since 1700 immigration had brought in a steady stream of Chinese from the mainland. In spite of sporadic prohibitions, hundreds of thousands of peasant farmers came to seek refuge from rural poverty in South China. Once arrived, they often reverted to this same condition, by reaching unfavorable terms with some of their countrymen already entrenched there as land speculators.

Poverty tended to reproduce itself among those who reached Taiwan, though there was also great wealth open to the few who rose from cultivation to commerce. Each settled family held an advantage over newcomers. This superior position placed new migrants in some competition for the more desirable lands near the coast. In order to maintain their accustomed manner of farming, many were forced to move inland, where they gradually dispossessed aborigines and the earlier Hakka settlers and pushed eventually to the foothills of the interior. These many-sided conflicts of interest gave rise to land tenures more complicated than those usually found in China. The result was a set of property customs that was to become confused and encumbering in later years.[1]

With agrarian land tenures, however, it is all too easy to mistake form for substance. The system of land tenures in Taiwan gained several features that are distinctive to itself, arising to incorporate new parties into an old system—the aborigines who first occupied the area, and Chinese who acquired land titles to profit from the arrival of immigrants. But, since these landed property relationships are of little interest to us from an antiquarian point of view, their lasting effects are more important: they contributed to a form of village organization that survived through the entire Japanese occupation down to the present.

The flow of migrants is remarkable in that it populated Taiwan, with little variation over the years, closely after the model of the South China coastal area.[2] The resemblance to the mainland went beyond forms of settlement and land utilization. Politically, under Manchu control the island was supposed to be assimilated into the administration of the rest of China. It was governed as a regular political division—first as a prefecture of Fukien and later as a province itself—by officials appointed directly from Peking.

Taiwan inevitably presented special problems of control. In the first place, it could be separated from easy communication with the continent; eventually it grew almost as accessible to the Western powers as to Peking. The device most relied upon to tie the area to China was a weak one. The authorities tried, futilely, to isolate it from all external contact. From time to time, they went as far as to restrict the entry of Chinese from across the Straits, though even this had little success.

[1] See Ch'en Cheng-hsiang (1950), pp. 41-43, and Kawada, Shiro (1928).

[2] The instances of alleged "radical transformation" of land tenures (Kawada, Shiro [December 1928], p. 88) were primarily fiscal measures to reassert the central government's share in revenues from the land. Such reforms often are superficial from the standpoint of village organization. By way of illustration, one of the early official acts of the Japanese in Taiwan was to sweep away a whole section of these archaic land titles. While these reforms cleared the way to regulate rural areas from outside, they scarcely made an impression on property relations within the villages.

Furthermore, higher officials were themselves aliens, responsible ultimately to the Manchu court. Their tenure depended on their standing in Peking. Special competence or energy in office was not an advantage—it could even be dangerous, by making them targets of rumor and innuendo. Careers were sometimes ruined on the suspicion that certain officials had separatist leanings or were friendly to foreigners. Personnel were transferred regularly, as in China, to remove them from temptations of familiarity with their offices. Their only safe path to success was to maintain stability in local affairs, and somehow to prevent civil discontent from turning into civil disturbance.

This system was calculated to engross its key officers in their personal relations with Peking. It proved to be more effective in ensuring loyalty than in promoting careful government or preventing corruption. There were few deterrents to peculation in office, which was respectable if prudently pursued, and surrounded by many opportunities—such as legal monopolies and illicit export trade—not present in China itself.

These limited and negative objectives of government invited continual lapses of internal rule. Being unfamiliar with local conditions, officials simply did not govern in rural villages. Throughout the countryside they kept the peace by intrigue with powerful families rather than through actual administration—families that relied heavily on property obligations among the peasantry to uphold their influence. The situation put a strain on the administration's own underpinnings, and led to severity in abuses and civil strife to which the mainland itself was unaccustomed. It is a testimony to the serviceability of traditional Chinese institutions that they survived this test.

Whatever its internal shortcomings, this scheme of political order was well suited to rebuff foreigners, at least foreigners whose advances were not backed by force. Acute frustration among the Western commercial agents in Taiwan stands as evidence that it was accomplishing this part of its purpose. They complained bitterly that officials had connived at Taiwanese violence against Europeans and had even incited such incidents.[3]

The best information available about Taiwan's external contacts is contained in the published reminiscences and travel accounts of foreign trading representatives. The literary interests of these men throw light on the main preoccupation of their trading activities.

[3] For example, see Pickering, W. A. (1898), Ch. 17.

Though their books have a wealth of illuminating anecdotes about the export trade, they provide almost no observations of any value about the ordinary affairs of the population. One might imagine from reading such sources that everyone in Taiwan was engaged in foreign commerce or some form of government service.[4]

These informants were, up to a point, honest men. They were not trying to mislead, and deserve credit for considerable acuteness and sincerity. The most likely reason for their failure to inform us about the Taiwanese is that they never had a chance to find out for themselves. Western merchants simply had no occasion to form more than special business associations with Taiwanese. Practically all of their transactions were conducted by contract merchants ("compradors") as middlemen. Foreigners not infrequently made efforts to interfere in internal affairs, but these all arose over specific issues. They were attempts to make the social order more nearly serve their ends, not to alter it.

As in China, trading relations carried on in this manner did not further the exchange of ideas along with commodities. They were contrived so as to minimize such interchange. This mutual aloofness worked both ways: it enabled outsiders to get along in ignorance of conditions prevailing in the island, and at the same time shielded the general population from contact with the outside world. Foreign commerce, the foremost potential channel for innovation until the conquest by Japan, was severely circumscribed by seclusiveness of the parties on both sides.

The reasons for this isolation are not all to be found in the hostility of officials or in the provincialism of Westerners. The foreigners were eager to obtrude their presence further into foreign trade, even if only on their own terms. Government officers were too inept as administrators, their conduct too deeply undermined by directives from above, to succeed in stifling any positive tendencies toward change if such had arisen. The real bulwark of conservatism behind

[4] These authors made better traders than ethnographers. They often did not go beyond expressing impatience that Taiwanese should not follow 19th century English trading conventions. The best and most comprehensive of these works (Davidson, James W. [1905]), out of a total of 32 chapters, devoted only a single superficial one to "The Inhabitants of Formosa," where the author did little more than describe the aborigines.

The apparent exceptions prove the rule. If good material about those Taiwanese of Chinese origin is scarce, books about the aborigines of the interior (of varying quality) are not. Few Westerners penetrated to the dangerous mountain regions of Taiwan, but all of them developed immense curiosity about the customs of these "savages," which was not held toward the Chinese. See, for example, the titles in Takekoshi, Yosaburo (1907), pp. 321-342.

this nominal government policy existed within Taiwan's rural villages. The bulk of the population was made up of peasant farmers and small tradesmen, who supplied the commodities for most of the export trade. The fact that their products were exported did not bring them into closer touch with outside markets. Farming and other village activities did not reach beyond local boundaries; the arrangements for disposing of farm produce, as we have seen, were in different hands.

The rural population led a settled existence. Taiwan being a small area, travel between places was not uncommon, but it was rare for families to change residence from one part to another. With poor roads and chronic banditry, even minor journeys entailed some hardship and risk and so were undertaken chiefly for exceptional purposes. The same difficulties hindered the movement of commodities. Internal markets had not been very effectively developed to transfer articles of ordinary use from town to town; reports tell of wide variation in prices for standard items such as food, and of prohibitive hazards to products in transit.[5] Often products could be shipped to the coast and on to China more easily than to points elsewhere in the island.

Local stability fostered local solidarities. The inconvenience of communication helped rural settlements to become close-knit communities, by segregating certain cleavages and antagonisms that the Chinese had brought with them from the mainland. Many had come from different localities in Fukien and Kwangtung, and had maintained their ancestral clan affiliations. Members of these groups frequently settled together and did not intermarry with others. Even many years after annexation by Japan, the Japanese found that several communities had kept themselves free of mixture with other groups. For these various reasons, village organization in many respects became self-contained and self-sufficient.[6]

Property institutions helped to buttress the stability in these small communities. In Taiwan, as in China, land ownership was the only durable form that substantial wealth could take. It was durable

[5] Takekoshi, Yosaburo (1907), pp. 252 and 269-270.

[6] The turbulent history of Taiwan has been carelessly represented as one of indiscriminate civil disorder, its early population as "unruly." It is noteworthy that most of the disturbances apparently followed the lines of cleavage above. Far from portending a breakdown of tradition within the Chinese settlements, these incidents were contests of strength between distinct parties—powerful clans, government forces, and aboriginal tribes. None was directed against the form of the social order itself, and none ever threatened that order.

against climate and short-term deterioration in use, against destruction through violence, and against decline in the income that it produced. Since the farming population was increasing within a fairly definite area, it had additional value in speculation. Land was also relatively safe against confiscation by the government; not only could its ownership be hidden from casual inspection, but the government itself depended on the obligations owed to landlords by tenants to uphold its authority. Under agrarian conditions of farming on a small scale it is impossible to cultivate large holdings of land under a single management. Hence, the only way to amass large wealth is to become a landlord—beyond some point, necessarily an absentee landlord. In early Taiwan, considerable concentration of landholdings was reported. Ownership tended to gravitate into the control of large and powerful families, whose influence was the only recourse of government officials in asserting their rule.[7]

On the economic side, this concentration of wealth was not given a chance to develop into industrial-type investment. The landed gentry, often landed on considerable scale, were the only group of persons who had access to sufficient income to become capitalists.[8] Practically, however, it proved more secure and profitable to let out their lands to tenant farmers. When they branched out into different enterprises, it was as an adjunct to their status as gentry. In South Taiwan, for example,

> ". . . sugar was manufactured from the cane grown upon the owners' plantations, or from that brought from elsewhere. The cane was grown by the tenants, or by those who through being heavily indebted to the landowner stood in the same relation as retainers . . . under it [this system] the master of the sugar factory secures a threefold profit.
>
> 1. As landlord, he claims from his tenants from 15 per cent. to 20 per cent. of the cane as rent.

[7] One might suspect that, as in China, members of these families *were* the officials at lower levels of administration. But there is no direct evidence on this point, aside from frequent references to the fact that *clan* solidarity, imported to Taiwan by the migrants from South China, was one of the few bases for organizing any kind of joint action by Taiwanese on a large scale.

[8] The government was unable to fill such a role itself for reasons already noted. Officials, who were not permanent fixtures in Taiwan, confined their acquisitive energies to foreign commerce, where returns were quicker and they did not need to make long-term commitments. For example, it is significant that the government almost never operated its own monopolies, but let them out to many private agents and taxed the products as they were exported.

2. As capitalist, he secures 14 per cent. to 24 per cent. interest on all the money he may have loaned to his tenant.
3. In order to cover the running expenses of the sugar factory he, as master, appropriates half the cane brought in by his tenants.

"These vast profits leave very little for the poor tenants, who have therefore no means of improving the soil, but fall deeper into debt, until at length they become mere slaves of the sugar factor. This system has proved the greatest hindrance to the growth of the business."[9]

Establishment of Japanese Authority

Japan's objectives in enlarging its Empire required a more energetic administration. With the background of past failures, it is understandable that the Japanese who first arrived in Taiwan met difficulty in trying to impose this kind of rule. It quickly became evident that neither profit nor political dominion was assured to them without some extraordinary measures.

Japanese first installed themselves in economic life exactly where outsiders had done so in the past—at the periphery of traditional marketing and property relations. They remained most active, as we have seen, outside the realm of agriculture proper. Through their steps in gaining access to the old agrarian institutions, we can now begin to see how far these changes impinged on agriculture itself. The Japanese did not proceed by sheer force, nor simply in a form of "economic penetration." The control was made effective by wedding the two channels—business and government—and by manipulating the pre-existing situation from a few vantage points at the outside. To make a success of this endeavor, the Japanese found it expedient to leave much of this rural social structure almost intact, and turn its basic features to their own account.

Histories of Taiwan over this period usually emphasize only the opposition to the new government that was overt and armed. But it was not by military conquest that the Japanese eventually secured the lowland area of the island. The military aspect was over quickly. Organized resistance collapsed by the end of 1895. Within a year or so after formally taking possession, Japanese became aware that direct attempts to alter the old rural state of affairs were too costly and slow, and were ineffectual against guerrilla bands that had wide-

[9] Takekoshi, Yosaburo (1907), p. 243.

spread local support. Their program to govern the countryside directly was a recognized failure as early as 1898.[10]

Starting with the issuance of *pao-chia* regulations in that year, the policy was revised with a view to getting less ambitious results, but more quickly. These were rules of conduct imposed on inhabitants of villages and smaller towns, under the threat of punitive action against the whole community. Virtually all Taiwanese outside the Aborigine Territory (with special provisions applying to certain cities) were assigned to household groups (*chia*), which were in turn grouped into village units (*pao*) for supervision. Responsibility for law observance and public order was allotted jointly among the households of each village. Positions of authority, carrying explicitly defined duties, were conferred on heads of prominent (i.e., wealthy and influential) families.

The system was based on a shrewd practical knowledge of those customary obligations that were most binding among Taiwanese. It was a move toward fitting the treatment of opposition to its roots instead of to its symptoms. By making the regulation of villages follow lines of kinship and property, these measures in effect were insinuated into the indigenous social structure of the population.

The rules placed a multitude of specific duties upon each *chia* as a group. The *chia*, through its head, was responsible for reporting all events such as births and deaths occurring within it, for reporting and controlling all movements of persons in and out of its area along with the conduct of the permanent residents; it put into effect the earnest health and sanitation rules that were often promulgated; it mobilized labor from its ranks for road-building and irrigation projects as directed from above; it was required to disseminate instructions for crop improvement and soil maintenance, bearing its own expenses; it supplied men for auxiliary police service, supported its own school facilities, assessed fines among its members, collected many taxes, and could be called upon to enforce additional rules decreed by prefectural governors.[11] These latter features in fact proved so attractive in avoiding the costs of more formal administration that the Japanese kept the regulations in full force throughout the entire span of their rule.

[10] Yanaihara, Tadao (1929), pp. 220-223.

[11] See OPNAV, Civil Affairs Handbook, *Takao Province* (1944), pp. 49-51; also Hsü Tzu-wei (1946), p. 160 ff. This latter author calls the *pao-chia* system "the most effective instrument for destroying organized Chinese resistance to the Japanese."

The arrangement had more than savings in the expenses of civil government to recommend it. It gave the new regime a channel of authority reaching into every village, however small. Perceiving the value of this, the Japanese took care not to let the system lapse through neglect. They kept a close watch over its functioning by means of a large and reliable force of their own police. More important, by insisting on rigorous enforcement of the regulations, they launched the *pao-chia* organization into full-scale and sustained operation from the beginning.[12] With the supervision of a trusted constabulary, it functioned through the medium of prior obligations and loyalties that were already present in every community, without the need to nurture affection for the central regime among the population.

Such a system—when it works—is a most efficient way of maintaining peace and order in a society already strongly bound by local custom. The Japanese originally adopted it as an improvement over the use of force, but never abandoned coercion in its operation. They merely utilized the structure of *pao* and *chia* to apply sanctions against wrongdoing more selectively and less frequently. Penalties fell on those persons in positions to exercise a deterrent influence on others.

As a further by-product, the refined coercive aspect helped to lessen the rewards that had to be granted for Taiwanese collaboration. This was important, for in rural areas such a form of control lends itself readily to keeping the avenues to individual betterment within an accustomed scope.[13] The impressive agricultural improve-

[12] A system like this one can function only where there are strong local solidarities. It turns communities into separate compartments for administration. This fact may be responsible for some of its success in maintaining order, for it inhibits organized opposition to established government from growing to any large scale. But the considerable success of the *pao-chia* system in Japanese hands cannot be accounted for by these divisive effects. They were also present in Nationalist and Imperial China, and there only helped to divide the society so far that no central administration was possible.

The essential difference was that in Taiwan the Japanese adopted it as an opportunity not for avoiding local government, but for effectuating central control over local affairs. Besides using it to enforce a minimum degree of legal conformity, they intermixed a host of other functions already alluded to. In addition, the Japanese incorporated a regular scheme of favors to be bestowed on active collaborators, in the nature of education, business opportunity, and appointment to government posts, and thus by-passed the usual effect of family connections in filling lower positions of authority.

[13] In later years many educated Taiwanese protested, and correctly so, that it worked as a levelling mechanism to impede all of them from rising very far above the status of peasants. In order to serve a central government at all, and not be merely a loose alliance of towns and villages, such a system must offer inducements to a gentry class for cooperation: this complaint by frustrated persons with schooling should properly be

ments, health program, and construction for public works all depended on generous amounts of labor. Without such cheap incentives to mobilize this labor, these projects could not have been pursued so effectively.

As obvious as these advantages of "indirect rule" may be, it should be as clear that it is a poor vehicle for introducing social change. The more it is used to wield authority, the stronger and more resistant to change it can become; the more it is undermined by altering local relationships that sustain it, the less remains of its usefulness. Hence, from adoption of this scheme initially as an expedient to "pacify" the island, Japanese authorities acquired a positive interest in preserving the same set of agrarian institutions that had existed in Taiwan before their arrival.

Thus they abandoned the idea of reorganizing the rural society—primarily because they tried and failed, but also because as it stood it gave them the best access to regulation of the agricultural population and farming practices. It was in some respects a ready-made instrument for exerting the necessary control with the least disturbance of customary affairs, having in the past enabled the various parties to the export trade to prosper at the expense of farmers. For better coordination of their policies, Japanese gradually did erect a more formal type of government administration, but the basis of the system in rural areas was not greatly affected by this modification.

The Impact of Improvements in Agriculture

The Japanese who were charged with remodeling Taiwan's economy gave first priority to long-range investments around the fringes of agriculture. The rural economy was already geared to exchange food and related products for special capital services. Certain of these services were soon altered under Japanese influence. Positions that provided them, or that could usurp them, gradually began to be occupied by Japanese nationals—official, private, and always an indistinct class in between that wielded quasi-official sanctions.

Those innovations that worked their way into agriculture were directed chiefly to raising crop yields per unit of tilled land. Another avenue of increasing the total agricultural product was by extending

---

construed as a lament that there were few opportunities for advancement outside the rural villages and towns dominated by petty gentry. Discontent from this source bore few signs of being the awakening of a popular movement for independence among the Taiwanese, as it is sometimes represented. See Hsü Tze-wei (1946), p. 161 ff.

the land area that yielded crops. From 34.2 per cent of all "level" land (under 500 meters elevation) in 1910, this area cultivated was raised to 43.7 per cent by 1940. The *effective* crop area was extended still further by irrigation, terracing and careful crop rotation. Irrigation converted many dry fields into paddy fields, as we found in the previous chapter. Improvement in irrigation made more of the paddy fields yield two or more crops each year (see Table 9). Evidently

TABLE 9

SPREAD OF DOUBLE-CROPPING IN IRRIGATED FIELDS, 1917 TO 1945

Area of Paddy Fields That Was Double-Cropped in Taiwan
(Thousands of Hectares)
Yearly Average in Each Period

				Per Cent Double-Cropped:	
Years	*Total Cultivated Area*	*Area in Paddy Fields*	*Area of Double-Cropped Paddy Fields*	*of Total Cultivated Area*	*of Total Paddy Area*
1917-1919	730	336	217	29.7	64.5
1920-1924	753	366	252	33.4	68.7
1925-1929	795	386	274	34.4	71.0
1930-1934	816	422	300	36.8	71.2
1935-1939	850	516	320	37.6	61.9
1940-1944	844	520	314	37.2	60.4

Sources: *Statistical Summary,* Table 196.
Ch'en Cheng-hsiang, *Land Utilization in Taiwan,* Appendix, Table 2.

much of the advance in crop production took the form of increasing the number of harvests from land already cultivated, which in Taiwan was already the "highest in the [Japanese] Empire."[14]

Land was not the only element of agriculture that was put to harder use. With a few exceptions,[15] cultivation continued to be carried on with little difference in ways of applying human labor to the land. Agricultural implements were improved, but remained similar in design; irrigation facilities opened new land, but their construction was itself labor-intensive; transplanting of rice became generally practised to save land, but it is inherently a very laborious process. One of the major problems of farmers in the Far East has long been that their work is distributed unevenly throughout the

[14] Nasu, Shiroshi (1941), p. 96.

[15] A few large-scale plantations experimented with the use of tractors in raising sugar cane.

year.[16] Double cropping fields not only uses land more intensively, but does the same for labor by spreading the intervals of greatest effort over a longer part of the year[17] (see Table 10).

TABLE 10

LABOR REQUIREMENTS FOR RICE CULTIVATION IN TAIWAN

Average Man-Hours Worked for One *Chia* of Rice*

Type of Work	*First Crop*		*Second Crop*	
	Man	*Man with Animal*	*Man*	*Man with Animal*
Seed Bed	6.3	0.8	1.9	1.4
Preparing Land	22.6	18.1	15.1	11.9
Transplanting	11.1	0.1	10.1	0.1
Fertilizing	7.1	0.9	4.0	0.1
Weeding	29.6	0.4	23.9	0.2
Irrigating	9.6	0.0	6.8	0.0
Pest & Disease Control	1.0	0.0	1.6	0.0
Making Windbreaks	0.1	0.0	1.8	0.0
Harvesting & Threshing	25.9	0.2	27.5	0.5
Total	113.2	20.5	92.7	13.1†

* Women's time was counted as 60-70 per cent of that of men, children's as 30 per cent. Figures represent averages from 36 farms, having a mean size of 1.6 *chia*. (1 *chia* = .96992 hectare) Table has no date.

† Published total does not check with sum of column.

Source: Mendiola, N. B. (1949), p. 72.

The data drawn upon thus far give no indication as to whether harder work and better techniques meant higher yields to farmers as well as to land. Fig. 9 helps in a rough way to settle the question. The number of farmers increased relatively more than the land area devoted to farms. It follows that the average gains in crop yields per person fell short of the gains in the yield of land. Fig. 9 also shows crudely the trends in the productivity of farmers, taking into account the major crops of Taiwan. They were unmistakably upward until

[16] If small-scale household farms are subject to two or three peak periods of work each year, shortages of labor tend to appear seasonally. When the seasons coincide for all or many farms, the shortages become general and cannot be met by hiring workers, since other available manpower is also in great demand. To maintain a household large enough to cope satisfactorily with this problem, the goal cherished by most peasant families is usually to bear the burden of supporting members who may not be fully occupied for the rest of the year.

[17] The net effect of double-cropping may even be to *increase* the amount of labor that goes into a given amount of output. However, some of the steps required to produce two crops where only one had been grown before are labor saving, i.e., involve the use of capital. The question of precise trends is too complicated to deal with here in these terms.

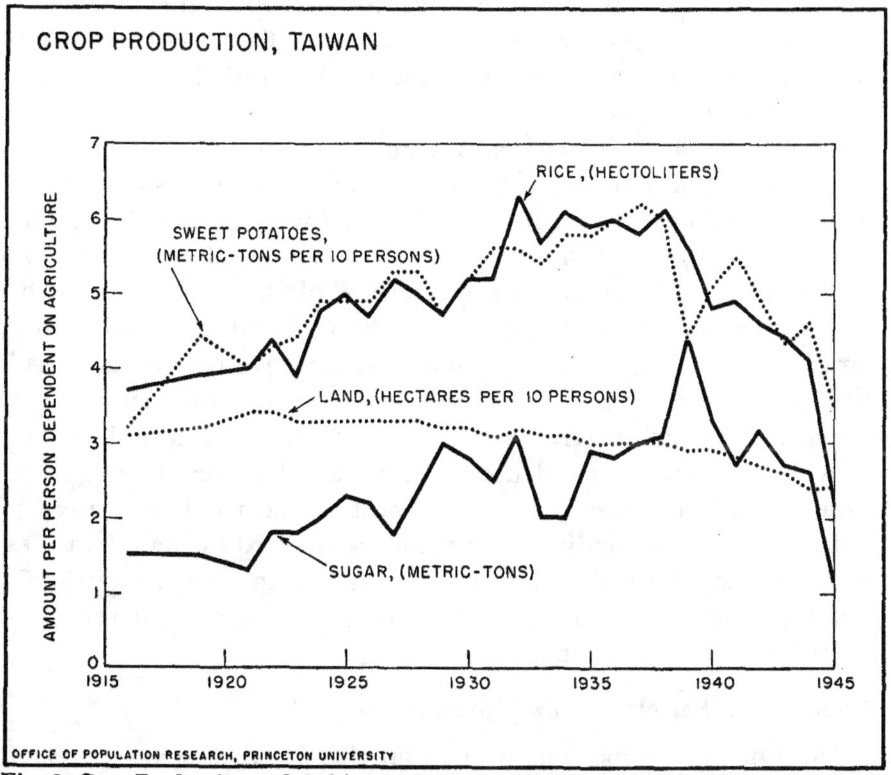

Fig. 9. Crop Production and Cultivated Land Per Person Dependent on Agriculture, Taiwan, 1916-1945.

the time of the war. But, considering the steady rise in the population dependent on agriculture, it is clear that the increased effectiveness of land use (discussed in Chapter II) did not owe so much to their colonial program as the Japanese themselves liked to believe. In part, it was merely a matter of more people working on the land.

Fig. 9 is based only on rice, sugar and sweet potatoes, and makes no allowance for the spread of some other crops during the late 1930's. In actual volume of crops produced, the product per person in agriculture therefore must have risen slightly more than the data imply. Diversification of this sort was of small benefit to most Taiwanese. Specialty crops like bananas and pineapples held a significance for the economy as a whole (they were export crops) greater than for individual farmers. Pineapples, for example, were grown entirely in plantations, and not by peasants as supplemental crops.

Trends in rice and sugar output were the trends for the rural economy as a whole; sweet potatoes are worthy of note because they have always supplied a large part of the Taiwanese diet. How well these three basic crops represent the whole of Taiwanese agriculture may be seen from their share in the total recorded value of farm produce (see Fig. 4).[18]

The spatial arrangement of crops discussed in the previous chapter has an important bearing on the question of persistence in organization of agriculture. Rice fields were found throughout the flat lowland area, overlapping in every civil division with the other types of farming. In its import for the nature of the rural society, this fact overshadows most effects of diversification and rationalization of farming. The types of social system that can give rise to paddy cultivation of rice seem to be uncommonly well equipped to resist change. They are centered around settled family relationships that provide for uninterrupted use of suitable fields over many generations. This is the case throughout most of the paddy-rice areas of Asia, where these conditions resemble what is to be found in Taiwan.[19] Hence, from this stability within farming itself, one should not expect to find that its social setting was greatly different as a result of Japanese occupation.

Changes in Pattern of Employment

Farming is so important to Taiwan that it has first been treated separately, with very little reference to its place among other activities. By viewing it in relation to the pursuits of the entire working population, we can take into account the nature of alternative opportunities outside of agriculture.

There would not be much point in looking for possibilities of non-agricultural employment if the economy could not have supported a larger proportion of people in other activities. This is where many agrarian countries have felt the effect of poverty to stand in the way of their industrial progress. From the start of its modern era, Taiwan's peculiar status as a food exporter suggests that food supply was no barrier. Since that time, special diligence in the matter made land and human effort more effective in producing crops. Advancing both of these aspects of productivity implied that at least some movement of people to pursuits outside of agriculture was economically feasible.

18 These trends, of course, indicate nothing about "well-being" of farmers, since large capital charges (for irrigation, fertilizer, and government administration) were being made against farm incomes.

19 See Taeuber, Irene B. (1947), pp. 21-43.

It is certain that Taiwan underwent some social changes under the Japanese. The colonial program itself was one, with consequences that were far-reaching. Moreover, the expansion of population and production could not have occurred without further adjustments in social institutions, for in the so-called natural environment men rarely succeed (under the most favorable conditions) in enlarging their works in exact scale. But to have left so much of the old society intact, these changes must have been distributed unevenly through the population; some portions must have been influenced more than others.

In ascertaining the facts of the case, the first step is to see how the working population became involved in new activities. The work of peasant farmers was least affected. Hence one should look for the largest results in alternative fields. The only way for specialization to have progressed very far, in view of what is known of the agricultural economy, was through the spread of employment other than farming.

Fortunately, there is reliable information to show who performed the principal economic activities at certain times. Five census enumerations were conducted with great concern for determining the occupational composition of the population. In four of these, up to 1930, tables were published classifying the people in detail according to occupation and other characteristics, using categories that are nearly if not exactly comparable from year to year.[20] The proportions of all working persons found among various classes of occupations have been assembled from these sources in Table 11. In 1940, the same information was collected and tabulated, but not published with full explanation of procedures; only the one table reproduced here has become available outside of Taiwan.*

Even as early as 1905 not everyone in the island was restricted to agriculture as a means of support. Slightly more than two-thirds of all persons with occupation were so engaged, with a group half as large remaining to be accounted for in other pursuits. These data

[20] Where the classification departed from previous practice, continuity can be preserved in broad groups of occupations by re-allocating occupations in the smaller groupings. Where such re-grouping has been possible, it will be appropriately noted in the text. Later, in cross-tabulations with other characteristics, the broadest categories often must be used as they stand.

* While this book was in press, a collection of tables from the census of 1940 was published in Taiwan. See *Results of the Seventh Population Census of Taiwan, 1940* (Taipei, Provincial Government of Taiwan, Bureau of Accounting and Statistics, March 1953).

TABLE 11

OCCUPATIONAL COMPOSITION, TOTAL POPULATION OF TAIWAN

Per Cents of All Occupied Persons Reported in Each Occupation,* 1905, 1930, and 1940. All Ethnic Groups, Both Sexes

Occupation†	*1905*	*1930*	*1940*
Agriculture‡	71.2	68.2	64.6
Fishing	2.2	1.8	5.4
Mining	0.5	1.4	1.9
Manufacturing	6.2	8.5	7.6
Commerce	6.7	12.0	10.0
Transportation	2.1	3.0	2.7
Gov't. and Prof.	2.3	4.9	5.1
Other	8.8	0.2	2.7
Total Occupied	100.0	100.0	100.0
Per Cent Occupied	45.8	38.8	37.6

* Persons classified as Domestic Servants have been removed.

† The data used in this table to represent the years 1930 and 1940 are not of precisely the same sort as those showing the occupational distribution of the population in other tables. The scheme for classifying occupations was greatly changed between the censuses of 1930 and 1940; as a result, the only basis for comparison between these two dates is the classification according to "Industry," of which the main categories remained the same. Hence the figures in Column 2 and Column 3 of this table represent the distribution of occupied persons by the "Industries" in which they worked, and not by their "Occupations."

‡ In all of these tables of employed persons, unless specified to the contrary, the category "Agriculture" includes "Forestry."

Sources: *Census of 1905, General Volume,* Table 45.
Census of 1930, Statistical Tables, Table 28.
Ch'en Cheng-hsiang, *Land Utilization in Taiwan* (1950), p. 62.

bear out the evidence of history during Manchu times, to the effect that a good many people had already been occupied in services connected with exporting and marketing primary produce.

Observations in 1905 cannot, of course, perfectly represent conditions ten years earlier—some Japanese were present in the statistics, and their influence in the economy was beginning to be felt. But these early census materials offer the closest approach to the pre-Japanese period that is possible. They depict a situation that must have been very similar to that of the final years of Chinese rule in Taiwan.

Table 11 summarizes the effects of major shifts in occupation throughout the entire working population, reaching to the eve of World War II. Though only an abbreviated picture, it belies any suggestion that the organization of livelihood in general had been profoundly altered under the Japanese. But any discussion of the problem very soon outruns crude data like these. Though Table 11 is comprehensive, covering all groups in the population, it lumps together people of too many kinds, and thereby hides many significant types of variation. The same material can be used more efficiently when refined by some of the controls at our disposal.

In the first place, not everyone in the population was equally well reported as to occupation. Asia being even more than the West a man's world, occupational data do not mean the same thing for males and females. Women are barred from many occupations and, whatever their duties, are not readily regarded in society as having regular employment. Whether a woman in Taiwan reported herself as being employed or not often depended on other attributes of her social position more than on the actual tasks performed—for example, whether she had yet been married, whether widowed or divorced, what work was followed by other members of her family, or simply local custom governing attitudes toward the work of women. For reasons that will be elaborated in the following chapter, we shall henceforth separate females from males in all occupational tables, under the assumption that the working activities of males more accurately reflect the composition of employment in the economy.

Omitting females from Table 12 has the effect of correcting the inflated appearance that they give to agriculture, especially in the earlier years. With this more meaningful series of observations, it is striking not merely that activities were so diversified in the beginning, but that they changed so little. In the 35 years that followed this first general census the structure of occupations among men remained about the same. By this more adequate criterion, agriculture lost almost no ground as a field of employment after 1905. Still nearly two-thirds of all working men were farmers as late as 1930, the terminal date for these figures. From Table 11 it is clear that the same thing must have been true in 1940.

And so, even including the Japanese, those who were caught up in the "industrialization" made up a minor part of all males in Taiwan. Demographically, this cardinal aspect of "economic development" was never anything but a small-scale operation.

Obviously, Table 11 and Table 12 cannot bring to light the full extent of trends accompanying events over this period. These figures indicate only shifts from one broad type of activity to another. They

TABLE 12

OCCUPATIONAL COMPOSITION OF WORKING MALES IN TAIWAN
TOTAL, ALL ETHNIC GROUPS

Per Cents of Occupied Males Reported in Each Occupation, 1905, 1920, and 1930*

Occupation	*1905*	*1920*	*1930*
Agriculture	67.7	64.3	63.1
Fishing	2.7	2.2	2.0
Mining	.6	1.5	1.3
Manufacturing	6.2	9.5	8.9
Commerce	7.8	8.3	10.9
Transportation	2.7	3.9	4.5
Gov't. & Prof.	2.8	4.1	5.1
Other	9.5	6.2	4.2
Total Occupied	100.0	100.0	100.0
Percent of Males Occupied	67.2	62.4	58.2

* Domestic servants have been excluded.
Source: Data of Table 16.

make no allowance for a more subtle kind of change—differences evolving within these groups of occupations.

These variations may take two forms. One consists of movement among the positions that comprise each broader group. This disturbance in the framework of positions can be taken as a result of innovations that actually altered the organization of work. It was noteworthy only in those lines where Japanese took a direct hand (see Table 13, below). Where it involved changes across the boundaries of the occupational groups tabulated in Table 12, the effects appear as occupational shifts from one census to the next. These one would expect to arise from such sources as the drawing of sugar workers from old into modern mills; from the wider shift toward factory work within the generic scope of "manufacturing"; the adjustment of commerce to the newer export industries; or the replacing of archaic transport or banking enterprises with wage-earning employees of Japanese concerns—though only a portion can be detected through the broad categories that we have used.

These differences also took a second form that cannot be conveyed in terms of the distribution of working activities. Many new skills were introduced within the existing arrangement or organization of work. The agricultural program was achieved primarily through this unobtrusive path, along with many of the spectacular improvements in productivity in other fields.[21] This form is the more elusive one to deal with, for it did not of itself produce shifts in employment. At the same time, the dimensions of economic achievement in Taiwan were too large to have been confined to the limits of occupational change shown in Table 12, unless they depended heavily on this second channel.

TABLE 13

RELATIVE GROWTH OF EMPLOYMENT IN DIFFERENT LINES
TOTAL POPULATION, ALL ETHNIC GROUPS

Occupation	*Ratios of Males Employed in 1930 to Those in 1905, by Occupation*
Agriculture	1.18
Fishing	.94
Mining	2.68
Manufacturing	1.81
Commerce	1.78
Gov't. & Prof.	2.28
Transportation, etc.	2.26
Other	.56
Total, All Occupations	1.27
Total Males	1.46

Sources: *Census of 1905, General Volume*, Table 45.
Census of 1930, Statistical Tables, Table 28.

Comparing the occupational structure at successive points of time is not the best measure of change. In some respects a better one is to indicate how the different lines of employment shared in the outstanding demographic trend, the growth of population. With 1905 as a base, the relative increase for each occupational stratum expresses more clearly the strides that were being made outside of agriculture (see Table 13).

These results would have been far different if none of the social changes under colonial rule had occurred—if, for example, the original situation had been fully stable, in the sense of being able to reproduce itself indefinitely, with no interference from outside or within save the single effect of population growth. (It is, of course,

[21] The two approaches were not independent. For example, introducing the use of fertilizers on a wide scale did not appreciably interfere with the management of peasant farms; but it did stimulate a lively business in supplying commercial fertilizer materials. The important point is that the two types of effect often fell in different places—in this case, the fertilizer trade went chiefly to Japanese importers.

nothing more than a hypothetical exercise to assume this course of events, since population growth itself presupposes some conditions that had not been present before.) Under these assumptions, presumably each occupational stratum would have received an equal share of the increase, and the ratios of expansion for all would have been identical. The fact that they grew so unevenly illustrates that the actual events departed considerably from this imaginary sequence.

Several conditions would be required in order to maintain this hypothetical stability. People would need to follow well-accepted rules in adopting occupations, customs that would impede any widespread transfers by individuals from one kind of work to another. Chinese have for centuries come close to this result by passing many types of work down from fathers to sons. In Taiwan, keeping the various lines of work in balance would have implied a close adherence to such traditions by most of the population, as it did in the past. In effect, the unequal ratios of increase between occupations meant that many men who would have become farmers did not, but entered some alternative employment instead.[22]

Table 13 also indicates which occupations were most affected. Employment expanded rapidly in some of the fields where Japanese capital was prominent. These were also the fields that employed technical specialists and made the least use of the traditional fund of skills existing among the Taiwanese. Growth in these lines did not necessarily broaden employment opportunities for Taiwanese. There were in all 26.6 per cent more occupied males in Taiwan in 1930 than in 1905,[23] but 2.3 times as many in professional and administrative positions and in occupations connected with transportation, 81 per cent and 78 per cent more in manufacturing and commerce respectively. The farming segment in the population lagged slightly behind the total of employed men; but it was so large initially that it could relinquish large numbers of actual or potential members to other occupations before showing signs of the loss.[24]

[22] This aspect of occupational transfers will be taken up in some detail in the next chapter.

[23] This ratio is less than the increase in the general population, because changes in the age composition over this period raised the proportions of children and aged persons in the total. The proportions of men occupied in the prime working ages—15 to 64—remained practically the same.

[24] Losses from agriculture did not supply all of the additional employment in the expanding fields. The group "Other Occupations" was the source of almost the same portion of the inequalities in these figures. Being a catch-all, this category is always a weak spot in occupational statistics. In Taiwan it was made up chiefly of "day laborers,"

These ratios measure how far each occupation increased irrespective of its size in relation to others at the start. Table 13 therefore expresses the force of events on each occupation, and not the force of occupational changes in the economy. This being the case, they should not all be given equal weight. The development of mining, by this criterion, exceeded any of the other fields. Though truly a creation of Japanese exploration and investment, the mining industry in Taiwan never reached any substantial size, and does not merit special attention as a field of employment.

Lacking detailed evidence for the period following 1930, some conjecture is needed. Official sources and more recent descriptive materials in English are unreliable, since they invariably exaggerate the extent of Japanese achievement. We have certain data, however, to suggest the dimensions of expansion in demographic terms. While Japanese planners tried to raise production in all lines, they concentrated on a few specific items that were especially important to Japan. They paid most attention to enlarging factory facilities for the processing of primary products. Hence, it should be possible to detect some of this flurry of new activity in the numbers of people working in factories.

Statistics of factory employment in Taiwan were begun in 1914, and published each year ending in 1941. They fell far short of being perfect indicators, being subject to many kinds of inaccuracy that a census enumeration can easily avoid.[25] Nevertheless as a series of observations they furnish very useful results. The rise of factory employment may be compared with growth in the total population in Fig. 10, where the numbers of persons employed in "factories" from year to year are plotted on a logarithmic scale. The growth in total population and in agricultural population is also shown, in hundreds of persons.

Factory employment rose steadily from the beginning to the end

---

not otherwise classified. Its decline represented some actual movement of workers and new recruits into new jobs, and in part merely assigning of new names to the same work. This circumstance tends to magnify the difference between agriculture and other occupations, but does not otherwise distort the picture shown in Table 13.

[25] They apparently paralleled the corresponding figures for Japan in covering all factories with more than five workers. They were published without explanation of standards or procedures, which were less rigorous than those used in the censuses. It is not specified whether factory workers were full or part-time workers; they are not shown separately by ethnic affiliation; their numbers must have increased (independently of any change in actual employment) by the adding of new enterprises to the reporting system; and their actual duties are not given.

of this period. There were only two departures from this growth—the prosperous days of 1920 and 1929 and their aftermaths. Overlooking these brief deviations from the trend, the average rate of growth from 1918 until 1935 was *no greater than that of the total population.* Only in 1936 did the force of economic expansion reach the population to the extent of diffusing factory work more widely through it.

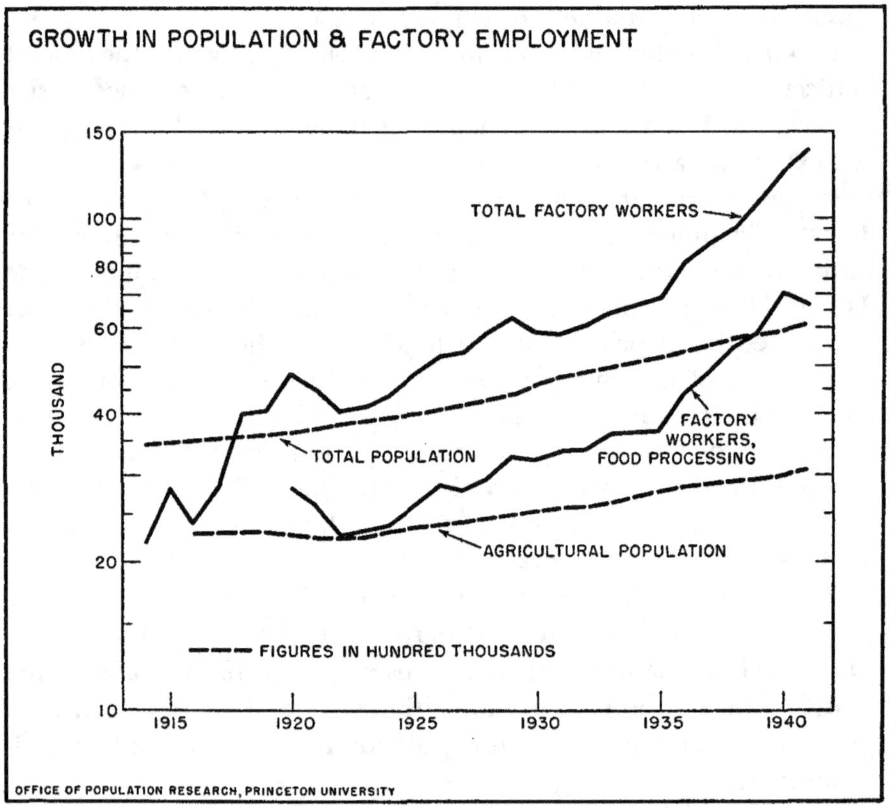

Fig. 10. Increase of Factory Employment and of Population in Taiwan, 1914-1941.

The largest part of the total (about 55 per cent) was made up of workers in sugar mills (see Fig. 10). The sugar industry kept its priority in the later economic planning. It serves as a reminder that the expansion of production continued to be dominated by this single industry, systematically nurtured and expanded as a source of alcohol for Japan.

The evidence for the spread of factory work can be supplemented by the annual registry of agricultural population (i.e., members of families dependent on agriculture).[26] The two major spurts in factory employment occurred during the first World War and just preceding the second. These were the only two periods of substantial slackening in gradual increments of farm population to the point of actual decline in the early 1920's. After 1940 this portion of the population resumed its usual rate of growth, suggesting that the opportunities for shifting the balance of employment had begun to disappear.

Occupational Shifts: Taiwanese and Japanese

The data up to this point illustrate some of the redeployment of manpower in the economy. They give no basis for considering the social changes that were responsible, for they do not disclose who were the participants. To understand how manpower responds to altered environmental conditions, one must know some of the affiliations that have shaped its members' decisions. Moreover, "economic development" is of no great interest here for its own sake, but rather for the nature of its reception and use by peoples not yet under its full influence. Therefore the Taiwanese are the important group to observe, and in a different sense the Japanese in their role of aliens on the scene.

Most of the apparent diversification in economic activities shown in Table 12 did not consist of movements in the Taiwanese population at all. It reflected primarily the special characteristics of Japanese in Taiwan. Though never more than one-twentieth of the total population, their nationals were so concentrated in certain special positions that they often outnumbered Taiwanese. Once this special group is removed (Table 14), Taiwanese appear to have contributed only a small amount to the total occupational shifts up to 1930. Separated from the presence of Japanese in these key posts, the part of Taiwanese in the modernized sectors of the economy was indeed a modest one.

[26] The total population and agricultural population have been reduced to one-hundredth of their size to fit into Fig. 10. They can consequently be used to show more than merely relative trends. Where either one intersects a trend line for factory employees, the ratio of the latter to the former is 1:100, or 1 per cent. (Of course, the scale being logarithmic, the same relation does not hold between points separated by larger intervals.) This circumstance helps to point out how small the total amount of work in factories was in relation to the entire population. At its peak, judged by these figures, it occupied less than 3 per cent of the population. It remained under 2 per cent for most of this period.

TABLE 14

OCCUPATIONAL COMPOSITION OF TAIWANESE
Per Cents of Occupied Males Reported in Each Occupation,*
1905, 1920 and 1930

Occupation	*1905*	*1920*	*1930*
Agriculture	69.9	68.9	68.0
Fishing	2.8	2.2	2.1
Mining	0.5	1.4	1.3
Manufacturing	5.6	7.9	7.6
Commerce	7.4	7.6	10.2
Transportation, etc.	2.2	3.2	3.9
Gov't. & Prof.	1.8	2.2	2.7
Other	9.8	6.6	4.2
Total Occupied	100.0	100.0	100.0
Per Cent of Males Occupied	66.7	61.8	57.7

* Domestic servants have been excluded. Occupations are adjusted in 1905 and 1920 to be comparable with 1930.
Source: Data of Table 16.

As for the Japanese, most who were old enough to work had been born in the Home Islands. All of these had arrived in Taiwan as a result of some decision to move, and presumably had some purpose in being there. Theirs was a highly selective migration. It brought in the promoters and technicians, the industrialists and clerical personnel, the officials and minor functionaries to operate this first colonial venture. As in most colonies, they enjoyed facilities and perquisites of a superior type—better, if not to conditions generally prevailing in the home country, at least to the standards that they as individuals could have expected at home.[27]

Much of the migration was coordinated with economic policy.[28]

[27] On top of better vocational opportunities, Japanese commonly received special bonuses for service in Taiwan. Rates of pay for comparable wage labor in Taiwan were consistently higher for Japanese (see *Statistical Summary*, Tables 301-303).

[28] This had not always been the case. For most of the first decade after 1895, Japanese were permitted to go to Taiwan with little restriction. The freedom attracted an "undesirable" element to the island, whose business activities were so unbridled and uncoordinated as to call forth a stricter government policy to deal with incoming personnel. Japanese looked back from the later ordered development on this early chaotic period with horror. The unsatisfactory results of laissez-faire may also have contributed to the decision to centralize the most profitable opportunities in state hands. Through official monopolies in the major export lines, it was possible to regulate continuously the conduct of Japanese businessmen as well as to make substantial levies in these enterprises for revenue.

Japanese drew lessons from the colonial experience of European powers in supplying the special skills and competencies that their program required. Government and private industry recruited their personnel from Japan, according to needs which they determined in advance. In one respect they learned the lessons of staffing their technical positions better than their teachers: they paid more attention to procuring lower levels of skills from their own ranks along with filling the top functions. Important implemental positions, like police, railroad technicians, and maintenance men, were heavily staffed with Japanese.

All Japanese nationals, regardless of whether specially recruited or not, were favored over Taiwanese when employed by Japanese concerns.[29] The best openings were in professional and official positions, as administrators in government and finance. Less coveted, but still bearing prestige over Taiwanese counterparts, were the jobs of technical and skilled workers in transportation and industry, and petty officials in the government bureaucracy. In every census Japanese appeared consistently in these occupations (see Table 15).

As a group, they were conspicuous in staying out of agriculture,

TABLE 15

OCCUPATIONAL COMPOSITION OF JAPANESE IN TAIWAN

Per Cents of Occupied Males Reported in Each Occupation,* 1905, 1920 and 1930

Occupation	*1905*	*1920*	*1930*
Agriculture	1.0	4.4	4.6
Fishing	0.6	2.0	2.1
Mining	5.0	1.9	0.5
Manufacturing	20.6	27.4	18.2
Commerce	16.5	15.0	14.6
Transportation, etc.	13.9	11.7	11.0
Gov't. & Prof.	41.3	37.2	45.6
Other	1.1	0.4	3.4
Total Occupied	100.0	100.0	100.0
Per Cent of Males Occupied	80.4	69.0	60.8

* Domestic servants have been excluded. Occupations are adjusted in 1905 and 1920 to be comparable with 1930.

Source: Data of Table 16.

29 Notwithstanding, the colony had its failures. The census reports list a scattering of Japanese as day laborers, ricksha pullers, longshoremen, and in similar occupations.

despite the fact that most were engaged in some capacity in helping the passage of farm products to Japan. Japan made almost no use of Taiwan as an outlet for its own growing agricultural population. From time to time the authorities announced projects for settling farmers from the Home Islands. These plans may have been designed to make a favorable impression among government circles in Japan itself; none ever proved feasible in Taiwan. Only a few thousand "colonists" of this type came to Taiwan and made a start in farming. In spite of manifold blessings of official support, subsidies, and special privileges, the settlements never managed to prosper. The families often left the countryside for better employment in towns and cities, and during the 1930's the whole idea was abandoned.[30]

Taiwan's economy was thus organized not only to export its narrow range of commodities to Japan, but to import its basic specialized skills in the persons of Japanese migrants. For the authorities this was an easy answer to the problem of staffing essential functions with people of appropriate training and experience. It avoided, among other things, the need to devise means for securing them from the human resources at hand in Taiwan. From the standpoint of Japan it was not an efficient solution. It drew upon types of manpower that the Japanese at home could not well afford to lose, and at the same time failed to make the best use of talents existing among the Taiwanese.[31] This anomaly in distribution of skills between the two areas is illustrated in Fig. 11. Japanese residents in Taiwan were a highly selected group even for Japan itself, where technical abilities were also scarce.

Possession of an external source of supply for specialized skills had

[30] Yanaihara, Tadao (1929), pp. 174-175, notes that it was already a failure before 1930.

[31] The founding of Taihoku Imperial University was an outstanding example of this policy. It was an institution of high caliber, well equipped and operated by men of repute in Japan. The University notably did *not* engage in training any considerable number of technical personnel among Taiwanese. It was organized to promote research rather than teaching, its classes were small, and Taiwanese students were not readily admitted. See Kerr, George H. (1942), p. 53 ff.

On a more practical plane, several technical schools were later established for limited training of Taiwanese. These, to use the common expression of educators in this country, were "vocational" rather than "professional" in that they taught manual instead of liberal skills. Enlargement of educational facilities came too late to provide the technical training needed for the war effort, though it did serve to advance literacy (in the Japanese language) among Taiwanese youth (see *Census of 1930, Statistical Tables*, Table 81). Once started, the spread of educational facilities made considerable headway. By 1943, 70 per cent of Taiwanese children of legal school age were attending some sort of school. In time this more liberal turn of policy might have paved the way for admitting Taiwanese into more responsible positions in the island's new industrial program.

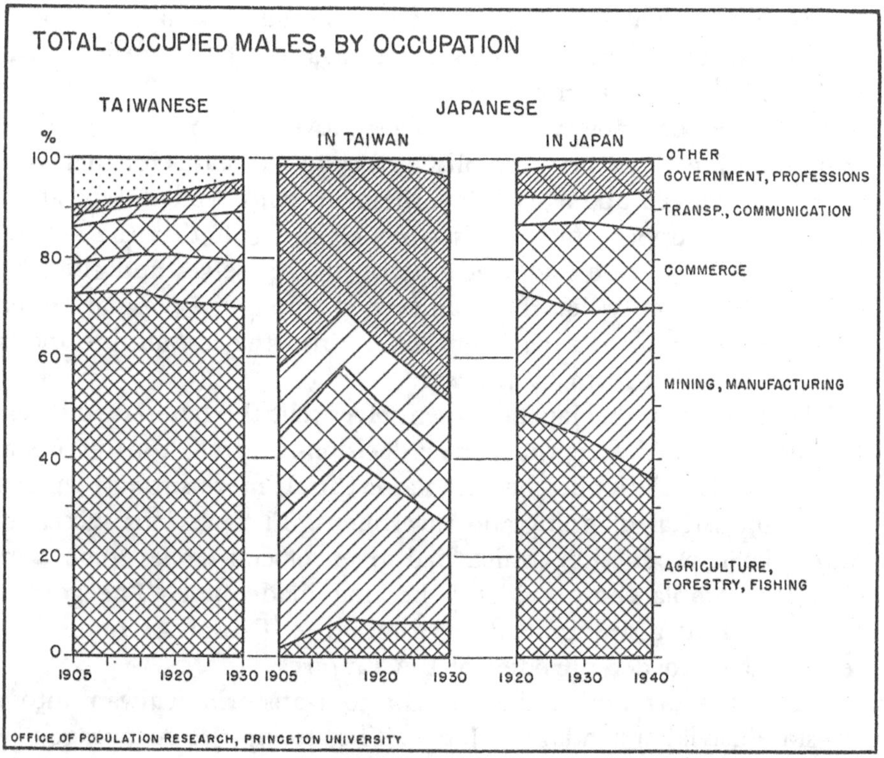

Fig. 11. Trends in Occupations in Taiwan and Japan, 1905-1940.

certain cogent advantages. The alien status of Japanese nationals was useful in keeping high standards of responsibility and performance among members of the public and private bureaucracies. This personnel could be interposed to administer Taiwanese affairs without becoming susceptible to local pressures. Though the Japanese had gained access to the rural society by manipulating its traditional institutions, they had to guard against subversion of their administration by influence from the Taiwanese side.

They did not succeed, as no large organization has, in making their officials completely disinterested and honest. There were scandals and reports of self-enrichment on the part of several of their highly-placed nationals. When it came to collusion with Taiwanese, however, they were all but incorruptible. The instances of improbity that achieved publicity in Taiwan were mostly between government and business interests. Irregularities of this sort did not threaten the objectives of the regime, for these parties had more at stake together than at issue in the economic expansion. Much of what was lost in this wasteful scheme of recruiting from abroad therefore must have been regained in the form of security against the conservative influence of tradition from within.

In one respect, however, this policy proved to be an unqualified loss to the Japanese. They established a caste-like status for their own nationals, hedged about with favoritism in employment, education, and business opportunity. This widened the gulf that the general severity of their rule had made between themselves and the Taiwanese. The enmity that they had earned among the population left them unprepared to bring it effectively into the last-minute industrial effort called forth by the war.[32]

We know from the Japanese themselves that the latter 1930's were for them years of exceptional new decisions and vigorous efforts at expansion. Official policy began to assert itself more strongly in matters of industrial planning and investment. The previous success in aiding farm production, which had given official circles some occasion for complacency, suddenly became inadequate. The government began at a strenuous pace to mobilize Taiwan's economy for serving the broader purposes of the Empire.

On very short notice they sought to transform Taiwan into a quasi-industrial appendage of Japan. The attempts to encourage new aptitudes and incentives among Taiwanese are as interesting to contemplate, in terms of their implications for manpower, as were the attempts to prevent this very development. The two objectives are of course incompatible, but they were fostered side by side by the Japanese under the stress of preparing for war. Yet by 1940, at the peak of all this energy, the portion of the working population employed outside of agriculture was scarcely greater than at earlier census dates—still only one-third, and this figure includes an undetermined number of Japanese residents (see Table 11). Only a tiny fraction of the people in Taiwan had taken up factory employment, and many of these were also Japanese. We are left with the conclusion that Japanese colonial policies and indigenous tradition had combined to restrict social change within a small segment of the population. Japanese comprised most of this segment. New activities were spread thinly among Taiwanese, and left the remainder engaged in the same pursuits as their ancestors for countless generations.

[32] During the quickened prewar mobilization of their resources in Taiwan, despite the crowded condition of agriculture, Japanese businessmen actually complained of a *shortage* of labor in industry.

TABLE 16

Taiwan: Total Males, and Males with Occupation Distributed by Occupation, at Census Dates, 1905 to 1930. Total All Groups, Taiwanese, Japanese, and Others*

Occupation	*1930*	*1920*	*1915*	*1905*
TOTAL MALES				
Occupied	1,369,877	1,180,842	1,155,777	1,081,667
Agr. and Forestry	864,884	761,047	776,181	731,473
Fishing (Excl. Salt)	27,709	25,858	26,911	29,465
Mining	18,345	17,240	9,741	6,843
Manufacturing	122,066	112,063	94,338	67,526
Commerce	148,847	97,726	93,171	83,815
Transportation	61,323	45,645	38,901	29,138
Gov't. and Prof.	69,644	48,018	34,737	30,568
Other	57,059	73,245	81,797	102,839
TAIWANESE MALES				
Occupied	1,265,185	1,100,297	1,088,199	1,045,667
Agr. and Forestry	860,613	757,917	772,437	731,102
Fishing (Excl. Salt)	25,916	24,261	26,150	29,260
Mining	16,970	15,629	8,319	5,203
Manufacturing	95,832	87,314	72,444	58,833
Commerce	129,372	83,600	79,823	77,060
Transportation	48,677	35,428	29,505	23,186
Gov't. and Prof.	34,260	23,811	19,177	18,923
Other	53,545	72,337	80,344	102,100
JAPANESE MALES				
Occupied	75,812	63,853	53,403	27,835
Agr. and Forestry	3,474	2,815	3,430	285
Fishing (Excl. Salt)	1,617	1,310	611	170
Mining	411	1,187	1,113	1,380
Manufacturing	13,796	17,530	16,482	5,739
Commerce	11,043	9,567	9,498	4,592
Transportation	8,360	7,466	6,273	3,871
Gov't. and Prof.	34,511	23,751	15,328	11,502
Other	2,600	227	668	296
OTHER MALES				
Occupied	28,880	16,629	14,169	8,165
Agr. and Forestry	797	315	312	86
Fishing (Excl. Salt)	176	280	150	35
Mining	964	424	309	260

TABLE 16 (continued)

Occupation	*1930*	*1920*	*1915*	*1905*
Manufacturing	12,438	7,209	5,410	2,954
Commerce	8,432	4,538	3,849	2,163
Transportation	4,286	2,727	3,122	2,081
Gov't. and Prof.	873	455	232	143
Other	914	681	785	443

* For comparability, Domestic servants are excluded at all dates; Ceramics workers are assigned to Manufacturing in 1905 and 1915; Salt workers are assigned to Manufacturing from Fishing in 1905, 1915, and 1920.

Sources: *Census of 1905, General Volume*, Table 25.
Census of 1915, Statistical Tables, Table 66.
Census of 1920, Descriptive Report, Appendix, Tables 51 and 52.
Census of 1930, Statistical Tables, Total Island, Tables 45 and 46.

CHAPTER IV

The Disposition of Manpower

THE human side of livelihood in the countries of Asia understandably attracts serious attention. For many years both Westerners and Asians have displayed increasing interest in the tedium of work in this portion of the world. Human labor under these conditions has variously been held the object of pity for its drudgery, praise for its industriousness, impatience for its low productivity, and admiration for the contentment it sometimes fosters and for its integration with cultural traditions.

Such impressions are not always a help in gaining a disinterested and factual grasp of the problem. They often are based on sentiment or feeling more than on actuality. Few of the commentators on the lot of the Asian peasant have ever come into contact with it at first hand, which may help to account for the diversity of views on the subject. Yet underlying all of them is a certain foundation of fact. No one will deny that work in these parts of the world is normally toilsome and arduous. It is, by our standards, conducted with such a lack of advantage from effective instruments that prodigious amounts of labor must be expended simply to keep alive. In addition, as compared with industrial societies, a person's usual work is more firmly imbedded in the social position that he occupies, which in turn may bear less relation to the income that he gains or the commodity that he produces.

No single project could properly cover all of these aspects of livelihood. For Taiwan the advantages of the data that exist lie in adopting a demographic view of work and discovering how laboring activities are distributed through the population. This approach does not enable us to answer all of the questions that usually arise about economic activities and their setting, but we can move from it to a more adequate conception of the connections between livelihood and the social structure. This point of view was introduced in the previous chapter in order to fill out the one-sided picture that resulted from taking Japanese policy at face value and surveying the economy through its specialized corporate structures. Since the body of facts to be covered was large, the evidence of the occupational statistics has up to this point been treated cursorily.

Economic activity is usually approached in demographic analysis by drawing attention first to the portion of a population that is involved. This group may be designated as manpower, or, more ambitiously, as the "labor force." It consists of those persons whom the influence of customary rules, the demand for labor in the economy, and expectations of others have induced to work for a living. In this chapter we shall take up some problems of determining the nature and size of this group in a population such as that of Taiwan, and to discover in greater detail some of the patterns that existed in its composition. Since this inquiry is also a means to observe the institutional environment of work, we shall be concerned only with the people whose society is reflected in these patterns, the Taiwanese.

The Nature of the Labor Force

By itself, the statement that the labor force is supposed to include people who work as distinct from others is not very useful. It is like knowing that humankind is composed of good- and bad-tempered persons—neither proposition gives any basis for assigning people to one class or the other. To classify a universe of individuals by any such principle requires a set of criteria for judging what activities should count as "work," and what degree of performance is necessary to qualify a person as being fully employed.

The first problem in specifying these criteria is a conceptual one: what purpose is the distinction intended to serve? This purpose may be to ascertain the usual state of affairs in a society where conditions of livelihood are relatively stable. One can expect that most of the population holds some employment status that is recognized in well-established usage. In this class the census procedure most likely to succeed is one that elicits a statement of the activities most commonly engaged in, according to this usage. Placing many arbitrary barriers in the way of such a response, like special rules for weighing levels of wages or exact units of working time, probably does not make the answers more precise. Such considerations may even obstruct the purpose by calling for facts that are irrelevant to the situation.[1]

On the other hand, the classification may be designed as a basis for estimating the volume of employment at a particular time (or of "unemployment," in the sense of people not working who would if they could), mobility between different types of labor, or short-term

[1] cf. United Nations, Population Division and Statistical Office. *Studies of Census Methods*, No. 4 (1948), pp. 14-38.

fluctuations in employment. If employment is to be regarded in this way, it needs a set of criteria that are more complex, more sensitive to particular circumstances, and better oriented to the activities of people at a given moment.

Census Procedures in Taiwan for Determining the Working Population

Even if the conceptual questions can be settled, there remains a group of procedural ones. Since information which might be used to measure the size of the labor force must cover the entire population, it is ordinarily secured as part of a general census enumeration. Consequently most of the issues in collecting such materials are encountered in connection with census administration, and they have usually been dealt with by official organs charged with managing a census. Until very recently, it has been in this procedural realm that most attention has been given to labor force measurement—how to establish definitions, etc.

In actual experience, some of these criteria of working status have always been incorporated into census data that are already collected and published. They are beyond the control of the persons who make use of the materials, who are as a rule not the same ones who gathered and compiled them. Most of them must be accepted as they are, save for slight alterations (like shifting or combining certain categories) which may or may not aid in comparing data from different sources. Often the best that can be done is to scrutinize carefully the standards that were used in any given instance, and to make whatever allowance is possible for peculiarities that may exist from case to case.

In Taiwan, where census practices in Japan were followed,[2] the first of the two concepts of employment was used with little variation from census to census. Some specific entry as to "principal occupation" or customary activity was required of each individual. This left it up to each person or household head to decide whether he held an occupation; if so, he was supposed to specify the usual activities that he actually performed, as distinct from the part of the economy in which the work was carried on.[3] The information was compiled

[2] The enumerations of 1905 and 1915 in Taiwan had been planned likewise to synchronize with Japan in every major respect, but were carried out actually without the intended counterparts in Japan Proper.

[3] That is, in the current census usage of the terms, the enumerations were "occupational" rather than "industrial." The compilation of occupational titles before 1930,

in detail, and transmitted to the central office, where it was reduced to groups of occupations by clerks. Here strict instructions were issued to ensure that the procedure of classification was uniform and consistent.[4]

The authorities were anxious to impress the outside world and their own superiors in Tokyo with their efficiency as a colonial government, and spared little trouble to prepare census reports that were documents of their competence. Thanks to elaborate and often exaggerated care in these matters, there is some possibility of checking on the modes of allocating people among groups of occupations. Every occupational census was published with at least one detailed tabulation showing the separate occupations of which the broader categories were composed. In 1905, for example, the census recognized 178 specific occupations. The number rose in the revised lists that appeared in later censuses, until some 376 were taken into account by 1930.[5] In fact, the zeal to gain stature for their work alongside the most modern Western enumerations carried Japanese census authorities still further. They prepared comprehensive glossaries of occupational titles to standardize the content of all categories that were tabulated. These translations contained up to several thousand names of occupations current in different dialects, and reconciled local usages with each other and with their conventional equivalents in Japanese.

It is not so clear how persons who had occupations were distin-

---

while designed to classify occupational roles as such, tended to group together many persons with different functions who worked in certain lines. For example, workers in retail stores selling a particular article, regardless of whether they were owners, hired sales persons, peddlers, or simply helpers, were often placed in a single group. The census of 1930 included a stricter classification of occupations, and introduced for the first time in Taiwan a separate "industrial" tabulation of occupied persons. With one or two exceptions explicitly noted, the former of these will be used throughout this study. It is the most nearly comparable from one time to another, and provides a more useful type of information for our purposes.

[4] For a short account of the administration of these measures in Japan in 1920 and 1930, see Taeuber, Irene B., and Beal, Edwin G., Jr. (1946), pp. 9-15. The execution of the census of 1905 is described in more detail in a descriptive report translated into English as *The Special Population Census of Formosa, 1905* ([Taiwan], Government of Formosa, Tokyo, 1909).

[5] The number of occupations included in any of these lists is in itself an important detail. Very likely the systems of classification were developed beyond the degree of specialization in the economy itself. This is especially true in the later years, for the occupational scheme was devised for use in Japan and transported bodily to Taiwan as part of the policy of coordinating their census practices. While useful in locating certain specific types of activities, these minutiae are relevant chiefly as evidence of the meticulous attention to detail in the compilation of the materials.

guished from those who did not. There were few rules covering this point. Once a person reported some employment on his census schedule, he could be assigned to an occupational class very simply by the central coding staff. But it was not easy, in terms of a "customary occupation," to control the basis on which a person might decide whether he was employed at all. The criteria for making this distinction ultimately rested on prevailing social standards of what constituted employment.

No society is lacking in definition of its own of what is useful and what is not, though the particular objects of such evaluations may vary widely from place to place. But as surely as standards of usefulness are universal among different peoples, census agencies likewise will inevitably tamper with them in the course of their duties. There is some practical necessity for this. These cultural definitions are not often explicitly formulated, nor are they consistent for all individuals in a society. Both clarity and uniformity need to be stressed in an occupational census, and so certain conventional rules are always established. The virtue of a notion such as "customary" occupation in use—and its greatest weakness—is that it serves well with little overt supervision. Hence, while an occupational inventory along these lines can be a simple matter, some of its basic categories are necessarily indistinct.

This type of inexactitude creates "fringes" of employment, especially among groups of people who are just entering or retiring from the labor force. Here are found the individuals whose exact occupational status would have to be decided on more explicit standards if all entries were to be made consistent. Customary occupations are generally suspected of being *inflated*, of retaining people who are temporarily out of work or who have retired from active work.[6]

The only procedure that census officials in Taiwan adopted to control this tendency was to specify carefully the circumstances for reporting *no occupation*, in order to settle the doubtful cases from this side. The "no-occupation" category thus had the most positive definition of all. All persons not reporting a regular occupation were required to state in detail their means of support.[7]

[6] Against this can possibly be set an honorific value, unusually strong in a Chinese society, that accrues to *leisure* activities, which may tend in the opposite direction.

[7] If living on income, the type of income was to be stated; if a family worker, the type and family status was to be included; for "dependents"—those for whom no separate source of income could be found—it was to be noted whether students, family

In publication, except for some special tables on households, this information was usually lumped into one single class ("no-occupation"). The census of 1930 was the one exception, when the census authorities tried to be more precise about all occupations than before. In that year the following separate types of status were tabulated as sub-classes of the major group "without occupation": those living on securities, living on tenant fees, living on house and land rents; students, "dependents," inmates of special institutions, persons on relief, prisoners, others and those whose occupations were not reported, and domestic servants.[8]

This policy towards the listing of all non-employed statuses should be kept in mind when interpreting occupational figures for Taiwan. It furnishes the only definite clue that we have of the boundary that was drawn to set off the labor force as a whole. The precautions taken to prevent the "no-occupation" category from being a repository for borderline cases may even have helped in exaggerating the amount of actual employment. Hence, while census data may give good evidence on the kinds and patterns of employment in Taiwan, they are not free from bias in indicating the total amount.[9]

Variation by Age and Sex

There is no way to clarify the meaning of data on occupations without investigating the purposes and problems of census-taking. But there are limitations. The outcome of these compilations depends also on how well the planning and execution of the censuses were adapted to the circumstances they were supposed to describe.

---

members, or other relationship to the household, and the occupation of the head of the supporting household.

[8] It has been necessary to reassign domestic servants arbitrarily to the "no-occupation" class. So few were enumerated that the category is meaningless, especially with reference to males.

[9] On conceptual grounds, there is not much reason to endow the "amount" of employment with much importance, for in demographic data one has to deal with units of persons and not of work. It is well known that a certain amount of temporary or partial unemployment is chronic in agrarian societies; it is taken for granted, expected, and institutionalized in some "hidden" form. Properly speaking, this is not unemployment at all: the persons involved would not necessarily work if work were available. In these circumstances the indistinct line separating these cases from the working force is not primarily a defect of the concept of "customary occupation," but reflects the facts of the real situation.

Other uses of such data are not necessarily impaired by this circumstance. The bias toward over-stating the number of working persons did not vary greatly in Taiwan over time, and therefore will not affect comparisons of the same population at different dates, such as those used in this chapter and in Chapter III.

In general, activities having to do primarily with livelihood are so important in human societies that they are always subjected to some special forms of coordination. Never are they treated casually in a society, as minor points of etiquette or personal friendship may be. Much of their importance arises from the fact that the same persons who engage in them also occupy other positions of social significance. This coordination, therefore, cannot be primarily a matter of regulation within the realm of economic behavior,[10] but consists of keeping such behavior consistent with the social order. Demographically, the problem is found wherever occupational functions overlap with other roles in the same individuals.

Two of the commonest regions of overlap in a population are with sex and age. Most of Asia, for example, is beset by such hazards to human existence that its peoples have maintained their numbers only by bringing forth abundant offspring. High fertility, which until recent centuries had been the universal offset to high mortality, has always necessitated a distinct kind of social position for women. Being the only ones capable of parturition, females in these societies come under the influence of family institutions that attach high priority and emphasis to the bearing and rearing of progeny.[11]

This circumstance has profoundly affected the part of women in economic activity. Most of the ways thought proper for an adult woman to have contact with the people beyond her family circle are in a married status. Few women escape marriage. Indeed, it is so normal an event that to pass the age of 25 unwed is considered a serious misfortune. To covet matrimony in vain does not carry with it any of the other possibilities (such as occupational careers) that exist in Western societies, and becomes a matter of anxiety if not humiliation for an entire family.

All this does not mean that women under these conditions do not work. The lot of a "home-maker" is a more laborious one in agrarian than in industrial countries, and may encompass more different sorts of particular activities from case to case. A wide range of tasks, including production of many physical commodities, is conducted as

[10] If it were, it would cease to present any problem, for it could be reduced simply to bureaucratic patterns of large-scale organizations.

[11] This does not mean that the particular family institutions are everywhere the same: such societies have long been renowned for the variety in such matters as marriage ceremonies, types of education of children, adolescent behavior and the division of labor in specific household tasks. We are not here concerned with superficial variation, but with the general features which are shared.

a matter of course within the households that finally make use of them—items which in industrial societies are ordinarily purchased in the market. In these activities women are occupied often from childhood to old age, and sometimes more vigorously than men. It is this economy of the household, and not real inactivity, that utilizes the efforts of females in useful pursuits but provides against their holding extra-familial occupations.

We can be certain that a goodly portion of the work done in Taiwan was concealed in the activities of women. When such is the case, estimates of manpower based on occupational data are necessarily distorted, especially when these data have been compiled without overt care to this problem. Here the only feasible procedure in measuring manpower is to exclude altogether this important segment—womanpower—and to concentrate only on the "male labor force" as representing the dominant working patterns of the population.

Even within the male population, however, not all of its members are eligible or able for permanent employment. Close to half of all males in Taiwan—practically all those without occupations—were consistently of ages in which employment was not customary. Age always has a great deal to do with whether a person follows an occupation or not, and often with the sort of work he may perform. Tasks that are looked upon as useful are commonly ones that infants and the aged, for example, lack the capacity for doing. In between these extremes, some males of certain ages are excluded from the labor force when sufficient value is attached to other activities such as school attendance, acquisition of special skills, patriarchy, or infirmity—either due to priority of the competing activities themselves (regardless of who performs them) or due to the kinds of persons involved.

These various factors determining employment are so closely associated with age that at any one time almost all of the men of young and middle adulthood in a population have some occupation. The exclusions are concentrated in the years of childhood and old age. For this reason it is meaningful to speak of the "population of working ages," and often more information is available about them as a whole than about the labor force itself.

The Labor Force in Taiwan

Let us continue this line of inquiry by inspecting the portions of the population that are employed in relation to sex and age. With some idea by this time of what the census standards of employment purported to be in Taiwan, one should then see how they are performed in practice. As a first step it is interesting to compare the occupied portion of the population with a corresponding group elsewhere. To judge from the proportions of men occupied by age in various countries—and under varied kinds of census administration—the extent of employment is approximately the same among the recorded populations of the world.[12]

In 1930, for example, these proportions in Taiwan closely resembled in most ages those for the United States, when a similar standard ("gainful occupation") was used in this country to assign status in the labor force. In Table 17, the figures for these two countries were nearly alike among all men above age 25, though they were markedly higher in Taiwan at younger ages. The parallel does not imply that "work" amounted to the same thing among men in both populations. Nor does their divergent use of young men suggest that Americans were necessarily more prone to idleness than Taiwanese. The chief significance of Table 17 comes rather from showing that work as defined for census purposes commands the energies of practically all of the young adult men in both populations,[13] despite the wide differences in economic organization between the two countries.

Granted the basic similarity, the principal difference in Table 17 deserves comment. In the first place men in Taiwan evidently begin to do regular work much earlier in life than in the Western world. Extension of general education into the years of later adolescence, as everyone is aware, is a recent and modern phenomenon and confined to a few countries, for it has just recently been felt to be indispensable to the skills that this new world requires. The luxury of being able to maintain these services is not readily appreciated without contrasting it with less fortunate areas. In Taiwan, as in most of Asia, practically everyone destined to have an occupation was already employed before age 20. Many, not shown here, even entered a permanent occupation, in which they remained, before reaching age 15.[14]

[12] Notestein, Frank W., et al. (1944), p. 118.

[13] It is interesting to note that the differences made by different criteria—i.e., more refined labor force measures—are slight, if not trivial, for our purposes. Cf. Durand, John D. (1948), Appendix A, pp. 197-200.

[14] The census data showing dependency of childhood up to 1930 do not tell the whole story. In the latter 1930's the Japanese made concessions toward the extension of schooling, until by 1940 Taiwan was perhaps better in this regard than most Asiatic countries

TABLE 17

THE LABOR FORCE IN THE TOTAL POPULATION, TAIWAN AND THE UNITED STATES

Proportions of All Persons in Each Age Group Who Had an Occupation, Male and Female, 1930

Age Groups	*Taiwan (Taiwanese Only*)* All Occupations	*Taiwan (Taiwanese Only*)* Occupied outside Agriculture	*United States (All Groups)* All Occupations
	Males		
15–19	85.4	24.4	47.8
20–24	96.4	33.6	89.9
25–34	97.5	35.9	97.3
35–44	97.3	33.9	97.6
45–54	93.8	29.0	96.5
55–64	81.8	21.6	90.2
65+	54.7	11.9	58.3
	Females		
15–19	38.0	5.6	26.6
20–24	32.0	4.6	42.4
25–34	31.2	5.2	27.8
35–44	31.2	5.7	22.6
45–54	23.3	4.4	20.4
55–64	13.4	3.0	16.1
65+	4.3	1.3	8.0

* Domestic servants among the Taiwanese, male and female, have been excluded.

Sources: U. S. Dept. of Commerce, Bureau of the Census, *15th Census of the United States, 1930, Population*, Volume V, *General Report on Occupations.* Chap. 4, Table 2.

Taiwan—Census of 1930, Prefectural Volumes, Table 15.

For reasons advanced above, data on occupations for women are less satisfactory. In Table 17, roughly one-third of the women in most ages up to 45 reported some occupation in 1930; but practically all stated that they were "farmers."[15] While superficially these figures appear to make a good showing against the data for the United States, the resemblance is misleading. In fact, on the basis of this information

besides Japan itself. But these events occurred too late to have much effect on the ages of starting work.

15 Even for the few women who acknowledged occupations outside of agriculture, the specific kinds of work that occupied the bulk of this group are, suspiciously, the very ones that are usually conducted in households. For example, most of the "industrially employed" women were engaged in handicraft production (wood and bamboo articles, food processing, Panama hats) typically conducted on a household scale.

one can really say next to nothing about the employment of Taiwanese women. Henceforth, except for special purposes, we shall confine ourselves to using occupational data for men only.

Occupational Composition of the Male Labor Force

With the outline of total employment among males of different ages now established, it is only a matter of course to follow up by showing the occupational composition of the same group. This amounts to a close view of the data in Chapter III, considered for the moment apart from the differences in age structure and differences in the extent of employment in various ages.

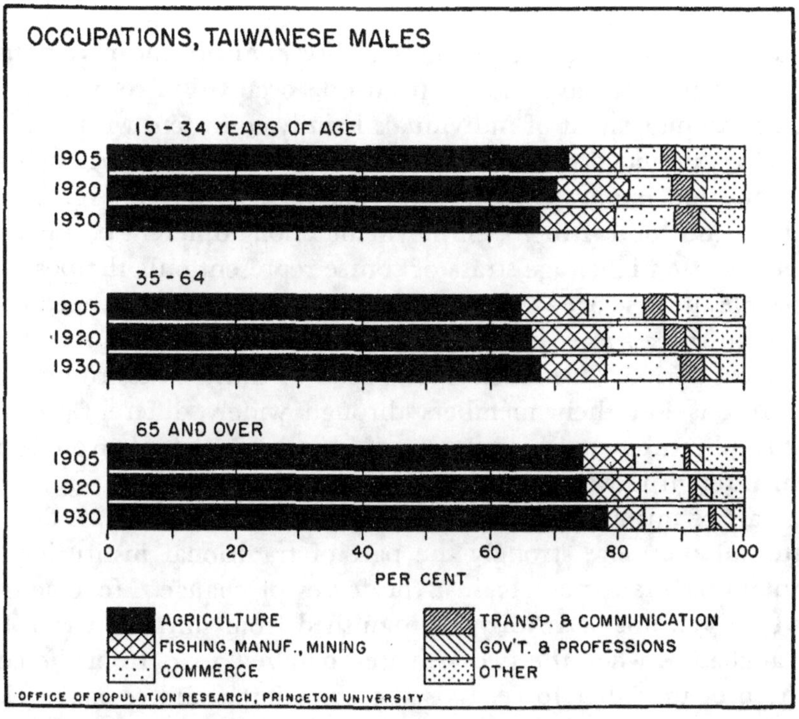

Fig. 12. Occupational Composition of Taiwanese, by Age, 1905-1930.

Even taken by separate age groups, Taiwanese men were performing the same types of work after 25 years of colonial rule as at the beginning. The situation can be efficiently summarized in Fig. 12, which bears out in some detail the evidence of the last chapter. As regards the whole of the male working population, the stability existing from one time to another was not exaggerated in Chapter III.

Broad features like these were reduplicated in a degree that overshadows all accompanying trends—in this case down to the disposition of manpower at all working ages at successive dates. Fig. 12 shows clearly that this society had, up to 1930, put new generations to work along lines very similar to those of the old.

That these proportions should remain almost constant through time implies great stability of the agrarian social order. But this evidence is of a nature that best illustrates the more prominent relationships, and does not give much weight to the shifts that did occur. Farming activities again appear predominant—as in fact they were—to the point of eclipsing the trends in growth of other types of employment. These can be brought out only through the use of more responsive measures.

Moreover, even this degree of stability does not mean that individuals could not have moved from one occupation to another. A circulatory movement of individuals is fully consistent with the data of Fig. 12, provided that the avenues remained unchanging. It is not only possible but implied by the data themselves. In Fig. 12 the swelling and contracting of employment among different occupations from lower to higher age strata of course represent only the positions of people in these ages at one time; but a pattern that is repeated so closely in three successive censuses can hardly reflect just the events of a short period. Over such a long span of time, unless the various occupations lost their members through widely different rates of death and retirement, this pattern could come about only from losing them through movement to other occupations.

If part of this movement is a matter of such circulation, it demonstrates all the more strongly the part of traditional institutions in maintaining the society against the forces of change. Movement of this type will not be readily distinguished from shifts as a result of actual change, when the two are later analyzed apart from the composition of the labor force. It is therefore important to make clear at this point that whatever the extent of such shifts (as yet undisclosed by these techniques), there must always have been a prominent element of circulation involved.

Movement between Occupations

The data of Fig. 12 are poorly adapted to illustrate the nature of occupational movements in the population. Agricultural employment is preponderant, and masks the shifts that individuals actually made between the classes of occupations that are listed. All movements in other lines of work hence appear small because they were absorbed in the numbers of all occupied persons, instead of being compared with the numbers that had been in each line before.

Some moves of occupation always occur in conformity with traditional usages—like entry into the labor force itself, moving from one position to another with gradual acquisition of skill, the advancement of successful men and the decline of failures, and eventual retirement from active work. Shifts such as these are found even among the peoples who are the most bound by custom, and do not depend on the existence of new social conditions. The problem in this section is to develop a more sensitive procedure to detect some of these transfers.

A more direct approach to this "hidden" movement is to locate persons in their later occupational careers after they once have started. Comparing the population in the *same* interval of age at two successive points of time meant that we were dealing with different people each time. Their selection of occupations might have been the same at both dates, since one of the functions of tradition is to perpetuate a given system of choice in new generations; but this type of comparison might not reveal what happened to any of them after the first observation was made. Uncovering this subsequent behavior rests on finding the same persons at a later date, which means also at different ages.

Age, as regarded by demographers, is one of the few characteristics carried by people that are predictable indefinitely into the future. Those who were in age 20 in 1920 will be exactly age 30 at the same time of the year in 1930. Accordingly, those persons who reported an occupation in 1920, and survived, can be located in an age interval exactly ten years higher in 1930. By the simple device of assembling the appropriate pair of figures and removing those who died during the interval, occupied persons in any age group can easily be compared with their survivors at the later date. One can then find whether, as a group, they still remained occupied, and to what extent.

The same basic reasoning applies as between one type of employment and another; the survivors of a group of farmers at one time, for example, can be compared with the number actually found at another. The difference in this instance would represent the net gain or loss to these farmers in relation to the remainder of the economy, including entries, retirements, and transfers to other classes of occupations.

As in all formal problems in which one seeks to determine the influence of some factors while removing others, this procedure requires that certain conditions be met. First of all, the population should be one in which some significance may be attached to "net movement" between occupations. In an industrial society, occupational transfers are frequent: over a period of several years an individual may make multiple moves, or certain occupations may be subject to many entries and exits among members of a given age group. If widespread, either of these types of event would make an estimate of net change meaningless, because they would distort it as an indicator of the true number of moves. In Taiwan, with foreknowledge that few people changed occupations after first adopting one, it is safe to assume that net movement is a good approximation to total movement across broad classes of occupations.

Second, it should almost go without saying that occupational categories used in this comparison should be comparable, if not identical, at the two points of time. This condition is moderately well satisfied among the different occupations as they are arranged here.[16]

Next, the risks of death at each age should, for perfect accuracy, be equal from one occupational group to another. It is unlikely that this condition could be strictly fulfilled in any population. In Taiwan, many of the pursuits that were conducted in cities, for example, were probably more healthful than farming, for the hazards of city life were not greater than those in the countryside. Here, the mortality estimates that are used must be derived from the average experience among all Taiwanese males. Since no allowance can be made for variations between different occupations, some unknown biases probably enter the computations from this source.

Age reporting must be very accurate in order to give assurance that the persons being compared are the same. By defining age in terms of the date of birth, the censuses of Taiwan developed age reporting that was more accurate and consistent than in most Western countries. While between 1920 and 1930 there was a slight change in

[16] With one exception, which will be pointed out below. There must also be reason to believe that the activities comprising a given occupation have themselves not greatly changed over the period. This is one condition over which the investigator has no control whatever. We can simply assume for Taiwan that it is met reasonably well for the period in question.

the technique of assigning age, it was systematic through all ages and cannot create bias either by age or by occupation.

Finally, because mortality estimates are usually applied to a population in the form of survival ratios, persons should be distributed evenly within the intervals of age that are used. When these intervals are broad, there is greater chance of introducing some inaccuracy due to uneven grouping within them, since mortality is known to vary with age. The intervals used for this manipulation all spanned 5 years of age, and some element of control is therefore lacking. This is especially true for occupied persons aged 15 to 19, the only group that departed greatly in internal composition from the general population.[17] There is no reason to believe that the imprecision arising from this source should create any appreciable bias by occupation. Even where certain occupations may have distinctive age patterns of recruitment or retirement that give them age groups with unusual internal structure (e.g., farmers aged 15 to 19), the bias is very small.[18]

These conditions would have to be met in order to apply the procedure we have outlined to make estimates that are precise in number. But the procedure itself is only an approximation. Nonfulfillment of any one of the conditions would not necessarily be serious, and could be foreseen and minimized by some arbitrary correction. No allowance can be made for the interaction of all of them, and for this reason some caution is appropriate in interpreting the following results.

With these qualifications, the way is clear to construct a set of comparisons between 1920 and 1930 according to the outline above. We shall estimate the balance of men entering and leaving ("retiring" from) the working force by subtracting the survivors of those who were already at work in 1920 from those who were found with employment in 1930. (The survivors from 1920 are advanced ten years of age: all ages given in the following tables represent ages achieved by 1930.) In the same way, we shall estimate the balance of

[17] The mortality estimates were formed by life table ratios of L_{x+10}/L_x. For convenience, and because it made no perceptible difference in the results, values were used for only the middle year of age in each 5-year interval. The values employed were taken from tables for actual cohorts, developed in connection with a later part of this study. They thus represent the actual mortality experience of the middle age cohort in each 5-year interval.

[18] Actually, to avoid *bias* by occupation from this source, the condition may be relaxed from that of *even* internal age distributions that are the same among occupations within a given five-year interval. This problem is therefore less serious than it would first appear to be.

movement into or exits from a given occupational class by subtracting the survivors of those at work in that occupation in 1920 from those found at work in that occupation in 1930. The results of these operations can be designated as "gain" or "loss"; the ratios of these numbers to the calculated survivors as "per cent gained" or "per cent lost."[19]

Drawing upon the range of ages from 15 to 64 carries the comparison through the span of greatest employment. The figures furnish in cross-section a picture of occupational movement in any selected categories with respect to all the remainder. While a cross-section, it is not an instantaneous view. Each entry in the table is based on the experience over a 10-year period for the given age group. Hence the number of age groups that can be usefully included is restricted by the length of this period. Older men have been dropped at age 70, which means that this last group was aged 55-59 in 1920. Similarly, the youngest age group is that of men 25-29, since in 1920 they were only 15-19, and too few of the boys under age 15 claimed occupations in 1920 for them to be of great interest.[20]

The *differences* between survivors and actual workers in 1930, and the ratios in which they stand to the numbers of survivors, are the most useful forms for interpreting these estimates. In Fig. 13 these are shown graphically in the arbitrary categories of "gain" or "loss," as explained above. The bar diagram in Fig. 13 shows the actual numbers of net entries and withdrawals, during the decade 1920-1930, of all occupations taken together. It is of some special interest in establishing the shape of these movements at different ages throughout the male labor force, and as a standard against which to compare the patterns for separate occupational groups.

More important here is the second part of Fig. 13, giving the *percentages* of the survivors of 1920 workers who had changed their occupational status between 1920 and 1930. Along the middle segment of the age scale, these percentages are practically zero (ages 30-44, covering the actual age span of 20-44). The working force as a whole was almost stationary over this entire interval, consisting of those persons who were already employed, with few entrants and few withdrawals in relation to the numbers who were already there. Over this span it is not likely that many entries and exits occurred

19 Where entries are still taking place, these are not true proportions: the numerator is not included in the denominator.

20 By a special arrangement, it will be possible somewhat later to deal more adequately with the males 15-19 and to include the group 10-14.

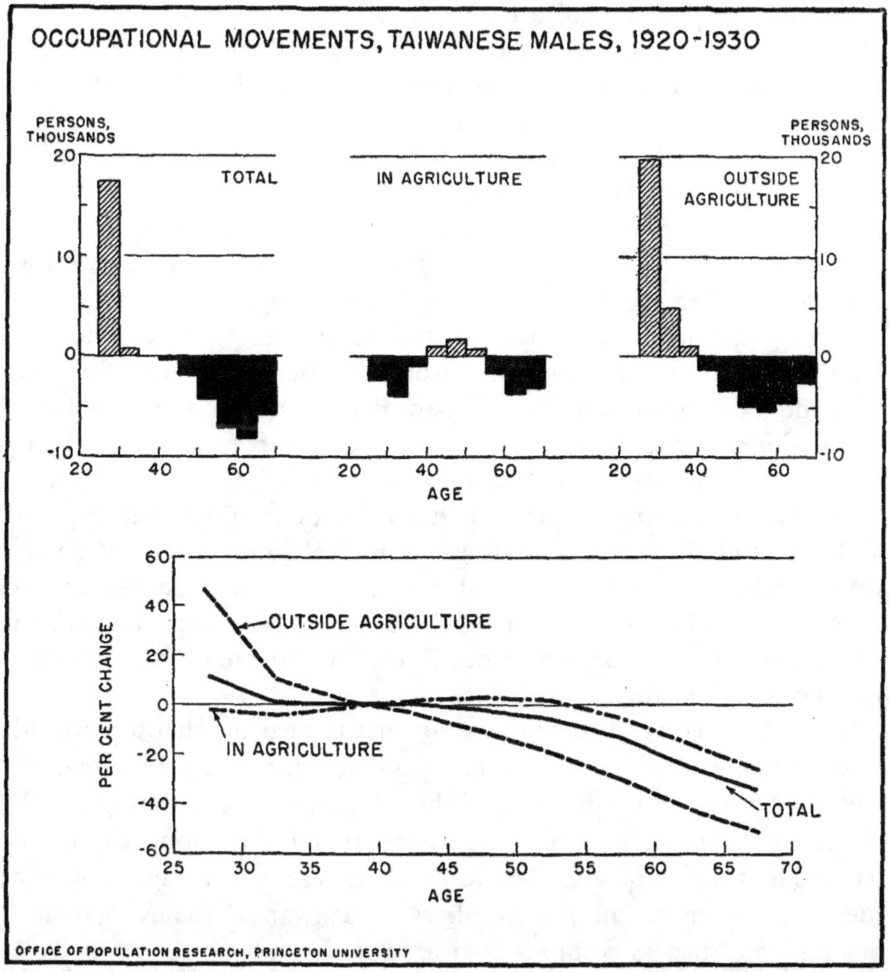

Fig. 13. Occupational Movement of Taiwanese Males, 1920-1930. Net "Gain" or "Loss" Inside and Outside of Agriculture, and in the Total Labor Force.

so as to balance each other; clearly few men began or left off work completely (except through death) in these ages, and what movement there was must have been limited to transfers from one occupation to another.

It was established above (Table 17) that the maximum degree of employment was reached by age 30. It follows from these data that in this decade almost everyone who was likely in his life-time to acquire an occupation had already done so at age 20.[21] By similar

[21] A small part of this pattern may possibly be a peculiarity of the unusual decade involved. The census of 1930 was taken during a world depression, which had a brief but severe effect in Taiwan. There are hints that this was reflected slightly in the pro-

reasoning, 90 per cent of all men who were going to become employed by 1930 must have held occupations already between ages 15-19 in 1920: since only 10 per cent of the employed survivors to this group had begun their employment later than 1920, though by 1930, at ages 25-29, the ones with occupations already accounted for almost all the population in that age.

One takes for granted that the boundary lines between being occupied or not were somewhat indistinct among young men entering and old men leaving the labor force. Even so, Fig. 13 gives a picture of the age incidence of retirement just as interesting as its evidence for the stability of employment through earlier adult ages. Starting with the men who reached ages 45-49 in 1930, the rate of exits from occupations over the preceding 10 years rose sharply with advancing age. Of the Taiwanese aged 55-59 in 1920, more than half the survivors had retired before age 70. Earlier ages exhibit what appears to be a gradual progression toward this rate of retirement. This would hold true even if we assume that the world depression in 1930 forced older men out of the labor force more rapidly than in normal times. The pattern would remain the same; only its age spacing would change.

These findings tend to conform to what the earlier chapters would lead one to expect. They do not provide much new information (except by way of verification of the procedure that is being used). Of greater significance are the patterns that hold among the occupations that make up the labor force. This is shown in Fig. 13 where the bars also represent the numbers of Taiwanese males "gained" or "lost" in 1930 as compared with 1920.

Agriculture is the most striking of these. There was an actual loss of several thousand young adult men who had been farmers between the ages of 15 and 30 in 1920. This does not imply that agriculture was failing to recruit new farmers. The losses in part reflect the fact that males undertook occupations at younger ages (at least in their census returns) in farming than in other pursuits. Agriculture gained many of its entrants *before* age 25 (the youngest age shown in these charts); by age 25 it may or may not have continued to re-

portions of older men claiming some occupation in 1930. Despite the tendency of the "customary occupation" census concept to resist inroads of short-term unemployment, these proportions are slightly lower in advanced ages than those in previous censuses. Even so, the "true" figure might make the proposition above even stronger, by revealing "normal" retirement to have been slower than Fig. 13 suggests.

cruit new workers—something that this procedure can never reveal—but was in any case exporting enough young men to the rest of the economy to outweigh these and create a net loss of workers.

Though substantial in the total number of workers involved in net movements among other occupations,[22] this rural exodus fades into insignificance when related to the number of men in these lower ages who remained in agriculture (Fig. 12). Obviously the standard against which to measure these events has much to do with assessing their importance. Losses of young men from agriculture supplied a fair share of all the entrants to other occupations in these ages. But this movement was not enough to make more than a slight inroad in the store of manpower for farming—and was more than offset by recruitments with agriculture between the ages 10-14 and 20-24. In this age interval, agriculture absorbed more than half of the total entrants to all occupations from 1920 to 1930.

If among the survivors of, let us say, all males 15-19 agriculture had merely matched its own recruitment to the scale of the total labor force (i.e., that of Fig. 12, above), two-thirds of the total entrants to the labor force in this age would have become farmers instead of entering other occupations as in fact they did.

No less important is the stream of older men—40 to 54 in 1930—who were entering agriculture. Though numerically not a large group, they reveal a degree of movement at least as great as that of the persons who abandoned farming at younger ages.[23] These were the ages in which "retirements" from other occupations were beginning. If we assume that the exodus of young farmers was a "normal" occurrence (and some of the earlier census data suggest this is so), it is almost certain that these older recruits to agriculture were re-entrants or "returnees" who had previously left.

The figures again reveal only *net* movement; if some farmers of these ages were "retiring" from agriculture, then returnees must have been more numerous than the actual figures here indicate. Evidently agriculture not only supplied young men to other parts of the economy, but reclaimed older workers that other occupations

[22] It needs to be emphasized frequently that the procedure we are following does not give an exact estimate of the total number of men who left agriculture for other work, even in the decade in question. Some of the actual exits were probably balanced by new recruits, though the number at these ages was undoubtedly smaller for agriculture than any other occupation.

[23] I.e., in view of the fact that not many men were alive in these ages, these entrants bear a larger proportion to the total number of farmers of the same age. Their significance in this respect can be read from Fig. 13.

had discarded. Re-entry to agriculture was thus for some men an alternative to ceasing work altogether.

The data for other occupational groups can best be examined in Fig. 14. The bar diagrams show the amounts of net gain or loss, which should be compared with the total amount in Fig. 13. The chart of percentages gain or loss gives the corresponding view of movement for each, taking into account at each age the number of persons who were already there. The first indicates the numbers of people involved; the second abstracts from this.

Due to changes in census practice, certain of the chief occupational classes must be lumped together so as to be comparable between 1920 and 1930. These consolidations make it impossible to say very much about activities in the non-agricultural portion of the economy that is not already implied by the relation of agricultural employment to all of them. This sector can be split into three main parts to compare their uses of manpower: industry and commerce (also including fishing and mining), professional positions and public administration, and transport and communications. Though not of the same size, all three of these classes absorbed and released workers in a similar age pattern, and all were distinct from agriculture and from the total labor force (see Fig. 12 and Fig. 13). All were most conspicuously users of youth, and taken together they obviously depended on people already working in agriculture for recruits. To some extent all, but especially transport and communications, tended to cast off older workers sooner than agriculture.

Evidently workers in transportation and in professional fields or the administrative bureaucracy were recruited more exclusively while very young. This is not surprising, in view of the fact that most Taiwanese held only junior positions in these fields, and frequently positions where some specific technical training put youth at a premium (for example, drivers of motor vehicles, railroad trainmen, school teachers, telegraph workers, clerks).[24]

Finally, a few words are required about the group of "other occupations." The steady "loss" of persons from this category is a fixed feature of Taiwan's whole succession of occupational censuses. Under the assumptions applied in the rest of the occupations, Fig. 14 would appear to indicate a flood of departures, in all ages, from these mis-

24 However, transportation workers also included a number of pullers of rickshas and other carts, who would likewise tend to enter this employment while young, but for different reasons.

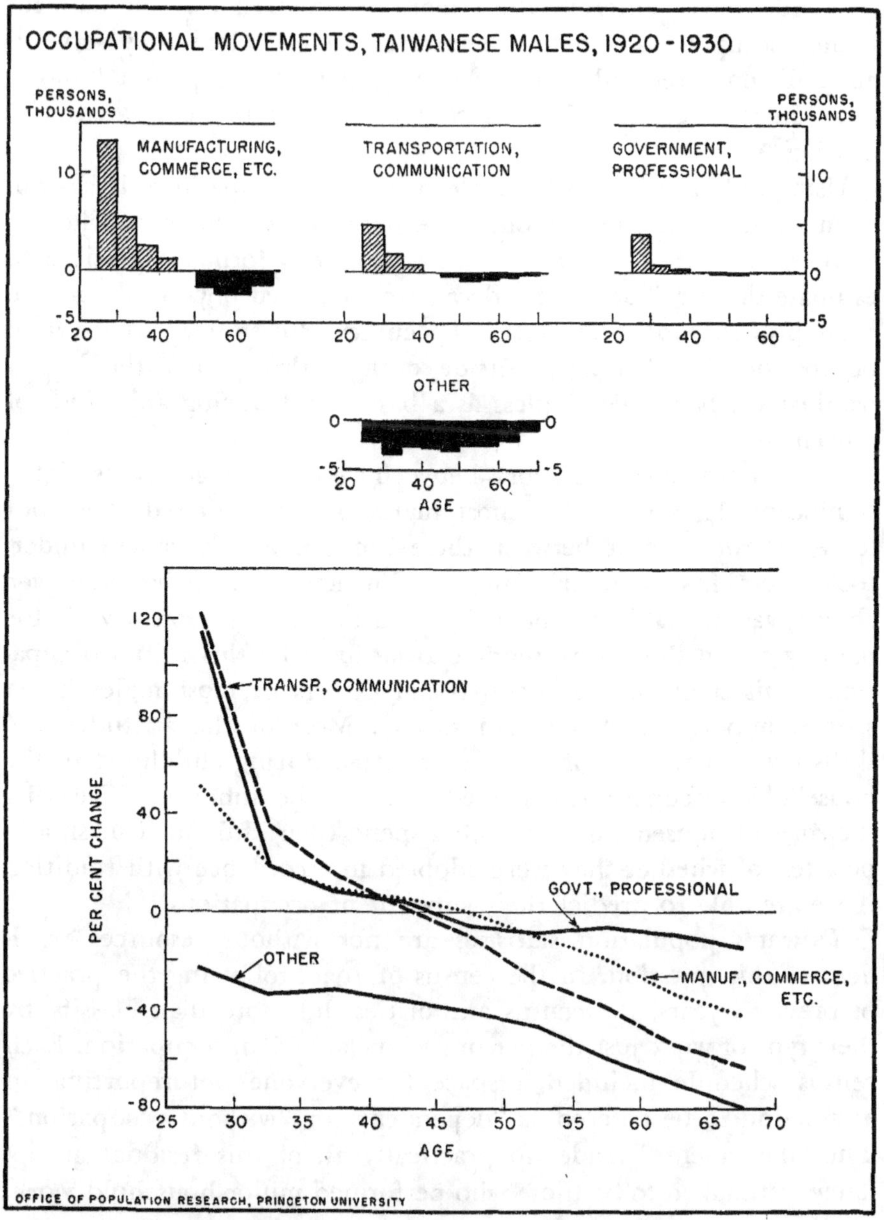

Fig. 14. Occupational Movement of Taiwanese Males, 1920-1930. Net "Gain" or "Loss" in the Occupations Outside of Agriculture.

cellaneous activities. More reasonably, it implies that most of these workers were shifted to more specific occupations merely by refinements of classification in 1930. Accordingly, these reclassified persons must have "entered" the remaining occupations. The data for "other occupations" are by themselves useless. Here they serve as an additional reminder that the estimates of occupational movement in this section are inexact, and deserve to be treated with caution.[25]

Using only the figures for males who held occupations, it has not been worth while to carry out these procedures with those who fell below age 25 in 1930 (age 15 in 1920). It is formally possible to estimate the survivors after a decade to employed boys aged 10-14 in 1920, probably to a fine degree of accuracy. But so few had acquired occupations by that age, outside of agriculture, that the results would have been meaningless as a basis for deducing any kinds of movements.

Yet this neglected age span—between age 10 and age 24—is highly significant. It is here that most males initially entered the labor force. At some point between these limits most Taiwanese undertook their first regular adult employment, exercising whatever choice was available to them. The nature of a person's work for many years in the future tended to be fixed by this initial occupation. This stage in the occupational careers of most males has a special import in an agrarian society. Most of the attitudes and skills pertinent to livelihood are imparted during childhood in the household—occupations, in effect, tend to be inherited. Knowing the sorts of households where boys spend their childhood, it should be a test of whether they were adopted in accordance with tradition if we are able to predict their subsequent occupations.

Taiwan's population statistics are not without resources pertinent to this question. In the census of 1920, following the practice of previous years, the census authorities did more than classify by their type of work just the persons who claimed an occupation. Each census schedule included a space for everyone not reporting an occupation to be entered as "dependent" or "without occupation." The "dependents" made up practically all of this residual group. They were taken to be those who performed minor household work,

[25] One can almost rule out the possibility that errors from this source have spuriously created the patterns derived from the data. In the first place, the men who have been reclassified from "other occupations" were not concentrated in any special age range, but rather spread more or less evenly over the whole span of working ages. Secondly, it is most likely that these persons were re-allocated to the *non-agricultural* sector of the labor force, and not within farming itself. They could in that case not affect the most important comparison of all—the differences between agriculture and the rest of the economy.

excluding ordinary domestic servants. Tables were published assigning all persons in this group to the occupation on which they depended—in most cases, that of the household head.

One such table, with this material cross-tabulated with age, can be used to supplement the data for men with full-fledged occupations. Here the "dependent" category amounts to a table of almost all the population outside those actually reporting occupations, classified by the type of work that they performed in the household. Virtually all of them (99.6 per cent) were members of the family of the household head. In other words, for young boys this table represents a division roughly along the lines of economic activity that supported their families.

All except a small fraction of Taiwanese males attained some occupation sooner or later during adulthood. Most of those who were recorded as dependents at the pre-adult ages of 10-14 and 15-19 would soon pass into some regular occupational group, and so were not far from such a transition at the time they were enumerated. This peculiarity makes it possible to treat the data as an approximate distribution of pre-labor force males according to the source of livelihood of their families. From this information we can count virtually all the males in these ages who would ever enter an occupation in the sense we ascribe to the term here, classified by the type of pre-occupational work they performed.

The same operations that were applied earlier in this section can be repeated with the male population thus tabulated (occupied and dependents combined), arranged by age. The results are plotted in Fig. 15 for the decade 1920-1930. No comparable tables of dependents were published after 1920. Hence, the survivors to occupied males plus dependent males of 1920, in each age interval beginning this time with 10-14, have been compared simply with men who had an occupation in 1930.

Fig. 15 supplements the findings of Figs. 13 and 14 by incorporating the group of males that reached ages 20-24 in 1930. It adds nothing new to the results at older ages. In fact, a small number of "dependents" are found among males even in adult age groups—a few men always remained in this status. In the "working ages," their proportion to all males was very slight—as low as two per cent. The survivors to workers and dependents taken together, therefore, were slightly more than the workers found in 1930. Fig. 15 is subject to

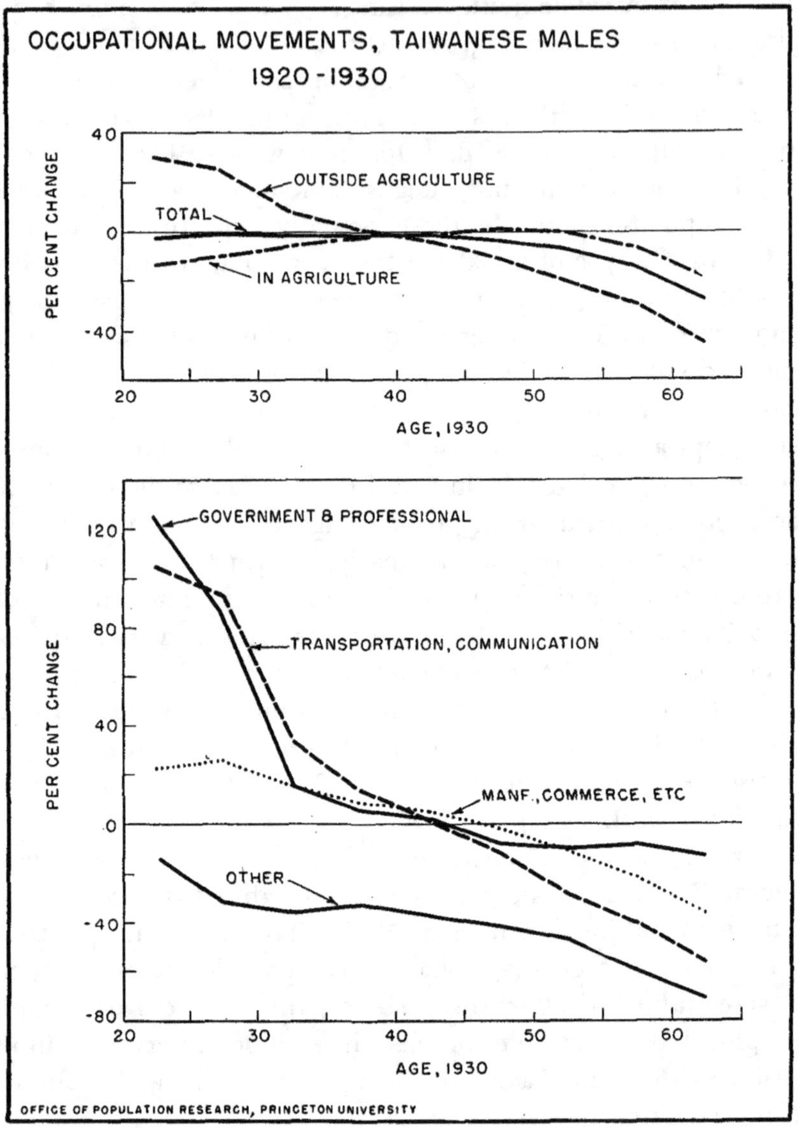

Fig. 15. Occupational Movement and "Inheritance" of Occupations by Taiwanese, 1920-1930. Net Movement between Occupations, and Movement into Occupations by Pre-Labor Force Males.

a small amount of exaggeration in the "loss" at all adult ages from this source.

For the total male labor force, the ratios of gain and loss over the decade 1920-1930 to survivors from 1920—by age in 1930—are connected in Fig. 15 by one continuous line. These ratios take into account the survivors of prospective as well as actual members of the labor force, starting with age 10 in 1920. This provision depicts a total occupational system that was self-sufficient with respect to the supply of young entrants during the decade 1920-1930. In the present set of data, next to no one was recruited into employment from outside. Therefore, deviations from this self-sufficiency in any occupational class implies some shifting—some failure to "inherit" occupations—and should also reveal the direction of the movement.

If the assumptions are correct, farming households apparently supplied a greater proportion of their males in these earlier ages to the rest of the labor force than did agricultural employment at later ages according to Fig. 13. Since boys in young ages were more numerous than men in their twenties, the *numbers* involved were much larger. Industry and commerce (also including fishing and mining) must have absorbed most of the young males who left agricultural households for other work. But they seem to have supplied an even greater number of their young workers over this period from their own families.

As in Fig. 13, the fields of transport and communications, and professional occupations and public administration, stand out as borrowers of youth from other families. Extending this test to younger ages only accentuates their debtor position in gaining manpower. This gain is evidence that these fields were expanding, but expanding by a very distinctive mode of recruitment. As before, "other occupations" indicate merely that the classification was inconsistent through time. But since the effect of this shortcoming is less among the ages specially discussed here, it need be of less concern than before.

Census data in this form have thus given a comprehensive picture of the principal flows of persons moving from one occupation to another in this decade. Even though the permanent result of the movement (in terms of changing the age-specific occupational structure of the population) was very small, these materials show that changes of occupation were actually more numerous and followed well-defined patterns. In particular, agriculture had a double role. It was the outstanding source of supply of young men in other occupations; and it was a pursuit to which many men returned when they were no longer youthful. From this we may draw the inference that some diversification of livelihood can be absorbed by an agrarian society with a minimum of lasting effect: rural agriculture "lends" workers to the rest of the economy in their young adulthood, and takes them back after their years of greatest contribution are past.

Manpower and Age Composition of the Population

Unfortunately for the conclusions of this chapter and the previous one, no population data on employment of any consequence have been published for Taiwan since the census of 1930. All that exist for the very interesting period leading up to World War II are the economic statistics reviewed in Chapter II (of quality far inferior to census figures), undisciplined travel accounts of a few foreigners, and the quasi-official reports of the Japanese themselves—half secretive and half boastful.

For this reason there is special value in observing the size of the population of working ages, from which the labor force is drawn, and its development as a component of the total population of Taiwanese. Requiring only detailed information by age and sex, this important measure can be derived from more recent census materials which were not published with elaborate occupational tables. It can be carried up to 1940 with exact figures, and extended beyond this date by the use of special assumptions.

All of the foregoing tables in this chapter have been arranged so as to represent occupational behavior of Taiwanese within certain age strata. This was a device for excluding temporarily two closely related aspects of labor force study: the age structure of the population at any one time, and trends in the size of different age strata. Insofar as these factors help to fix the supply of labor and the amount of dependency in a society, they exert a profound and subtle influence on economic activities.

At a given moment, among male Taiwanese some form of occupation was almost universal in most of the span between ages 15 and 60. Narrowing attention to the men between ages 15 and 64, as the "population of working ages"—to follow a common convention—will obviously include all ages of extensive employment. Not many boys younger than age 15 held occupations, and few people survived at all after age 65 (not all of these remaining occupied). Therefore, the group of men aged 15-64 also contained practically all working males.

Viewed as representing their region in the world, the Taiwanese are not one of the "major" populations of Asia. Consequently, we are free to analyze their composition without introducing the idea of vast numbers, and the global problems that these tend to raise. Compared with some of these more familiar examples, in Asia and

TABLE 18

AGE COMPOSITION OF TAIWAN AND SELECTED OTHER COUNTRIES, *CIRCA* 1930

Both Sexes

	Percentages of Total Population in Each Age Interval						
Age	*Taiwan**	*Japan*	*British India*	*U.S.S.R. (incl. Ukraine)*	*United States*	*England & Wales*	*Sweden*
0–14	41.0	36.6	39.9	37.2	29.4	23.8	22.1
15–39	39.0	38.3	41.1	41.3	41.2	40.4	41.7
40–64	17.5	20.3	16.8	17.5	24.0	28.4	27.0
65+	2.5	4.8	2.2	4.0	5.4	7.4	9.2
Total	100.0	100.0	100.0	100.0	100.0	100.0	100.0

* Taiwanese only.

Source: Institut International de Statistique, *Aperçu de la Démographie, 1929-1936*. The Hague, 1939. Table 7.
Statistical Summary of Taiwan, Table 58.

the West, Taiwan ranked with India, a land of proverbial "population problems." Together these two areas illustrate an ironic historical circumstance: those areas that for other reasons are most handicapped by poverty are also the ones with the greatest burdens of dependency, and with the smallest proportions of their people in working ages. The differences are outstanding in the ages of maturity, near the range between age 40 and age 65, when Western nations have been in a position to make far better use of the accumulated training and experience among their people (see Table 18). While next to nothing is directly known of its earlier demographic history, Taiwan was already in this situation when it entered its census era, and was placed still more at a disadvantage as time went on.

Through time, the population of these various ages in Taiwan has not shifted so signally as it has grown. From 1905 to 1940, each of these age strata almost doubled in size. In the same period, the important span 15-64 underwent slow but steady changes in relation to the rest of the population, older and younger. Its share in the total was reduced, though its numbers grew by more than one-half. On the other hand, the proportion of aged (always small) did not greatly change, though their numbers doubled. But most signifi-

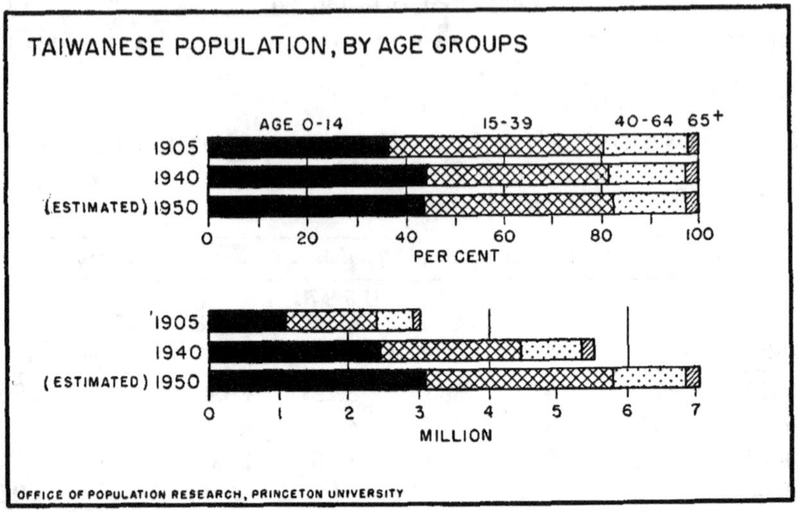

Fig. 16. Taiwanese Population in Working and Dependent Ages, 1905, 1940 and Projected to 1950.

cantly, infants and children, represented by all persons under 15 years of age, expanded into an ever larger part of the total population (see Fig. 16).[26] This young and dependent segment did not advance its share in rapid strides; only by 1940 did it reach 44 per cent of all Taiwanese. A glance at Table 18 will show how extremely this departs from the composition of populations in industrial countries. There is little reason to suppose that the trend would have continued much further, even with the large numbers of births that contributed to it each year and the efforts at health control already sponsored by the Japanese.

On the purely hypothetical assumption of continuance of mortality and fertility through the 1940's as in the period 1936-1940, a bar has been added to Fig. 16 for 1950. It gives an indication of what these same circumstances might have produced in ten more years. As an actual estimate it is of no value, since conditions did not in fact remain so favorable after the end of Japanese rule. The resulting figures are nevertheless of interest, for they suggest that without new improvements in longevity this trend might have progressed already as far as it could go.[27]

[26] Fig. 16 is based on data for males and females combined, since when it comes to dependency of childhood and old age both required support. It is implicitly assumed that women in prime adult ages are not dependent in this same sense.

[27] It is interesting to note that the age composition of Taiwanese in 1940 was almost identical with that of the "stable population"—i.e., the age composition that would

With continuance of these demographic conditions—and infinite resources for their support—the Taiwanese could probably have expanded in this same scale forever. But, while the pattern of occupational movement that we have observed was also a stable one that did not contain many elements of change, it could not have perpetuated current conditions indefinitely, any more than the actual growth has been allowed to continue without setback. The phenomenon of growth itself was an underlying factor of instability for the society. If the Japanese had remained in control, they would have been forced to recognize the problem sooner or later, and either provide additional opportunities for livelihood or risk disruption of their program from other sources. Their efforts toward industrialization were too small and too selfish to have made any difference in the result.

---

have resulted from indefinite persistence of the fertility and mortality rates of the same period, 1936-1940. The rate of increase implied by the structure of this hypothetical stable population is somewhat higher than that which was actually recorded at the time.

CHAPTER V

Migration and the Growth of Cities

DEPENDING on the way one looks at it, the history of colonial rule in Taiwan can give the appearance either of having brought great transformations to the island or of having left the indigenous social structure virtually intact. This apparent contrast comes from shifting attention between the two principal groups of people that were involved—from the Japanese, who had little to do with the archaic customs and usages of the population, to the Taiwanese, who had only small acquaintance with the modern changes that were being introduced. Here we shall be concerned with those of the latter who came into contact with the new elements.

Though the full force of these developments passed them by as a group, the Taiwanese were not all uninfluenced. The organization of farming, to be sure, continued as before with little modification. The activities most affected were those outside of agriculture. Hence the people must have moved to the new conditions, since the innovations did not move to them.

The Territorial Frame of Migration

Taiwan is a small island, and recording the migration of its people should not be a task of great magnitude or difficulty. Japanese regarded such a record as essential in keeping a close watch over the population. It was so important that they inaugurated continuous population registers for every village, every group of households. These reports were compiled in fine detail by the authorities and published in a single volume each year.[1] A certain amount of adaptation is needed to make these registers answer questions that are germane to our interests.

Japanese conquest began to provide not only the first reliable data for assessing movement in the population, but also a new type of control over it. It put an end to the historic influx of people from China that had been responsible for populating most of the island.

[1] The data proved to be more efficient for their purpose than for ours. The system faithfully counted the arrival of new persons in a community (the most important information from the standpoint of regulation) but did not expunge the records of all persons who left. The result was a more or less consistent bias toward *over*-estimating the number of people living in a given locality, and of course a somewhat distorted view of total migration.

On a much smaller scale, Japanese replaced Chinese as immigrants. Chinese arriving from the mainland were given a distinct legal status as aliens. Their activities were restricted, and they were no longer allowed to merge with permanent Taiwanese residents. Practically all movement by Taiwanese thenceforth consisted of internal migration, redistributing the population that was already there.

Only a part of the island is level enough to have encouraged heavy agricultural settlement; almost half of the total area is more than 500 meters above sea level. For administration, and therefore for the census, Taiwan was separated from 1920 on into seven main divisions. Two of them, plus an eighth for P'enghu (the Pescadores Islands) off the West coast, were technically under a different sort of political organization; but for convenience we shall refer to all eight as *Prefectures.*[2] Most types of census and registration statistics were tabulated for each of these political units as well as for the total island.

Beneath the level of Prefectures, local administration was organized around a set of Districts and a smaller number of Municipalities. In the population statistics, these formed two parallel units: no District contained a Municipality, and both were subordinate to Prefectures.[3] There were seven Municipalities at the census date in 1930, raised to nine before 1935, and 53 Districts in both years; in comparisons of different years, all will be standardized to the arrangement in 1935. Inside each District were towns and villages. Few materials are available for these individually; for most purposes the smallest divisions that can be studied are the Districts.[4]

Finally, the mountainous interior region—the Aborigine Terri-

[2] If not literally accurate, the term is appropriate in that authority below the Government-General was highly centralized in the subordinate governors of these divisions. How they are designated here is a matter of no consequence, as it made little difference in the actual administration. P'enghu, scarcely known to Westerners except as the Pescadores Islands, was in 1926 made a separate division under the Government-General. Prior to this it had shifted between separate status and a subdivision of Kaohsiung Prefecture. Hence there is no unbroken series of data for it.

[3] Again, the details of political organization were not uniform, but that need not concern us here. Both terms are arbitrary: "District" for the term *chün* (in its Chinese reading), and "Municipality" for *shih.* It was the practice to form new municipalities by removing some important town of sufficient size as a unit from its surrounding District, sometimes adding some former villages, also intact. This practice gives a basis for identifying the population of cities for comparison over a period when such administrative changes were taking place.

[4] The area of towns and villages exhausted the entire area of Districts, leaving no space between their boundaries. Therefore they do not always refer to meaningful units of settlement, and the terms are not consistent.

tory—was put under special control (though it nominally fell inside some part of each prefecture). This area must be considered as a separate division of the island. Its actual conditions and the quality of its population data are distinct from the remainder. Japanese were secretive about their treatment of the Aborigine Territory, and we have little information about it that is dependable.

These civil divisions were the outcome of some experimentation in government administration. The scheme just described was put into essentially its final form in 1920. Accordingly, most comparisons involving internal boundaries cannot be carried back beyond that year.

The Distribution of Total Population and of Migrants

In 1930, the population of Taiwanese was divided among the Prefectures as indicated in Table 19. Data in this form do not readily

TABLE 19
TOTAL POPULATION OF TAIWAN, 1930
By Prefecture, Inside and Outside the Aborigine Territory
(All Ethnic Groups)

	Area of Regular Administration			*Aborigine Territory*		
Prefecture	*Population*	*Density: Persons Per Sq. Km.*	*Density As % of Average For Total Island*	*Population*	*Density: Persons Per Sq. Km.*	*Per Cent*
Taipei	896,380	328.0	141	17,151	9.4	4
Hsinchu	641,479	243.9	105	23,232	11.8	5
Taichung	990,571	279.3	120	24,975	6.5	3
Tainan	1,155,287	233.9	100	4,359	9.0	4
Kaohsiung	601,547	210.5	90	31,772	11.1	5
Taitung	46,182	46.2	20	12,619	5.0	2
Hualien	72,555	53.7	23	14,304	4.4	2
P'enghu	60,124	473.9	204	—	—	-
Total Island	4,464,125	232.7	100	128,412	7.6	3

Source: *Census of 1930, Statistical Tables*, Table 11.

reveal relative concentration and dispersion of people. The real centers of population, if we disregard for a moment the dense settlement in the largest cities, were in portions of Taichung and Tainan

Prefectures, and in Taipei. A thin belt of level land along the east coast was only freshly settled; people were extremely sparse in the interior region (see also Fig. 2). Separating the Aborigine Territory removes the greatest variation in terrain and land use. On this basis the more populous sections of the island can be roughly distinguished, though only in terms of Prefectures (which were not evenly settled throughout). To facilitate this comparison, the density of total population (per square kilometer) in each Prefecture is expressed in the final columns of Table 19 as a percentage of the density over the entire island with the Aborigine Territory excluded.

One can get a quick glance at the total effects of migration by examining the disposition of people among the smallest civil divisions at two separate dates. This information is prepared, for the years 1920 and 1935, in Table 20. The intervening period covers

TABLE 20

TAIWAN. TOTAL POPULATION BY SIZE OF CIVIL DIVISION, 1920 AND 1935

Excluding the Aborigine Territory

Size of Civil Division	1920 Population	1920 Civil Divisions	1935 Population	1935 Civil Divisions
	A. Numbers			
Under 10,000	765,772	116	1,244,749	130
10,000-20,000	1,980,510	141	2,262,691	118
20,000-30,000	409,149	19	606,831	22
30,000-40,000	166,543	5	119,785	3
40,000-50,000	47,921	1	469,151	7
Over 50,000	239,342	2	384,973	2
Total Island	3,609,237	284	5,088,180	282
	B. Per Cents			
Under 10,000	21.2	40.8	24.5	46.1
10,000-20,000	54.9	49.6	44.5	41.8
20,000-30,000	11.4	6.7	11.9	7.8
30,000-40,000	4.6	1.8	2.3	1.1
40,000-50,000	1.3	0.4	9.2	2.5
Over 50,000	6.6	0.7	7.6	0.7
Total Island	100.0	100.0	100.0	100.0

Sources: *Census of 1920, Descriptive Report,* Appendix, Table 8.
Census of 1935, Statistical Tables, Table 3.

fifteen years of uninterrupted growth in the island's population. This is a short span, but it is the longest one for which appropriate figures exist. Before 1920 the territorial divisions were not the same, and for the census of 1940 no full reports have been published.

Apparently, from Table 20, the fact that there were more people in 1935 made little difference in their mode of settlement. At both dates more than two-thirds of all people (here including Taiwanese and all other groups) were living in places of less than 20,000 in size. Some of the larger civil divisions shifted upward from one group to a higher one; this is to be expected from the mere fact of general population increase. What is surprising is that the biggest cities—and as late as 1940 Taiwan boasted only three larger than 100,000—failed to advance substantially over the rest of the island. Subsidiary centers of less than 50,000 population made the most headway in relation to other places. A certain amount of administrative reorganization enters into these figures, since evidently a few of the minor units were split up into still smaller ones. But these changes were confined to units of the smallest size, and did not encompass many people. Viewed in entirety, migration therefore did not have a marked effect in redistributing the population growth that was in progress among the Taiwanese.[5]

Economic activities had changed so little, however, that migratory movements could hardly have been large. Besides, no large areas of new lands were available to farmers after 1900. Most of the additional space brought under cultivation since that time was converted to agricultural use within the settled area. Expansion of agriculture along these lines did not open opportunities of wider settlement.[6] In the absence of empty lands, there was little for peasant farmers to gain in changing residence unless they also changed their livelihood. In general, if they remained agriculturists it was advantageous also to remain in localities where they were well known, where their families were well established, and where they did not suffer the invidious treatment commonly accorded to strangers.

[5] Differences in natural increase, which might have hidden the effects of some migration in these figures, bore almost no relation to the differences in actual population growth between civil divisions.

[6] The exception to this rule was the rugged east coast of Taiwan. There the authorities brought in "colonists," first Japanese and later Taiwanese, to establish special settlements in the limited plains area for cultivation of sugar and other crops. Though making up a large part of the population later found in this region, this migration was small and of a very special nature.

On the basis of the previous chapters we should know in advance some of the reasons why people moved. If movement was difficult and uncommon within agriculture, then permanent migration was presumably a matter of going to new jobs. Occupational movement and spatial movement were two interconnected parts of the same process. This meant, for the society, a shift in its economic base; for individuals, it amounted to a change in status, together with exit from rural life and activities.

Bearing in mind that the migrant population was small, we can try to discover where these people went and who they were. For the aggregate of those who crossed local boundaries, both origins and destinations can be found by estimating the balance of persons who moved into or out of each civil division.

This measure is suited to detecting various types of migration. In its results much depends on the types of areas and the period of time chosen for making the estimates. Districts and Municipalities are the places that will be used here; they are small enough not to hide very many moves of more than ten or twenty miles. The smallest time interval is set by the fact that census data give the best indication of total population change by place (i.e., the difference in the people counted from one census to the next in each unit of enumeration). This fixes the period to be used at five years. It is probably sufficient to cancel out some short-term migration and give a certain amount of weight to permanent shifts of residence.

But intercensal population change represents the effects of both net migration and the net amounts gained by births and lost by deaths or natural increase. Since only a tiny fraction of births or deaths went unregistered, they give a good basis for taking out the component of natural increase. The residual term that remains from intercensal population change can therefore be regarded as "net internal migration" in any given civil division.[7]

From 1925 to 1930, net migration viewed in this fashion did not vary greatly among Districts. It is interesting, however, to see the regional groupings of Districts, in terms of per cents of their Tai-

[7] That is, it is practically zero for the island as a whole. Discrepancies are possible for local areas if the chances of dying have been affected by whether or not some of their people were migrants, or if deaths were registered in a previous place of residence. There is no direct evidence available as to the error from those sources. Because Taiwan's population records were of high standard, and because migration was not heavy, it seems safe to assume that these distortions are minor in any particular place. The procedure used for estimating net migration may, however, increase the amplitude of errors in the residual values.

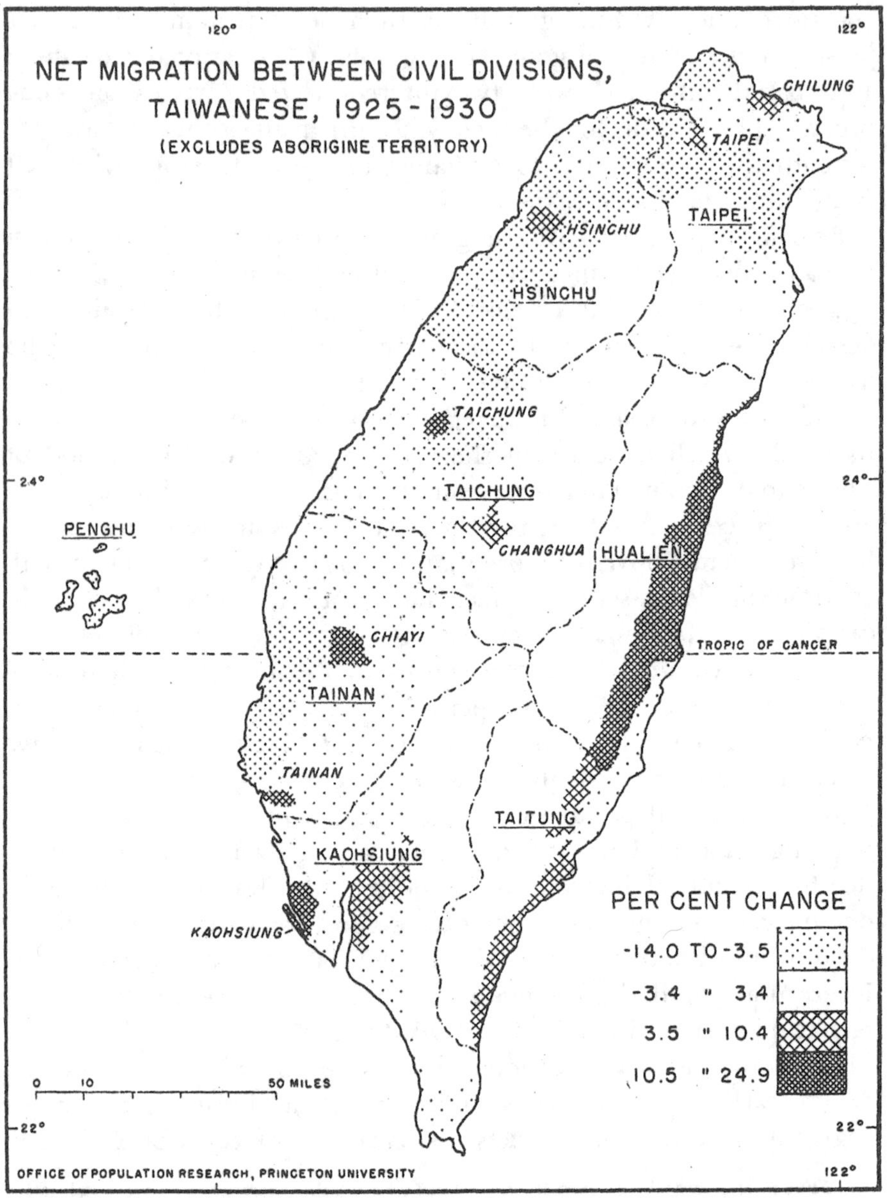

Fig. 17. Net Migration of Taiwanese between Civil Divisions, 1925-1930.

wanese inhabitants received or lost in this way from 1925 to 1930 (see Fig. 17).[8] These groupings divided the rural areas into two parts—a zone of out-migrant Districts in the north, and a more or less neutral region having almost no increase or loss through migration. A process of rapid settlement was beginning in the habitable parts of the eastern coast, where the authorities and a few private companies encouraged people from other Districts to go. This settlement was carried on partly through government design, and was not entirely spontaneous. It grew rapidly from a small start, but did not shift large numbers of people.

These transfers of people were extraordinary. The only other noteworthy exceptions to near-immobility over the rest of the island were cities. On the map these appear as the several isolated points with relatively high gain in migrants.[9] They were interspersed in rural areas of migration deficit, suggesting that much of the movement covered only the short distance from one civil division to the next.

The same data used for Fig. 17 yield more information in terms of the relation of intercensal change with natural increase and net migration. Fig. 18 illustrates the pattern of association that holds in either case, taking each District and Municipality simply as a unit, equally weighted. Against total population change as the standard of comparison, the percentage of natural increase varied from District to District more or less at random, and within a narrow range. Net migration, on the other hand, contributed most of the variation in population change from one civil division to another. The gist of Fig. 18 is summarized in Table 21, this time with each civil division weighted by the number of persons. In a somewhat different way, Table 21 reinforces what we have just learned about the components of population change: natural increase was nearly the same in all quartile groupings of places according to total population growth. Only net migration varied consistently with total change.

[8] Strictly speaking, ratios of estimated migrants to 1925 population. The Aborigine Territory has been excluded in these data, as it was only in the process of being "pacified" at this time; the ratios therefore show the total area illustrated in Fig. 17 to have a net out-migration, presumably because some people moved into the fringes of the interior area as it was gradually subjugated.

[9] In addition, part of one of the Districts was marked by exceptional growth among its neighbors due to the influence of a city that it contained. This was P'ingtung City, slightly to the east of Kaohsiung. It was elevated to a Municipality in 1932 and separated from the surrounding District.

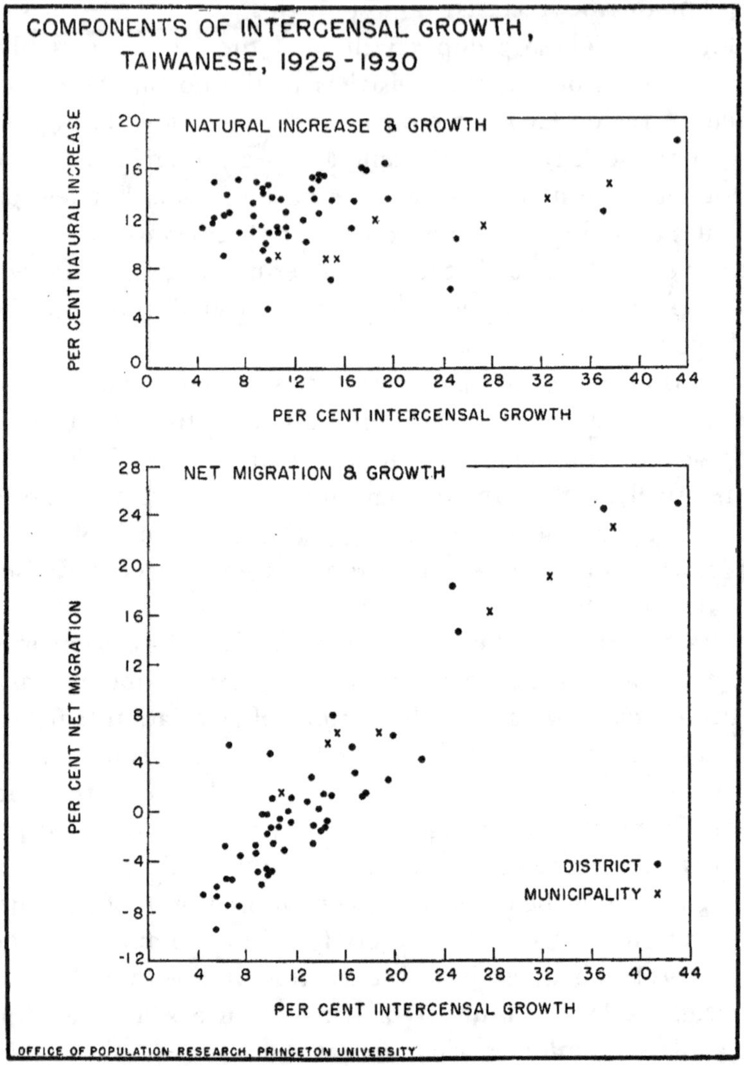

Fig. 18. Net Migration and Natural Increase by Civil Division, Related to Intercensal Growth of Population, 1925-1930.

The residual estimates of net migration above indicate that city populations gained the most from migration. This fact does not of itself imply that they gained the largest numbers of migrants, for we have not yet established that the cities were large enough next to the rural population to have such weight. All that these data reveal about the migrants is, in an aggregate sense, the places of origin and destination. For some idea of the numbers of people involved,

TABLE 21

NET INTERNAL MIGRATION OF TAIWANESE, 1925-1930

By Districts, Grouped in Quartiles According to Total Intercensal Change. With Municipalities Shown Separately*

	Per Cent Intercensal Change	*Per Cent Natural Increase*	*Per Cent Net Migration*
First Quartile	6.2	12.4	—6.2
Second Quartile	9.5	12.1	—2.6
Third Quartile	12.7	13.1	— .5
Fourth Quartile	17.3	13.9	3.3
Municipalities	19.1	10.3	8.9

* Percentages are ratios based on population of 1925 in each civil division.
Sources: *Census of 1925, Statistical Tables*, Table 1.
Census of 1930, Statistical Tables, Tables 1 and 2.
Vital Statistics, yearly volumes, 1926-1930.

and of the proportion of migrants who went to cities, we should rather deal directly with those who migrated.

The census reports for 1930 contain a special table showing persons born in a Prefecture other than the one in which they were enumerated—i.e., who had travelled across a prefectural boundary at some time after birth. This material is not in sufficient detail to establish the broad pattern of migration illustrated above,[10] but forms a valuable supplement to our estimates. In particular, it supplies a fuller answer to the question of relative drawing power between country and city.

Very few Taiwanese shifted residence across prefectural boundaries—obviously fewer than those who moved across District boundaries. The ones who did are a specially selected sampling of all people who moved. Most changes of residence in an agrarian society may be expected to be over short distances. These involve the least break with the past and exposure to unfamiliar conditions. They contain much "normal" movement of people having nothing to do with social change, for they are often bound closely to stable local

[10] It is, for example, an independent source of corroboration for the general spatial pattern of migration shown above. With it we can locate those migrants whose travels happened to cross prefectural boundaries (and who survived to the census date) according to their place of destination. By this criterion, the places of highest immigration are mostly the same as those shown by the measure of "net migration" above in the text. These census data lack, however, any information about the District of origin of the migrant population, which is just as essential to know.

customs.[11] Since the Prefecture in Taiwan was a fair-sized geographical unit, much of this short-distance movement regularly occurred within these boundaries and would never come to light in such coarse tabulations. The rural Districts receiving most migrants from other Prefectures were, not unnaturally, those which lay on the border of an adjoining Prefecture.

The growth of each Prefecture through migration was therefore strongly conditioned by this fact. Cities were not so affected. Unless they were located near the edge of their Prefectures—and none was situated at a boundary—they had less chance of receiving short-distance migration from another Prefecture than did their rural hinterland.

Every Municipality in 1930, however, had a larger proportion of inter-prefectural migrants in its population than the remainder of its own Prefecture (see Table 22). These migrants, of course, were not necessarily people who had entered within a definite period of time, but those who had ever migrated. The east-coast Prefectures (Taitung and Hualien), which were non-urban, had the largest proportion of people from other Prefectures; but we have already seen that they were exceptional cases.[12] Significantly, the attraction of cities for people of other Prefectures tended to favor males more than that of their surrounding areas. In Hsinchu Prefecture (which on balance steadily lost migrants), the difference is greatest of all: the sex ratio of migrants to Hsinchu City was 167, to outside the city 72 (see Table 22).

These facts are put into better focus in Table 23. When migration data of this type cover a complete area, they have the special virtue of enabling one to count the migrants by place of origin as well as place of destination. Part A in Table 23 more nearly corresponds to the residual approach that was adopted above. The column next to the number of in-migrants shows their proportion among all residents; the final column gives the proportion of all in-migrants who went to cities. At the same time when 23.5 per cent of all inter-prefectural migrants had gone to cities, the cities themselves held only 10 per cent of all Taiwanese. A more appropriate comparison than over the entire island is to examine the cities of each Prefecture

[11] As, e.g., the "marriage migration" in certain countries. Cf. Davis, K. (1951), pp. 111-114.

[12] And Hualien contained a growing city of moderate size, which was made a Municipality in 1940.

TABLE 22

INTER-PREFECTURAL MIGRANTS IN TAIWAN, 1930

Taiwanese Residing in Prefecture Other Than That of Birth, Enumerated in Rural Districts and Cities

	A. Rural Districts				*B. Principal Cities (Municipalities in 1930)*				
		Migrants from Another Prefecture (i.e., Born in Other Prefecture)				*Migrants from Another Prefecture (i.e., Born in Other Prefecture)*			
Prefecture	*Total Taiwanese Residents*	*Number*	*% of All Residents*	*Sex Ratio*	*Total Taiwanese Residents*	*Number*	*% of All Residents*	*Sex Ratio*	*Name of City*
Taipei	588,165	18,443	3.1	95	147,620	8,395	5.7	124	Taipei
					51,337	3,353	6.5	145	Chilung
Hsinchu	611,145	6,989	1.1	72	39,361	928	2.4	167	Hsinchu
Taichung	943,314	36,247	3.8	111	39,431	5,040	12.8	106	Taichung
Tainan	989,591	21,678	2.2	100	76,073	5,101	6.7	110	Tainan
					47,615	5,114	10.7	103	Chiayi
Kaohsiung	552,243	24,985	4.5	121	45,288	15,698	34.7	127	Kaohsiung
Taitung	53,684	7,411	13.8	140					
Hualien	72,103	25,670	35.6	136					
P'enghu	55,936	554	1.0	—					
Total Island	3,866,181	141,967	3.7	—					

Source: *Census of 1930, Prefectural Volumes,* Table 30 in each.

separately, where their drawing power stands in clearer contrast to that of their surrounding rural area.

Part B of Table 23 is an interesting supplement to the information already at hand. The deficit standing of Hsinchu is more conspicuous here than in Fig. 17, for the other Prefectures retained most of their own migrants inside their boundaries. P'enghu Islands, in addition, had lost relatively more people to other parts of Taiwan than any other Prefecture. These islands experienced disastrous storms and rural poverty for many years, and had no adequate economic base for many people to follow pursuits other than farming. Through the years P'enghu supplied an unbroken stream of people to Taiwan proper, most of them going to Kaohsiung City.

TABLE 23

TOTAL SURVIVING MIGRANTS BETWEEN PREFECTURES, AND THOSE WHO WENT TO CITIES*

Taiwanese Enumerated in 1930 Whose Place of Residence Was Different from Place of Birth

	A. By Prefecture of Destination Resident in Prefecture, Born Elsewhere			*B. By Prefecture of Origin Born in Prefecture, Resident Elsewhere*		
Prefecture	*Number Who Migrated*	*% In-Migrant of All Persons Resident in Each Prefecture*	*% of the In-Migrant Who Went to Cities*	*Number Who Migrated*	*% Out-Migrant of All Persons Born in Each Prefecture*	*% of the Out-Migrant Who Went to Cities*
Taipei	30,191	3.9	38.9	28,665	3.6	19.2
Hsinchu	7,917	1.2	11.7	91,360	12.4	16.3
Taichung	41,287	4.2	12.2	16,569	1.7	20.6
Tainan	31,893	2.9	32.0	19,950	1.8	27.4
Kaohsiung	40,683	6.8	38.6	9,719	1.7	26.0
Taitung	7,415	13.8	—	2,066	4.3	3.4
Hualien	25,650	35.6	—	1,681	3.5	6.1
P'enghu	544	1.0	—	15,570	21.9	74.7
Total Island	185,580	4.3	23.5	185,580	4.3	23.5

* People living in boats are excluded.
Source: *Census of 1930, Prefectural Volumes,* Table 30 in each.

Movement to Cities: The Rate of Growth

These census materials above all emphasize one important fact: cities were the outstanding recipients of people from the rest of the island. The data regrettably can be used to demonstrate the case in only a limited way. The limitations are, however, of a nature that make this testimony an understatement—the total number of migrants to cities was much larger than merely those who had crossed the borders of a Prefecture. Lacking further data directly for the people who moved, we may find out more about them at their destinations as members of the urban population in Taiwan.

Since these several cities took such a large share of all migrants, they must have grown more rapidly in population than the rest of the island. The Municipalities were only a part of all the cities and towns in Taiwan, for the distinction was one of administrative convenience. Not all had equally developed economic services. They are a makeshift way of distinguishing urban places from rural Districts. Many subsidiary market towns, for example, must be overlooked for lack of data.

But in a population that was predominantly rural, these cities were the most "urban," the farthest removed from traditional peasant agriculture. Under the watchfulness of the Japanese, a town could not enlarge its economic importance for the rest of the island very far before it was given regular municipal administration. Hence we may treat them as representing the most extreme departures from rural conditions to be found in Taiwan, and can proceed to find out how far they deviated from the rest.

In 1932, two more cities were raised to municipal rank. The earlier and later population figures for all nine that were Municipalities in 1935 have been sorted out from the respective census reports, and appear in Table 24. It is clear that the cities of Taiwan were not great metropoleis. These nine were the largest, and many Westerners would regard only the foremost among them (Taipei) as being urban. One cannot gainsay their importance to Taiwan: they differed consistently enough from the rest of the island not to be lightly dismissed.

One distinction that is obvious in Table 24 is in the rate of growth. Though the cities varied considerably among themselves, every one increased its Taiwanese inhabitants more than the entire island did. Most cities maintained steady rates of growth, and therefore tended to keep their differences with the others.

The data are condensed and plotted on a logarithmic scale in Fig. 19, so as to contrast the rates of increase of city and non-city Taiwanese and Japanese. The inequalities in growth stand out clearly. Those cities that were expanding more slowly are likewise the ones that had relatively fewer migrants in the data above. They did not outgrow the non-city population by much of a margin, either in Taiwanese or Japanese. The differences in increase persisted over the entire recorded period, and carried over into the later years of accelerated economic growth. Indeed, from these data on population redistribution one could scarcely guess that the tempo of economic life had changed after 1935. Whereas these same cities had held 10 per cent of all Taiwanese in 1920, they contained only 14.7 per cent as late as 1940. For all their growth, cities did not greatly surpass the increase of all Taiwanese.

TABLE 24

POPULATION OF TAIWANESE AND JAPANESE IN NINE MAJOR CITIES AT SUCCESSIVE CENSUS DATES, 1915-1940*

	1915	*1920*	*1930*	*1940*	*Ratio: 1940/1920*
TAIWANESE					
Taipei	98,495	108,107	147,620	221,602	2.0
Chilung		33,692	51,337	69,578	2.1
Hsinchu		28,951	39,361	51,060	1.8
Taichung	18,444	22,250	39,431	64,884	2.9
Changhua		32,810	40,747	54,741	1.7
Tainan	56,297	62,115	76,073	122,173	2.0
Chiayi		31,392	47,615	80,828	2.6
Kaohsiung		27,153	45,288	96,588	3.6
P'ingtung		18,420	28,917	46,961	2.6
Total, All Cities		364,890	516,389	808,415	2.2
Total Taiwanese		3,466,507	4,313,681	5,510,259	1.6
JAPANESE					
Taipei	37,974	45,211	67,687	91,550	2.0
Chilung		11,898	18,541	24,815	2.1
Hsinchu		2,649	5,102	7,504	2.8
Taichung	6,817	8,817	13,214	16,300	1.8
Changhua		786	1,977	2,977	3.8
Tainan	9,708	12,140	14,955	16,654	1.4
Chiayi		5,445	8,575	9,960	1.8
Kaohsiung		8,840	15,437	28,336	3.2
P'ingtung		3,112	4,814	6,747	2.2
Total, All Cities		98,898	150,302	204,843	2.1
Total Japanese		164,266	228,281	312,386	1.9

* Cities not yet formed before 1935 have been reconstituted for previous years according to their 1935 boundaries from the detailed census tables. Cities changed after 1935 have been adjusted to 1935 boundaries.

Sources: *1915 Population Register* } (Both of these volumes contain the census fig-
1920 Population Register } ures for minor civil divisions.)
Census of 1930, Statistical Tables, Tables 1 and 2.
Census of 1940. (Figures secured from the Gazette of the Taiwan Government-General, April 22, 1941.)

Japanese on the whole had stronger preferences for the same cities as did Taiwanese. But the functions of urban growth were not the same in the two groups. Taiwanese moved to cities as the most promising alternative to farming. Japanese, coming from outside to city and countryside alike, held technical and professional positions in

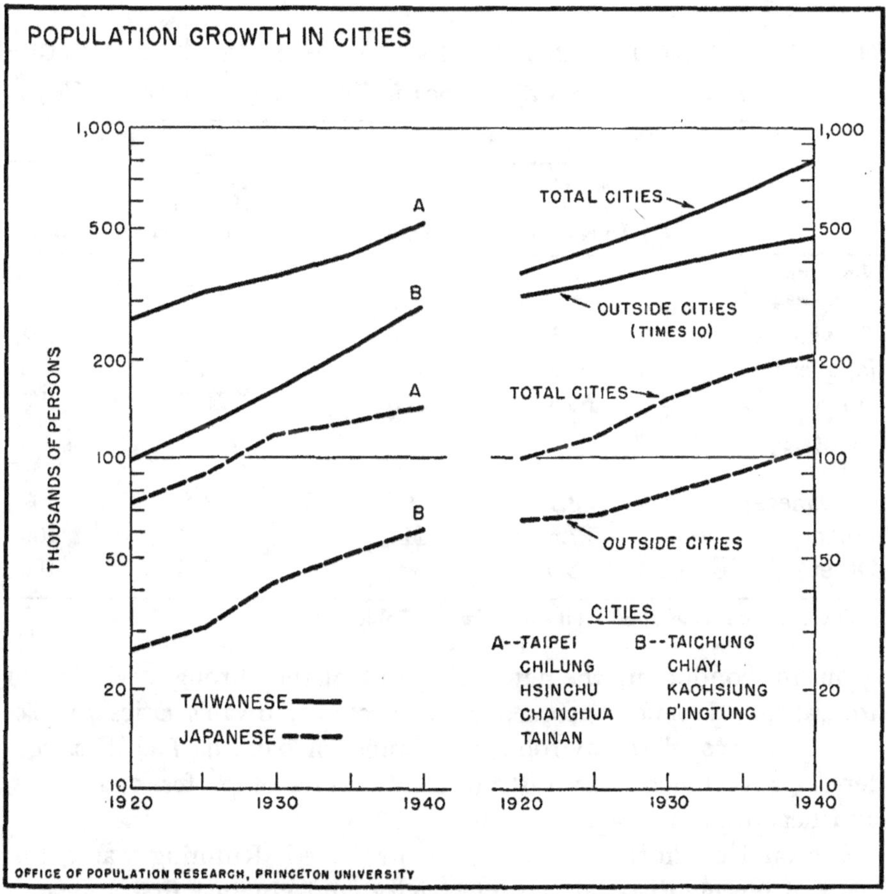

Fig. 19. Growth of Population in Major Cities of Taiwan, 1920-1940. Taiwanese and Japanese.

both places. They certainly esteemed urban more than rustic life; but work of a similar nature was also available to them outside the cities. For them the place of residence had less influence on their type of livelihood.

Ethnic Composition of Cities

The growth of cities depended on only a small part of all Taiwanese to supply the necessary migrants. It was not so with the Japanese. In a sense, the majority of them were migrants, having been born outside of Taiwan. More important, however, nearly two-thirds of all Japanese took up residence in cities and presumably stayed there (see Table 25). They found an urban setting most advanta-

TABLE 25

PROPORTIONS OF TAIWAN'S POPULATION OF EACH ETHNIC GROUP Living Inside the Nine Major Cities in Taiwan, and in Taipei City

	1920		*1940*	
	Per Cent of Total Population	*Sex Ratios*	*Per Cent of Total Population*	*Sex Ratios*
Nine Cities Combined				
Taiwanese	10.5	106	14.7	104
Japanese	60.2	119	65.6	105
Other	68.4	345	59.8	175
Taipei City Alone				
Taiwanese	3.1	102	4.0	99
Japanese	27.5	117	29.3	100
Other	38.6	364	26.8	166

Source: *Census of 1930, Statistical Tables,* Table 1.

geous for conducting the new activities that they brought with them to Taiwan. Japanese proceeded to develop Taiwan's cities to provide an appropriate environment of modern banking facilities, centers of government administration, reservoirs of professional skills, and headquarters of private business.

Personal comforts, too, were not neglected. Running water, systems of sewage disposal, gas, electricity, and cinemas first appeared in these cities, and did not spread far beyond them. For those who could afford the time and expense, life in Taipei was graced by a nearby golf course and several fashionable vacation resorts. Japanese were energetic in constructing large public buildings conspicuously of Western architectural styles, thoroughfares and parks for their gratification and diversion. The section of Taichung City that was occupied by Japanese was referred to fondly as "little Kyoto."[13] Cities understandably were attractive places for Japanese to reside.

The Japanese affinity for urban life was exceeded only among the mainland Chinese that were found in Taiwan.[14] The explanation in their case is somewhat different. These people were admitted to the island as small merchants or as laborers in many of the modern enter-

[13] OPNAV, Civil Affairs Handbook (1944), *Taichu Province*, p. 149 ff.

[14] These made up almost all of the category "Other Nationalities" in Table 25 and in published census tables.

prises that flourished wherever there were Japanese. In this respect they were distinct from Taiwanese, as their occupational composition indicates (see Table 16). Otherwise they merged in language, customs, and sympathies most closely with the urban population of Taiwanese.

The Chinese tended to remain in cities or commercial towns. The authorities held them under suspicion and close scrutiny, and often confined them by labor contract to menial positions. On the whole they did not become permanent residents of Taiwan; by their sex ratios they appear as a relatively transient group (though some of them intermarried with Taiwanese). Many were merely seasonal workers who remained in Taiwan for only part of the year.

The ethnic composition of the urban population was, like its increase, a product of migration from outside cities rather than growth from within. Different cities did not all exert the same attraction for people according to ethnic background. Variations between cities in ethnic composition (see Table 26) were scarcely a matter of *Taiwanese* being drawn less into some cities than into others, for they comprised the broad population base in every one. These differ-

TABLE 26

ETHNIC COMPOSITION OF MAJOR CITIES IN TAIWAN

Per Cent of Total Population in Each Ethnic Group

1920, 1930 and 1940

	Taiwanese			*Japanese*			*Others*		
*Cities**	*1920*	*1930*	*1940*	*1920*	*1930*	*1940*	*1920*	*1930*	*1940*
Taipei	66.4	64.1	67.9	27.8	29.4	28.1	5.8	6.6	4.1
Chilung	70.3	68.4	69.5	24.8	24.7	24.8	4.9	6.9	5.7
Hsinchu	90.7	87.4	86.3	8.3	11.3	12.7	1.1	1.2	1.0
Taichung	70.5	72.8	78.9	28.0	24.4	19.8	1.5	2.8	1.3
Changhua	97.0	93.6	94.0	2.3	4.5	5.1	.7	1.9	.9
Tainan	81.1	80.5	86.0	15.9	15.8	11.7	3.0	3.7	2.3
Chiayi	83.8	82.3	87.4	14.5	14.8	10.8	1.7	2.9	1.8
Kaohsiung	74.1	72.2	79.8	24.1	24.6	18.6	1.8	3.2	1.6
P'ingtung	84.2	82.8	85.8	14.2	13.8	12.3	1.6	3.4	1.9
Total	75.9	73.9	78.0	20.6	21.5	19.2	3.5	4.5	2.8

* Boundaries of all cities have been adjusted to those of 1935.

Sources: *1920 Population Register*, Table 2.
Census of 1930, Statistical Tables, Tables 1 and 2.
Census of 1935, Statistical Tables, Table 1.

ences are to be explained primarily by the preferences of Japanese for certain cities as opposed to others.[15]

We may thus regard the proportion of Japanese in the population as the major element in the variation between cities. The ethnic composition of each city was remarkably stable from 1920 to 1940, though almost all doubled in population. Taipei, Chilung, Taichung, and Kaohsiung were all more than one-fifth Japanese at each census date. This is least surprising in the case of Taipei, for it was the administrative hub of the entire island, and a thriving center of foreign trade as well. Chilung because of its natural harbor became established early as the principal port of access to and from Japan. It kept this position even after the harbor no longer handled heavy traffic, by possessing some of the key industries intended to complement Japan's war effort. Taichung was in the fertile middle section of the island, and prospered enormously from the collecting, processing, and marketing of agricultural produce. Kaohsiung was the center from which the Japanese mounted their most extensive efforts at modernization: in the city itself and its immediate environs were concentrated the major processing industries of the island. Large sums were spent in improving its harbor to facilitate the passage of this new production out of the island.[16]

The remaining five Municipalities were more typically Chinese in atmosphere, with the alien features of Japanese presence kept more in the background. Whatever their types, these cities of Taiwan were the most important places where Japanese residents mingled with Taiwanese. Japanese nationals were scattered over the rest of the island in administrative and technical posts, public and private, but only in these cities did they associate regularly with Taiwanese. Only there did many Taiwanese who were non-farmers come into frequent contact with Japanese. Consequently, one would expect that the urban environment was the principal channel of modern influence.

Even in these cities there were certain obstacles in the way of such contact. The barrier was not entirely one of language, for Taiwanese soon acquired the rudiments of the Japanese tongue through school-

15 Mainland Chinese varied almost as much as their share in the total population by city. But they were so few, and their stay in Taiwan so impermanent, that they cannot be considered a very important part of even the urban population.

16 Kaohsiung City was also built up as a base for southward expansion in the Pacific Ocean, but did not have the opportunity to fulfill the promise of this investment.

ing and practice. Japanese did many things to discourage free intercourse between the two groups, and raised exaggerated fears of animosity from the Taiwanese among their own kind.[17]

The Japanese maintained high levels of living in Taiwan. Their wealth did not create the separation between the two groups, but helped to enlarge it. The opulence of Japanese was more than simply a matter of superior income (which the Taiwanese might have emulated); it was also founded on privilege.

For example, wherever possible they lived apart in special portions of each city. These sections were arranged so as to provide the facilities that they were in a position to command—Japanese shops, entertainment, and cleanliness, one of the greatest of all luxuries in Asia. Influential Japanese strove to put themselves in such surroundings, whereupon they allowed poorer sections to develop as Taiwanese residents could best afford. Owing to this combination of jealous care and neglect, the central districts of most cities were elaborately laid out with efficient street patterns and handsome landscapes—but with residential finery and modern public buildings concentrated in a few blocks and the indescribable slums that Asia often produces spread over the remainder.[18]

It is easy to see the nature of residential segregation in Taipei City, where it was carried farthest (see Fig. 20, based on 1935 census data). There were two large concentrations of Taiwanese, at the north and the southeast corners. These were the sites of the original pair of settlements that grew into the present city. The space in between had been gradually built up before 1895 as the seat of Manchu administration for the island. It was razed and replaced by the Japanese (following a destructive typhoon in 1912) to make way for new construction that they planned. The Japanese built this central area themselves, and therefore to their own design. It had a core in which almost none but Japanese eventually lived, surrounded by a

[17] One can say that these fears were exaggerated without implying that they were without foundation. By their repressive administration, Japanese invited widespread ill-will in the population. Much of this might have been allayed if they had not on the one hand advertised the benefits of their rule and, on the other, systematically cut off any opportunities for Taiwanese to compete with Japanese on equal footing. This ambivalent policy even undermined some of their foremost objectives by impeding their use of the local labor supply in the most effective ways for war production.

[18] The enforcement of health and sanitary regulations held the two groups in complete equality before the law. In looking back at the severity of these measures, Chinese have remembered them as instances of oppression by the Japanese. But by such means the authorities were able to avoid the unhealthful conditions usually associated with urban crowding in Asia. See Hsü Tze-wei (1946), p. 444 ff.

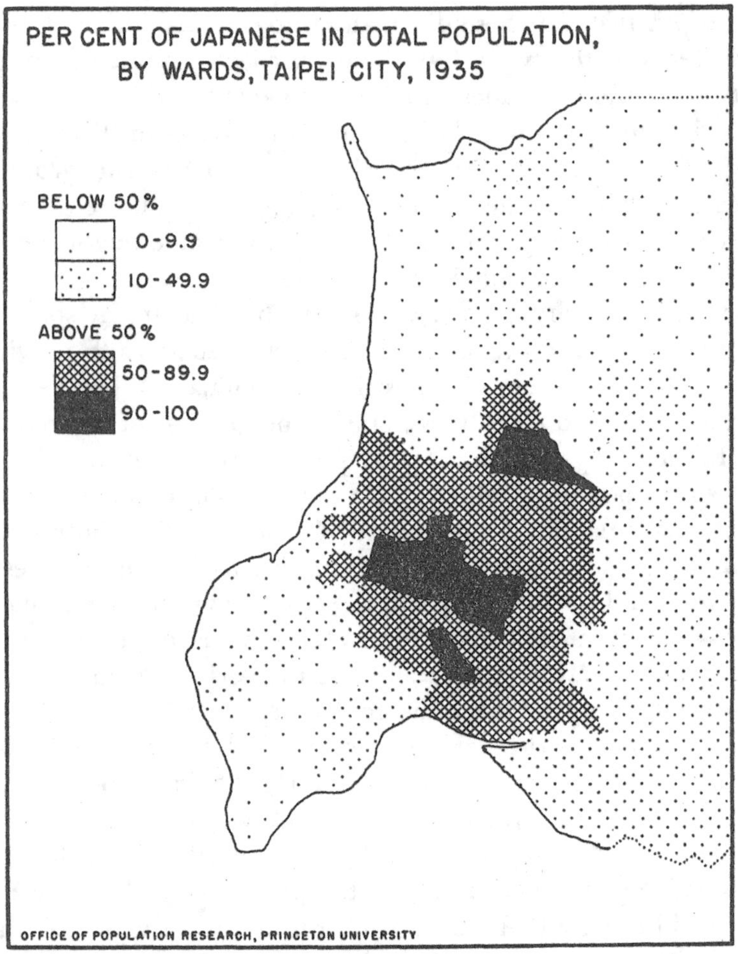

Fig. 20. Residential Segregation of Japanese in Taipei City.

substantial area where Japanese residents predominated. Around the fringes of this modern district, other Japanese (reportedly those of lower income and social status[19]) lived more thinly mixed with Taiwanese. Almost one-half of the city's surface was taken up by poorer districts composed entirely of Taiwanese dwellings, shops, and open markets.

There is also another way to see how the separation of living quarters kept the two groups apart—in terms of persons rather than the space involved. Table 27 illustrates this aspect of segregation for

[19] OPNAV, Civil Affairs Handbook (1944), *Taihoku Province*, p. 133. A more comprehensive account of the growth of Taipei City, in relation to the surrounding region, is given in Ch'en Cheng-hsiang (1952).

TABLE 27

RESIDENTIAL SEGREGATION IN TAIPEI CITY, 1925 AND 1935

Taiwanese and Japanese Population Distributed by the Proportion Japanese in Each "Ward"

Per Cent Japanese in Each Ward	1925 Number	1925 Per Cent of Total	1935 Number	1935 Per Cent of Total
		Taiwanese		
0– 9.9	94,551	73.4	109,309	62.5
10.0– 49.9	25,681	19.9	48,815	27.9
50.0– 89.9	7,964	6.2	16,508	9.4
90.0–100.0	606	0.5	384	0.2
Total Taiwanese	128,802	100.0	175,016	100.0
		Japanese		
0– 9.9	3,069	5.8	3,640	4.5
10.0– 49.9	11,462	21.5	18,173	22.2
50.0– 89.9	24,926	46.7	48,775	59.7
90.0–100.0	13,884	26.0	11,116	13.6
Total Japanese	53,341	100.0	81,704	100.0

Sources: *Census of 1925, Statistical Tables*, Table 2.
Census of 1935, Statistical Tables, Table 2.

Taipei City in 1925 and 1935. Here both Taiwanese and Japanese have been grouped according to the degree of concentration of Japanese in each "ward." While the non-Japanese wards held the bulk of Taiwanese, there was some considerable area of overlap where the two groups were relatively mixed. From the evidence of this table, many Japanese who were arriving in Taiwan were forced to go to residential areas that contained some Taiwanese residents. This is shown by the relative gain of Japanese in the sections that were not purely Japanese, but where Japanese residents were in the majority. With its members increasing, the Japanese community eventually had to mix more widely with Taiwanese, since the areas that were already more than 90 per cent Japanese could not absorb any newcomers. They moved into wards with only the "better element" of Taiwanese, however, and managed to keep this mixture to a minimum. The proportion of Japanese living in predominantly Taiwanese wards actually fell off very slightly.

From the Taiwanese side, moving into mixed sections was carried somewhat further. Taiwanese were beginning to spread into wards that were not purely Taiwanese, sections closer to the center of the city which they had occupied together with Japanese. Because there were more of them, and because they had been more concentrated among their own kind before, the Taiwanese moving into these areas contributed more to the mixture than the Japanese. The data here do not signify that it was very extensive. But it makes some difference which of these two aspects of segregation we choose to use as a standard of comparison.

This trend in the segregation of urban residents was of some significance in the other cities during the years when they were growing rapidly, for the system was put under strain by the continuous arrival of new immigrants. On the whole, the Japanese were successful in housing most of their people in residential wards that were predominantly Japanese, and well-to-do Taiwanese were moderately successful in entering sections containing some Japanese, but not into the sections most prized by the Japanese.

For Japanese, no other city offered living quarters and facilities so exclusive as those of Taipei (see Table 28). In every one of these six other Municipalities they lived more widely intermixed with Taiwanese (though not necessarily at the same levels of comfort). Kao-

TABLE 28

RESIDENTIAL SEGREGATION IN SIX CITIES OF TAIWAN, 1935

Taiwanese and Japanese Population Distributed by the Proportion Japanese of Each Ward

Per Cent Japanese in Each Ward	*Chilung*	*Hsinchu*	*Taichung*	*Tainan*	*Chiayi*	*Kaohsiung*
			Taiwanese			
0– 9.9	56.6	68.5	52.7	50.0	58.2	56.1
10.0– 49.9	34.2	30.7	42.7	48.3	41.5	36.2
50.0– 89.9	8.9	0.7	4.5	1.7	0.3	7.7
90.0–100.0	0.3	0.1	0.1	0.0	0.0	0.0
Total Taiwanese	100.0	100.0	100.0	100.0	100.0	100.0
			Japanese			
0– 9.9	5.7	16.4	6.8	11.0	15.7	7.9
10.0– 49.9	35.6	54.3	53.0	69.9	80.0	38.6
50.0– 89.9	50.9	16.6	34.9	11.1	4.3	53.5
90.0–100.0	7.8	12.7	5.3	8.0	0.0	0.0
Total Japanese	100.0	100.0	100.0	100.0	100.0	100.0

Source: *Census of 1935, Statistical Tables,* Table 2.

hsiung and Chiayi had not a single ward with as high as 90 per cent of its population Japanese. For Taiwanese, on the other hand, Taipei consisted neither more nor less of mixed wards than the other cities. In all, at least nine-tenths of the Taiwanese population of every city stayed in districts in which less than a majority of the inhabitants were Japanese.

The Taiwanese in Cities

Of all Taiwanese, so few went to cities that one is prompted to ask whether there were not some special factors present restricting the size of this migration. The effects of such a selective process over many years should produce differences in the characteristics of persons living in cities and of those living outside.

Since few if any newcomers had an opportunity to take up agriculture in the cities, a prominent feature of cityward migration was a movement to new work. To the extent that it was, one would expect that the migrants were the types of persons who usually undertook new occupations in Taiwan—for example, men rather than women, primarily in the ages of young adulthood. If the migrant population had been limited to these categories, cities with large proportions of migrants in their populations must have had disproportionate numbers of young men as compared with the rest of the island. Such a tendency has characterized rapid urbanization elsewhere.

In addition, cities frequently offer opportunities for employment that are considered superior to those found in the countryside. This is especially true of many agrarian societies, where rural poverty sometimes reaches extremes that make the meanest of urban jobs seem attractive. Where such conditions exist, movement to cities very often serves to drain off large numbers of men in young working ages who have lost or overcome their attachment to farming.

In 1935, these effects of age and sex selection were hardly perceptible in Taiwan's urban population taken as a whole. The age composition of all their males combined was nearly the same as the rural population (Table 29). Surprisingly, urban females likewise had almost the same age structure as those outside of cities. Hence, there could have been no sweeping dislocation of persons of different age and sex groups as a result of urbanization in Taiwan.

There are special circumstances in which it is not hard to imagine some movement of single individuals in an agrarian society; this has

TABLE 29

AGE AND SEX COMPOSITION OF TAIWANESE, INSIDE AND OUTSIDE OF NINE MAJOR CITIES, 1925 AND 1935

Per Cent of Total Population in Selected Age Intervals, Male and Female

Age	*Males* Inside	*Males* Outside	*Females* Inside	*Females* Outside	*Males per 100 Females* Inside	*Males per 100 Females* Outside
			1925			
0–14	36.5	40.2	37.5	40.0	101	105
15–39	44.1	40.6	39.5	37.6	116	113
40-64	17.8	17.4	19.5	18.8	95	96
65+	1.6	1.8	3.5	3.6	47	52
Total	100.0	100.0	100.0	100.0	104	104
			1935			
0–14	41.0	43.2	41.1	42.9	103	103
15–39	41.6	38.5	39.0	37.0	110	107
40–64	15.9	16.5	16.8	16.8	97	101
65+	1.5	1.8	3.1	3.3	50	57
Total	100.0	100.0	100.0	100.0	103	103

Sources: *Census of 1925, Statistical Tables,* Table 3.
Census of 1935, Statistical Tables, Table 7.

been known to occur in the form of contractual servitude by children, of young men (though not frequently young women) shifting to non-agricultural employment, and of movement by old persons to reside with emigrant kin. But it is inconceivable that these deviant events might have occurred jointly in chance coordination so as to reproduce the rural age structure so closely in cities. Such a migration as this could have been possible only if many people travelled to cities in family units and not as isolated individuals. A great many migrants therefore must have moved merely because they were members of migrant kinship groups.[20]

This situation did not hold with equal force in all cities. Variations in composition among separate cities were as great as the distinction between city and non-city. Assuming the age group 15 to 39 among males to be the most responsive to new opportunities for

[20] Estimates for the age composition of the *migrants* lend weight to this supposition. Survivors to 1935 of people who were already in cities in 1925 can be estimated at every age by subtracting the deaths that one would expect of them; the amount by which these survivors fail to account for the people actually found in cities in 1935 gives a fair idea of the persons gained through migration at each age. Though migrants measured in this way were somewhat concentrated in young adult ages, there were also impressive numbers in younger and older ages.

TABLE 30
DIFFERENCES IN AGE AND SEX COMPOSITION OF TAIWANESE BY CITY, 1935

Cities	*Per Cent 15-39 of all Taiwanese Males*	*Sex Ratios 15-39*	*Sex Ratios all Ages*	*Growth of City: Ratio of Taiwanese Population 1940/1920*
Taipei	41.8	106	98	2.05
Chilung	42.4	112	103	2.07
Hsinchu	38.2	101	100	1.76
Taichung	43.2	115	107	2.92
Changhua	39.0	102	100	1.67
Tainan	40.6	110	105	1.97
Chiayi	42.2	112	105	2.58
Kaohsiung	42.8	120	110	3.56
P'ingtung	43.5	118	108	2.55
Total, All Cities	41.6	110	103	2.22

Source: *Census of 1935, Statistical Tables,* Table 7.

employment, we can use this group to summarize the differences (see Table 30). The cities of rapid growth—i.e., with relatively large proportions of immigrants—were the cities with more young men. Cities that grew faster did so in part by attracting more men in young working ages, and thus separated many of them from normal family life. Significantly, the age composition of females was nearly the same in *all* the individual cities, and thus was similar in each to rural communities.

The non-rural character of Municipalities in Taiwan, therefore, did not of itself make for non-rural age structure, but the same factors that were behind the more rapid growth of some cities tended to draw selectively from the population of different ages outside cities. One should always bear in mind that the greatest of the differences in Table 30 are moderate when considered alongside societies in which urban growth has been associated with sweeping modernization.

Something in addition can be learned about the particular characteristics of separate cities from the nature of economic activities in each. One single census table of persons with occupations was published in 1930 for individual cities, with the males of all ethnic groups lumped together. Cities were farthest removed of any civil

TABLE 31

INTER-CITY DIFFERENCES IN OCCUPATIONAL COMPOSITION

Per Cent of Occupied Males in Selected Types of Occupation in Each of Seven Municipalities, 1930

All Nationality Groups

Cities	*Manu-facturing*	*Commerce*	*Trans-portation*	*Govern-ment*	*Agri-culture*	*Other Occupations*
Taipei	26	30	10	18	6	10
Chilung	16	21	23	9	4	27
Hsinchu	21	25	10	13	20	11
Taichung	23	28	10	19	14	6
Tainan	28	28	13	18	5	8
Chiayi	22	29	10	12	20	7
Kaohsiung	24	19	20	11	13	13
Total Seven Cities	24	27	13	15	9	12

Source: *Census of 1930, Statistical Tables,* Table 40.

divisions from rural conditions. Nevertheless, large blocs of Taiwan's urban population still supported themselves by farming. Only three Municipalities in 1930 had as few as one-twentieth of their working males engaged in agriculture. It is small wonder that these cities had failed to show symptoms of advanced urbanism in other respects.

Other types of employment in these cities also had certain special features. Government administration in Taipei, transshipping of seaport cargoes in Chilung and Kaohsiung, and sugar processing in Taichung and Tainan were reflected as important activities in their share of all male employment. These figures, pertaining to 1930, reveal nothing of the intensified industrial activity in these cities in the succeeding decade. They are the only available indication in demographic terms of the peculiarities of individual cities. In any event, we are less interested in these peculiar elements than in the relations between types of employment and urban settlement among Taiwanese. Since Table 31 does not show Taiwanese separately, it is affected by differences in the proportions of Japanese and in their work among the various cities. Hence the information, while illuminating, is less useful than one might wish.

More information is available for the population of all seven cities combined. By means of some estimation, we can find the occupational

TABLE 32

OCCUPATIONAL COMPOSITION IN CITIES OF TAIWAN BY ETHNIC GROUP, 1930*

Distribution of Occupied Males by Occupation and Nationality

	Taiwanese	*Japanese*	*Other Nationalities*
A. Per Cents by Occupation			
Agriculture	13.1	0.9	0.2
Fishing	2.1	2.2	0.5
Mining	2.1	0.2	1.1
Manufacturing	22.8	18.6	43.8
Commerce	29.1	19.6	27.8
Transportation	13.7	10.2	19.1
Govt. & Prof.	6.4	44.4	3.3
Other	10.7	3.9	4.2
Total Occupied	100.0	100.0	100.0
Per Cent Occupied of All Males	54.4	58.0	76.8
B. Per Cents by Ethnic Group			
Agriculture	97.5	2.4	0.1
Fishing	70.8	27.2	2.0
Mining	89.9	3.8	6.3
Manufacturing	65.0	19.0	16.0
Commerce	73.2	17.8	9.0
Transportation	69.1	18.5	12.4
Govt. & Prof.	28.2	70.0	1.8
Other	84.7	11.1	4.2
Total Occupied	67.4	24.0	8.6

* Includes the seven cities of Municipal rank in 1930.
Source: Estimated from *Census of 1930, Statistical Tables,* Table 39.

composition of each ethnic group separately (Table 32).[21] Taking account only of males with occupation, these data represent the urban Taiwanese at less of a disadvantage next to the Japanese than was true over the entire island. Of course, one must remember that Taiwanese (and Mainland Chinese) in the same type of work with Jap-

[21] The necessity to "estimate" arises because the occupational data *by ethnic groups* were given in "Occupation" units (i.e., persons with a principal occupation plus persons with a secondary occupation), and counted some persons twice. In the tables shown here, the ethnic composition of "Occupations" has been applied to the total of persons (males) in each occupation.

anese usually had subordinate positions. Nevertheless, it seems conclusive that by moving into cities Taiwanese were able to narrow the gap that separated their forms of livelihood from those of the Japanese.

The ethnic composition of occupied persons (appended to Table 32) indicates how the differences in occupational structure among these ethnic groups were weighted in the urban population. Taiwanese, of course, predominated in all lines except in government service and professional activities. Keeping these coveted positions in their own hands was one of the ways in which Japanese were able to live side by side with the rest of the population and avoid the pressure of competition.

Chinese nationals ("Other Nationalities" in Table 32) in these cities also appeared in a few types of work far more than in the working population as a whole. Their specialties were of an opposite kind: many worked as laborers in small manufacturing enterprises and as longshoremen, accounting for their large share of all "Manufacturing" and "Transportation" workers.

TABLE 33
OCCUPATIONAL DISTRIBUTION OF TAIWANESE MALES REPORTING AN OCCUPATION, INSIDE AND OUTSIDE MAJOR CITIES, 1905, 1920, 1930

	1905		*1920*		*1930*	
	*Inside**	*Outside*	*Inside†*	*Outside*	*Inside‡*	*Outside*
Agriculture	2.3	72.1	13.2	71.9	13.1	74.0
Fishing	.6	2.9	1.2	2.3	2.1	2.0
Mining } Manufacturing }	28.4	5.4	1.1	1.4	2.1	1.3
Manufacturing			27.1	6.9	22.8	5.9
Commerce	37.7	6.4	28.9	6.4	29.1	8.2
Transportation	10.4	1.9	11.2	2.8	13.7	2.8
Govt. & Prof.	5.6	1.7	6.7	1.9	6.4	2.3
Other	15.0	9.6	10.6	6.4	10.7	3.5
Total Occup.	100.0	100.0	100.0	100.0	100.0	100.0

* Comprises the cities of Taipei, Taichung, and Tainan. The boundaries for Taipei in this tabulation were smaller than the city as subsequently organized.

† Cities of Taipei, Taichung, and Tainan, with the same boundaries used at later census dates.

‡ Cities of Taipei, Chilung, Hsinchu, Taichung, Tainan, Chiayi, Kaohsiung.

Sources: *Census of 1905, Detailed Tables, Prefectural Volume*, Table 17.
Census of 1920, Prefectural Volume, Table 16.
Census of 1930, Statistical Tables, Table 39.

Finally, the role of migration in social change can be clear only if we can make comparisons at different points of time. Occupational profiles of city and non-city working males are available in not quite the same form for three separate dates. The census reports of 1905 and 1920 each included a table of occupied persons in three cities (Taipei, Taichung and Tainan). Placed next to the corresponding figures in 1930 (Table 33), these early data are reasonably similar in all three years.

Not all of the same cities are included, and so the occupational distributions for cities alone do not stand close comparison with each other. One's attention is therefore drawn to the structure of occupations *outside* the cities involved. In Table 33, it appears that by removing the small group of urban working persons from the total population of Taiwanese, one in effect also removes most of the diversification in employment over time, and consequently a large share of the social changes that occurred in Taiwan. In other words, the new activities that resulted from Japanese occupation remained sealed up in the few urban centers. The Taiwanese population outside of these cities remained essentially as agrarian as at the beginning of Japanese rule.[22]

Even if as centers of innovation we did not consider Taiwan's cities important, a study of migration would have made them so. Permanent migration was rare among Taiwanese; but of those who migrated, a large proportion went to a few cities. Even though these cities were not growing fast enough to enlarge their share of all Taiwanese very substantially, they did the greatest part in redistributing the population.

The real significance of these shifts of residence arose from the fact that they were also shifts in activities. For the most part withdrawal from agriculture meant exit from rural communities. People departed every year to large towns or cities that had some provision for more diverse kinds of livelihood. It was primarily in these centers that the Japanese fostered modern enterprises and developed a need for labor. Migration was one of the forms of the response to

[22] Obviously, since more cities are represented in the 1930 figures, the figures themselves are biased and there is some chance of bias in the conclusion that we have drawn. By taking occupied men of all ethnic groups, the same comparison can be made based on the *same three cities* at all dates. This is possible because the table for all ethnic groups was published for each city separately (cf. Table 31, above). The result is the same, in that the data indicate no change in occupational structure outside even these three cities.

these new opportunities for employment. It steadily brought more Taiwanese into contact with the modern side of the Japanese economic program.

Yet even though movement to the cities did widen the horizons of a few Taiwanese, it was surrounded by circumstances that tended to minimize this effect. The familial character of the migration made the break between country and city less sharp than it might have been. Removal to a city did not expose migrants very readily to whatever new influences were there. These were all dominated by Japanese, who kept most of their innovations to themselves and erected barriers against free intercourse with the rest of the population.

Urban growth therefore did not promote general social change among the Taiwanese. It removed into cities those who were to feel the strongest effects of contact with these alien elements. Migration thus helped to absorb the modern aspects of economic development so that they did not intrude into the affairs of rural communities.

CHAPTER VI

Public Health and the Risks of Death

In the preceding pages, we have given attention to various features of intercourse between Taiwanese and Japanese in Taiwan. Most of the evidence has been in agreement on one point—the policies of Japanese as rulers of the island failed to make any substantial difference in the social structure of its people. The more it seemed to change in some particular, the more it turned out to be essentially the same thing. As a matter of official design many innovations were concentrated in the hands of a favored few. Even when it came to implementing their aims, Japanese found ways to meet the population on its own terms. Much of their success in colonial administration was due to the ability to make the social system serve their purposes without changing its form.

The most significant exception was their effort on behalf of the health of the inhabitants. Japanese have never received full credit for their achievement in this realm, either on the part of the Taiwanese (who resented the intrusions that it involved in their lives) or from Western students of population and public health (who mostly ignored or belittled it). The "benefits" of rationalizing Taiwanese agriculture may be a matter of dispute, for it enormously enriched a few Japanese at the same time that it broadened standards of consumption in the population. The motives of Japanese in introducing to Taiwan some of the advantages of scientific discovery from the outside world may likewise be suspect, for they managed to keep control over most of the fruits of improvement. But there is no doubt that in the field of public health Japanese rule added many years to the expected lifetime of Taiwanese. This, in an environment of opinion that looks with approval upon any postponement of death, deserves to be given adequate attention.

Early Health Conditions in Taiwan

Prior to 1895, Taiwan was renowned as an unhealthful place to live. It presented special hazards to survival in addition to those which its people had learned to accept in South China. Unusual efforts had been called forth in expanding settlement into the relatively empty area, and these entailed unusual risks of death. Early Chinese migrants to Taiwan had to attend to clearing new lands, and to contend with many types of hardship not found on the mainland. As they pushed toward the island's foothills, they also suffered the consequences of many bloody incidents of violence that they provoked among aboriginal tribesmen.

Even in the lowlands, where activities were comparatively settled and routine, life itself was a very uncertain thing. From their environment people were subjected to attack by several kinds of fatal sickness. Through certain traditional practices they unwittingly exposed themselves to many others. The semi-tropical climate of Taiwan favored the spread of a multitude of disease-producing agents. Accustomed methods of cultivating the land—especially those having to do with the conservation of human wastes as fertilizer—encouraged the transmission of these organisms to humans.[1]

Through conditions such as these, the population harbored many body parasites and other sources of infection. As a result, many people passed their lives chronically enfeebled, and others remained constantly exposed to the onset of illness. Certain types of disease often spread over the island, restrained only by the isolation of many localities and the difficulty of travel. From time to time, some would grow to spectacular epidemics in which thousands perished. Disease even proved to be one of the best defenses that Taiwan had against attack by the troops of Western powers, and delayed the Japanese in taking control of the island.

Plague was the foremost among these epidemic diseases.[2] Taiwan was repeatedly swept by attacks of this illness, with heavy fatalities. An uncontrolled traffic of shipping from the mainland and from elsewhere in Asia, much of it illicit, made it easy to introduce infected rats and persons. Conditions of knowledge and sanitation in Taiwan were wholly inadequate to cope with the problem.[3]

Cholera was the second most important disease that occurred in epidemic proportions. Lacking knowledge or facilities to control the spread of cholera, Taiwanese sometimes suffered the full course of epidemics throughout a whole season without being able to take counter-measures.[4] Cholera also was well known and feared in the

[1] For an able popular account of some of the connections between custom and the "food cycle" that propagates these organisms, see Winfield, G. F. (1948), p. 112 ff.

[2] See Hsü Tze-wei (1946), p. 444.

[3] For some of the futile steps adopted against plague by the people, see Campbell, W. (1915), p. 77.

[4] Drinking water was usually taken from the rivers or from shallow wells, making them easily subject to pollution. See Takekoshi, Y. (1907), p. 285.

early Western contacts with Taiwan. It all but wiped out some of the military expeditions sent there as tentative colonial ventures by European powers, and later helped to persuade the Japanese to embark on large-scale measures of control.

Malaria was ordinarily endemic in Taiwan. The moist heat, and the practice of admitting water into fields for irrigation in pools that were left to stagnate, helped to nurture the mosquitoes that spread the disease. Occasionally malaria broke out in epidemic form. It was likewise impossible to control, but was simply allowed to run its course. Even in the more fortunate years it served to undermine the strength of Taiwanese during much of the year, and probably also their resistance to other sickness.

In addition to these major diseases, Taiwanese were widely afflicted with the more common debilitating ailments that tend to shorten life and lead to complicating illnesses in Asia. Enteric diseases and internal parasites were always prevalent, as in China. Tuberculosis and venereal disease were later found to be widespread, and presumably had existed also at this earlier period. Superficial skin and eye maladies were frequent. Taiwan's position as a transshipping point in the opium trade introduced a plentiful amount of the drug for local consumption, which impaired the health of the inhabitants still further. In the census of 1905, it was found that nearly one-fifth of all Taiwanese men over age 30 were known users of opium, and there were probably others who managed to conceal the fact. As external trade increased, surreptitiously and openly, Taiwan became exposed to a wider variety of diseases and a greater number of transmitting agents from outside. At the same time, the official policy of seclusion also kept out the techniques that the West was evolving to deal with them.

These baneful health conditions added new hardships for the people who migrated to Taiwan. The risks of death thus engendered became a formidable feature of everyday living. Moreover, under the pressure of poverty many families apparently eliminated certain unwanted offspring, either through exposure or deliberate neglect. As a result, a large proportion of those who were born into the population never survived to adulthood. The dangers to life were such that probably Taiwan gained few if any people through natural increase; very high fertility was needed merely to offset the losses through death.

The Japanese and Public Health

The Japanese military forces that first set out to subdue Taiwan met no firmly organized resistance among the people, but were nearly overcome by sickness in their own ranks before taking possession of the island. Out of an undisclosed total number of troops taking part in the campaign, the Japanese acknowledged only 154 combat fatalities, but over 4,000 died of disease within the first several months, and 27,000 had to be hospitalized (most of them in Japan).[5] Epidemic illness did not, like poverty, stay confined to the Taiwanese population and leave the new rulers unmolested. Mosquitoes that carried malaria, for example, did not observe this distinction. The Japanese liking for raw fish was said to make them even more vulnerable than Taiwanese to the parasites that infested the food. Among the garrison alone, annual deaths of more than 40 per thousand were reported during the first decade of occupation, probably a higher figure than in the adult population of Taiwanese. In order to make this region of the world safe for imperialism, the Japanese found that they had to take drastic measures to curb the spread of disease.

They started almost at once to devise ways of counteracting the most serious sources. The steps that they adopted are instructive, for the result was a marked success with only a modest outlay. The campaign against sickness was launched when scientific knowledge as to the nature of these diseases was by present standards still rudimentary. Its weapons were crude and sometimes misguided. Moreover, there were many other goals of administration that competed with public health for attention. The authorities were never in a position to divert large blocs of funds to make their program elaborate or munificent. It lacked the grandeur of projects sometimes contemplated by those who draw up plans for "backward" areas today. The whole approach of the Japanese to the problem of disease in Taiwan was an austere one. They avoided every possible expense in equipment and physical facilities, and depended on intensive use of all the administrative resources at their command.

In slightly over a decade the authorities almost eradicated plague as a major disease, through strict vigilance for suspected cases of infection, rigorous quarantine regulations, and careful inspection of incoming ocean cargoes for infected rats.[6] Cholera was similarly pre-

[5] Davidson, James W. (1903), p. 354.
[6] Naito, Hideo (1937), p. 84 ff.

vented from spreading in the population by incessant search for afflicted persons, and quarantine of those cases that were found. Inoculations gradually were developed into an indispensable preventive measure against both of these diseases.

The cities, where crowded and unsanitary living conditions invited some deterioration of health standards, were made less favorable to cholera by piping in water from mountain streams and from specially constructed wells. In nearby localities, regulations were issued—and enforced—requiring villagers to tap sub-surface sources of water with deep wells that were kept covered.[7] Contamination of food supplies in the larger cities was minimized by crude provision for sewage disposal—a few septic tanks and public sewers were built, but most municipal authorities merely supervised the removal of sewage by cart. Agencies of the Sanitation Bureau regulated food handling and butchery in the public market places.

Malaria had to be attacked indirectly, and hence proved more stubborn to keep in check. It remained a source of widespread enervation and an important cause of death even during the 1930's, when measures for its control had become most effective. There were then no very satisfactory ways to kill mosquitoes or to check their breeding under conditions in Taiwan. The government drained many swamps, but the irrigation procedures necessary for the island's food supply depended on open water storage and flooding of fields.[8] The localities most frequently affected soon became known, and the authorities relied on detection and compulsory treatment of cases that were discovered. They sent special medical personnel to these districts, backed up by police power, and forced all suspected individuals to undergo blood tests and compulsory treatment with quinine. In the later 1930's, over three million examinations were regularly being performed each year. By unremitting and energetic insistence on these devices, the Japanese managed at least to prevent any large epidemic outbreak of malaria during their stay in Taiwan.

With these few outstanding dangers under control, the principal remaining causes of ill health and death were respiratory ailments and enteric disorders. As the former ceased to produce epidemics, these more common types of sickness came to account for an increas-

[7] U.S. War Department. *Technical Bulletin* (TB Med 30) (1944), p. 2.

[8] It is moreover alleged that certain types of mosquitoes bred in streams of the interior foothills. See U.S. War Department, *Technical Bulletin* (TB Med 30), p. 9.

ing share of all deaths.[9] They were diseases that could readily be avoided by individuals whose livelihood did not continually expose them to contact with likely sources of infection, and whose income permitted them to observe simple precautions. Most Japanese were consequently protected by the nature of their occupations from the common forms of fatal illness in Taiwan. These diseases did not jeopardize their possession of the island as had epidemics in the past.

Even so, the Japanese conducted among the Taiwanese population a wide program of education and instruction in some of the simpler techniques of contending with these sources of ill health. They issued countless sanitation rules, and utilized much of their apparatus of government to enforce their observance.[10] Administratively, the health and sanitation functions of government were coordinated in several departments. In practice most of the regulations were put into effect under the authority of the police. Some trained specialists participated, bringing elements of Western medicine to Taiwan where formerly there had been none except for scattered and uncoordinated efforts of missionaries.

The level of skill among the personnel at their disposal suffers by comparison with that of modern Western countries, and it probably also fell below the standards of the more restricted public health work in some of the tropical dependencies of European powers. The strength of the system established by the Japanese, however, was in its organization and generality, and not in its equipage. It was a comprehensive program rather than a piecemeal offering of the most elaborate medical treatment.[11] Though the physical facilities of sani-

9 For reasons that we shall come to presently, the statistics on causes of death are hard to interpret in Taiwan. They show clearly, however, a decline in malaria and the epidemic diseases, and a relative increase in deaths due to these other more insidious ailments.

10 Indeed, it sometimes almost appeared that they used these objectives to cement their control over the population. The enforcement of public health regulations provided an excellent occasion for the police to enhance their authority over everyday activities. The Taiwanese who protested that these measures were mere excuses to interfere in the private lives of the people probably had a certain amount of justification for their charges. See Hsü Tze-wei (1946), p. 444.

11 The Japanese did not ignore training, but assigned it a special role in their general health program. Various medical schools were established for medical instruction of Taiwanese, the first as early as 1902. The staffs of these schools and part of the faculty at Taihoku Imperial University included some competent medical specialists, but these men were retained primarily for research that had no close bearing on public health in Taiwan. Through such limited educational facilities as these and the licensing of local doctors and midwives, Japanese managed to give elementary instruction to many Taiwanese practitioners. Though superficial, the training was distributed widely enough for a striking effect on mortality.

tation were confined to some of the major cities, the influence of these broader health measures gradually spread evenly over most of the island. In this way Japanese gained results that were very substantial through the use of none but crude techniques.

The Japanese policy toward opium addiction was less consistent, for here they found welfare goals to be in conflict with profit motives. They made the manufacture of opium a government monopoly, and closely regulated its sale. The announced purpose for this control was to eradicate the use of the drug, but the Taiwanese occasionally complained that officials secretly abetted its consumption. The truth of the matter is not clear, but their success in other tasks suggests that opium addiction could have been stamped out far more quickly if they had made a determined effort to do so. Some of their own records show that new users of opium were being granted licenses as late as the 1920's. It is likely that the Japanese appreciated the effectiveness of addiction in enervating the resistance to their rule among wealthy families, and they made no secret of the steady public revenues that they derived from opium sales.[12]

The Evidence for Measurement of Mortality

There is not much point in describing the purposes and methods of public health work without having some independent appraisal of results. Such efforts have often been sponsored elsewhere with much fanfare and little accomplishment. The only trustworthy way to view the results of economic and sanitation policies in prolonging life is through some form of measurement; this is likewise the only precise way of comparing the risks of death in Taiwan and in other areas.

Fortunately the data that exist to gauge mortality in Taiwan are excellent. The occurrence of many kinds of illness involving danger of contagion was required by law to be reported to the authorities. Partly as a means of avoiding contamination of the living by the dead, and partly just as a means of tightening official control over the reporting of disease, the Japanese also strictly regulated burials and cremations.[13] The rigors of enforcing these rules led to concealment of some illness and evasions by mis-stating exact causes of

[12] A careful study of opium addiction in Taiwan and its relation to mortality is contained in Tu Tsung-ming (1935 and 1938).

[13] See Hsü Tze-wei (1946), p. 449.

death;[14] but at the same time they led to registration of deaths that was virtually complete.

A person while living had a legitimate civil status only by being entered in an appropriate police register. Deceased, his absence could be legitimized only by removal from these rolls, and his burial could be permitted only by following this prescribed procedure. All of these records were kept by the police or by affiliated agencies. The police were alert and well-deployed to prevent evasions. Since such records were useful to them in surveillance of the population, they employed the *pao-chia* system to make the registration effective. The people in each locality were thus compelled to accept conformity with these requirements as a matter of their own collective interest. Consequently a person's identity in these records from birth till death was almost never subject to confusion or concealment.

This consistency of information in all the population registers has a special significance for demographic research. It means, for example, that each person's death record was matched to the record of his birth, so that the exact number of years elapsed between the two events can be calculated. The same legal identity of a person formed the basis for his entry in every census enumeration. "Age," as a census category, was not set down according to an individual's recollection of the number of birthdays experienced. Instead, the pertinent fact that was entered was his date of birth, and age was ascribed to him in the process of tabulation at the central census office.

Age in Taiwanese population statistics was therefore explicitly defined: it was a classification of equal intervals, in which each person ideally had one and only one "true" position at a time. It was possible for age to correspond perfectly in the recording of all three kinds of events of interest here—birth, enumeration at census date, and death. An unambiguous scheme of this sort for reckoning age is especially important in a population of Chinese, because most Chinese compute their ages in a manner that cannot be reconciled to Western usage. Starting with age one at the date of birth, it is customary for them to add a year of age with the passage of every (lunar)

[14] Once cases of smallpox, scarlet fever, typhoid fever and certain other diseases were discovered, the people were forced to undergo disinfection of lodgings and personal effects that was often destructive. Hence, it has been alleged that diagnoses were deliberately falsified to avoid these consequences (see OPNAV, Civil Affairs Handbook, 1944, *Shinchiku Province*, p. 54; U.S. War Department, TB Med 30, p. 6). A more important source of inaccuracy was probably (in the case of deaths) ignorance as to the nature of a decedent's illness. Tuberculosis was said to be very prevalent, and yet few deaths were ever diagnosed as due to this cause.

New Year thereafter. The Japanese system of ascribing age completely avoided bias from this source.

Moreover, in this system the year of age that a person occupied at any date did not depend on his personal conception of it at the time. Such subjective conceptions of age often do not change through an individual lifetime exactly as "true" age does. Misstatement of age is always a source of error in census procedures that rely on people to report their own ages directly. The recorded ages of people in Taiwan at census dates and at death were determined at the date of birth. If the birth had been registered on the proper date, it was next to impossible for the reporting of age in a census enumeration to be incorrect. Even when the date of birth was reported wrongly, there was strong pressure to be consistent later when reporting it in the census and at death. For purposes of constructing life tables, the system thus made an automatic adjustment for these errors by shifting the age at death by exactly the same amount.[15] Decedents at a given year of age were registered according to the particular calendar year in which they were born; persons enumerated in a census of the same year at the same age were the survivors of births in that prior calendar year, from January to December. It follows that both registered deaths and census of population belonged to the same group of people. With these two figures, it is a simple problem in arithmetic to compute the number of persons who entered that year of age, the number who died before reaching the next higher age, and the proportion who died out of the first group.[16] This proportion is the most important element in the construction of life tables, and it places Taiwan's mortality data in this respect among the most remarkable that exist. The applications of this special feature are discussed in the next section.[17]

15 The census of 1905 enumerated Taiwanese with birth dates as far back as the year of Meiji Restoration and earlier. Though evidence like family records and land titles were often called upon by the authorities in order to substantiate this information, some inaccuracies must have been present. They could not have been numerous, for they do not appear as "heaping" in census age distributions of people.

16 Of course, the census population must be brought up to December 31 if the census was taken earlier (which has always been the case in Taiwan). Also, the figure for deaths must be re-constituted from the vital statistics reports of two years, since many of the decedents died later than December 31 of the census year. These two details do not alter the principle explained above.

17 In the earlier census enumerations, before 1930, age was ascribed by calendar year of birth. Persons born after January 1 in the census year were placed into the first year of age, those born in the calendar year preceding the census into the second, and so on. To this peculiarity of the system we owe the possibility of making accurate early life

A welcome feature of Taiwan's mortality and census data is that they lend themselves to a detailed test for accuracy. First, they can be checked against the number of people counted in one census who died before the next one. For any given cohort of births, if the data are all correct, this should be equal to the number of survivors counted in the earlier minus the number counted in the later census. The censuses of 1905 and 1920 are compared in these terms in Table 34, for males only; the result is almost identical for females. The column of ratios indicates the degree to which registered deaths account for the difference in the numbers of survivors counted at successive census dates.

If all records were complete and accurate, the ratios would be unity at every age. If the differences in census survivors are assumed to be correct, then apparently a few deaths went unregistered in certain years. It is obvious that the records were not perfect. As it is, they were so nearly complete that there is little if anything to be gained from trying to make corrections for the discrepancies. Since this is simultaneously a test of census enumeration and vital registration (and an extremely sensitive test of age reporting), it is not possible to decide whether the discrepancies arose from deaths that were omitted or people overlooked from the earlier census.[18]

Since mortality in the first year of life is usually measured on the basis of the number of live-born babies, it is necessary also to know how adequate the birth statistics were in relation to death and census records. A test for births, similar to that above, is shown in Table 35; the results give an excellent account of the birth registration. The registration of birth entered a child permanently in the police lists, and was an almost inescapable bond during his later life. By this criterion, the chances of evading subsequent controls allied to

---

tables for Taiwanese, for the yearly intervals had the same upper and lower limits as those of the vital statistics.

Japanese were apologetic about the deviation of this system from the Western mode of age reporting, and beginning with 1930 "modernized" the system so that its special virtue was eliminated. Starting with the census of that year, census-year rather than calendar-year intervals were used, making the system identical with the Western conventions in design. For dates after 1930 it is no longer possible to relate deaths precisely to enumerated census population.

18 There is reason for not putting all the blame on registered deaths, for the area of effective administration was expanded slightly after 1905, and by 1915 and 1920 had brought more people into the registration and census system than the survivors of those enumerated in 1905. This being the case, it is possible that both measuring instruments were nearly perfect, and that the discrepancies arose entirely from the expansion of administration.

TABLE 34

TEST FOR ADEQUACY OF DEATH REGISTRATION OF TAIWANESE

Males by Year of Birth, Surviving at Census Dates in 1905 and 1920, and Intervening Deaths as Registered

Year of Birth	*Survivors 1905*	*Survivors 1920*	*Difference*	*Registered Deaths 1905-1920*	*"Completeness" of Death Registration**
1904	48,859	38,257	10,602	11,602	1.094
1903	43,432	35,769	7,663	7,768	1.014
1902	43,340	36,392	6,948	6,718	.967
1901	41,658	35,523	6,135	6,087	.992
1900	41,910	36,224	5,686	5,564	.979
1899	38,149	32,899	5,250	5,099	.971
1898	40,913	35,409	5,504	5,257	.955
1897	34,183	29,707	4,476	4,801	1.073
1896	33,855	29,149	4,706	4,872	1.035
1895	35,579	30,148	5,431	5,177	.053
1894	32,338	27,187	5,151	5,052	.981
1893	32,581	27,062	5,519	5,444	.986
1892	34,122	27,945	6,177	6,224	1.008
1891	32,421	25,963	6,458	6,263	.970
1890	31,626	24,672	6,954	6,540	.940
1889	32,164	25,479	6,685	7,273	1.088
1888	34,355	25,907	8,448	8,040	.952
1887	35,471	27,101	8,370	8,584	1.026
1886	33,697	25,254	8,443	8,587	1.017
1885	33,445	24,708	8,737	9,016	1.032
1884	36,969	27,156	9,813	10,023	1.021
1883	34,750	25,257	9,493	9,911	1.044
1882	32,431	23,034	9,397	9,922	1.056
1881	35,951	25,034	10,917	11,100	1.017
1880	31,335	21,484	9,851	10,242	1.040
1879	31,345	21,230	10,115	10,287	1.017
1878	29,016	19,036	9,980	9,961	.998
1877	27,669	18,379	9,290	9,988	1.075
1876	31,238	20,263	10,975	11,239	1.024
1875	27,991	17,880	10,111	10,741	1.062

* Ratio: Deaths/Difference.

Sources: *Census of 1920, Descriptive Report*, Appendix, Table 15.
Vital Statistics, yearly volumes, 1906-1920.
Statistical Summary, Table 58, for population by age in 1905.

TABLE 35

TEST FOR ADEQUACY OF BIRTH REGISTRATION OF TAIWANESE

Births from 1906 to 1920, as Registered and as Estimated from Survivors Enumerated in Census of 1920 and Intervening Deaths

Year of Birth	*Survivors 1920*	*Registered Deaths Since Birth*	*Estimated Births (1) + (2)*	*Registered Births**	*"Completeness" of Registered Births†*
			Males		
1920	46,832	7,725	54,557	54,064	.9910
1919	55,006	12,993	67,999	70,349	1.0346
1918	52,260	18,219	70,479	71,764	1.0182
1917	52,245	19,854	72,099	73,430	1.0185
1916	46,234	19,805	66,039	65,837	.9969
1915	48,109	22,322	70,431	70,855	1.0060
1914	49,637	23,109	72,746	72,755	1.0001
1913	48,427	21,550	69,977	70,170	1.0028
1912	48,810	20,961	69,771	69,990	1.0031
1911	48,388	21,159	69,547	69,558	1.0002
1910	46,609	20,806	67,415	68,042	1.0093
1909	44,540	20,780	65,320	65,666	1.0053
1908	41,626	20,353	61,979	61,993	1.0002
1907	43,003	20,074	63,077	63,290	1.0034
1906	41,598	20,008	61,606	62,120	1.0083
			Females		
1920	46,017	5,815	51,832	51,410	.9919
1919	53,950	10,346	64,296	66,358	1.0321
1918	50,328	16,028	66,356	67,701	1.0203
1917	49,315	18,099	67,414	68,984	1.0233
1916	44,230	18,658	62,888	62,768	.9981
1915	45,348	21,372	66,720	66,814	1.0014
1914	46,245	22,279	68,524	68,695	1.0025
1913	45,434	21,281	66,715	66,797	1.0012
1912	45,403	21,090	66,493	66,632	1.0021
1911	45,373	20,805	66,178	66,100	.9988
1910	43,251	20,262	63,513	64,099	1.0092
1909	41,268	20,187	61,455	61,620	1.0027
1908	38,292	19,737	58,029	57,807	.9962
1907	38,594	19,981	58,575	58,466	.9981
1906	37,323	19,824	57,147	56,987	.9972

* In 1920, deaths and births have been taken only from January 1 to October 1.
† Ratio: Registered Births/Estimated Births.
Sources: *Census of 1920, Descriptive Report*, Appendix, Table 15.
Vital Statistics, yearly volumes, 1906-1920.

the registration system were very slight. The same result is found for births of more recent years.

With very few exceptions, these events—births, deaths, and presence at each census date—were nearly all recorded and were recorded accurately. The pattern of omissions is itself significant: whatever their source, they contained practically no age or sex bias. Therefore (with one reservation)[19] we shall accept all published deaths and all population figures as complete and correct for the measurement of mortality. The differences would be trivial if they were distributed as adjustments over all the years of deaths; and the tests give no clue as to how such adjustment should be distributed.

The Decline of Mortality

The simplest question that arises about the trend of Taiwanese mortality is also the easiest to answer: what happened to the prevalence of deaths in the population during colonial rule? Unfortunately for judging this trend, no one can say what was the level of mortality in Taiwan when the Japanese first arrived. The Manchu government did not even know the number of its subjects, far less their behavior with respect to births and deaths. The colonial regime founded by the Japanese started a thorough system of vital statistics only after a decade of control. Consequently the very earliest usable record began at a time when life had already been made more secure.

The trend of annual death rates after 1905 appears clearly in Table 36. It was not only downward, but was rapid in its fall. Over the same period there were scarcely any recorded instances to equal the speed of this decline. Supposing that there were over 40 deaths per thousand persons in 1895 and before, the yearly incidence must have dropped by more than one-half in the next fifty years.

Thanks to improved drugs and newer approaches to the problems of health, such a feat has since this time become fairly easy in countries of high mortality. Crude death rates of 20 are no longer considered low. But subsequent advances in medicine should not be allowed to detract from this performance. With the resources and

[19] The only reservation is in the case of infants. This requires special attention, and is discussed in the section on infant mortality.

In reality, the ambiguity is a more fundamental one than any amount of "correction" can remedy. It arises from an inherent difficulty in making a precise definition for a "live" birth in a society where infants are delivered without skilled medical care and where the chances of surviving the first day of life are very poor. Where families regard mere discussion of deceased offspring as inauspicious, the prospects for developing precise measuring standards for infant mortality are poor.

TABLE 36

CRUDE DEATH RATES OF TAIWANESE, 1906-1943*

Years	*Deaths per Thousand Persons*
1906–10	33.4
1911–15	28.6
1916–20	31.0
1921–25	25.0
1926–30	22.1
1931–35	21.2
1936–40	20.6
1941–43	18.5

* Unweighted averages of annual death rates for each year. Before 1915, deaths have been adjusted slightly on the basis of the internal pattern of infant mortality in later years, as explained in the text.
Source: *Statistical Summary*, Table 64.

knowledge available in these earlier years it was a far more noteworthy achievement than it now appears. Almost entirely through the reduction of mortality, the annual natural increase of Taiwanese rose to 25 per thousand, which even today is rarely found.

The fall of mortality was not unbroken. It was interrupted in quick succession in 1915, 1918 and 1920 by waves of fatal illness over the island. The first occasion was accompanied by an unusual number of malaria deaths,[20] when the program of malaria control was only in its second year. In 1918 and 1920, the Taiwanese were visited by a part of the world-wide influenza outbreaks at the end of World War I. In all three years the cause-of-death data, defective as they were, revealed exceptional fatalities due to malaria and respiratory ailments respectively, but no serious recurrence of the old epidemic diseases.

None of these setbacks quite matched the initial years of statistical record. Since mortality in 1906 undoubtedly was already lower than it had been in the pre-Japanese period, one can say that for the island as a whole these later reversals were minor and transitory (see Fig. 21).

Taiwanese Life Tables

The life table is a device that represents mortality in a special conventionalized way. Conceptually it is an instrument of precision,

20 And reportedly some civil disturbance, though such instances are always exaggerated and difficult to evaluate.

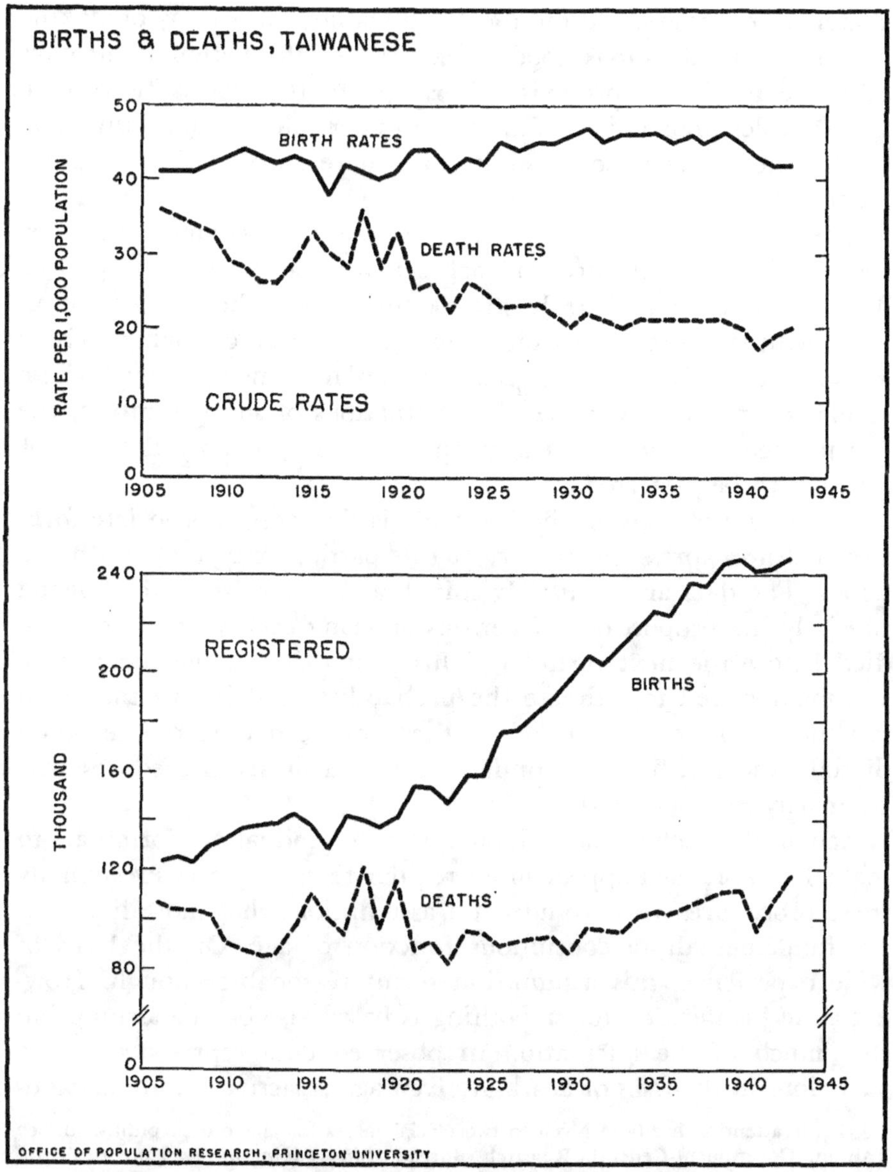

Fig. 21. Crude Birth and Death Rates and Total Registered Births and Deaths of Taiwanese, 1906-1943.

for it allows one to speak in terms of probabilities of dying, which is what we mean here by the notion of mortality. Being conventional, it lends itself easily to comparison with data from other places independent of differences in age structure, even when the procedures of computation are slightly varied. Some caution, of course, must be exercised in this application, for the life table is also a way of making poor mortality data look good. Since precise information about mortality has not heretofore existed for a population consisting of Chinese,[21] tables prepared for Taiwanese under differing mortality conditions should be of some additional interest from this standpoint alone.

Life tables are very convenient as a way of summarizing age-specific risks of mortality for each sex in a specified short period. They can also be used to illustrate one aspect of the course of mortality with the passage of time—the age incidence of change. There are more efficient ways of expressing secular change *per se*;[22] where secular change is interrupted by fluctuations of short duration, the age incidence of deaths in a given period is probably the sort of measure to be preferred.

In the case of Taiwan the life table is the most appropriate form in which to express the import of this particular type of death statistics. The data are peculiarly suited, as we have seen, to showing precisely the proportions of persons entering each year of age who died before the next birthday. This proportion is the figure conventionally used to estimate the probability of dying in the given year of age. Having such data as these, one can prepare life tables directly and not by the roundabout and arbitrary procedures that ordinarily must be used.[23]

Actuarial practice has adopted strong graduation formulae to make life-table data appear more regular than they are. Presumably these procedures are grounded on assumptions that mortality risks are fundamentally a continuous function of age. On the basis of wide experience, this assumption seems reasonable enough. However, the justification for smoothing is based also on the assumption that much of the fluctuation in observed data represents chance variations in the risks of death at given ages;[24] actuaries, understand-

[21] Little attention has been given to two official tables that have been published. See Taiwan, Government-General, Research Bureau. *Life Tables of Taiwan, 1926-1930* (First Issue) (1936), 160 pp.; Taiwan, Provincial Government, Department of Statistics. *Life Tables of Taiwan, 1936-1940* (Second Issue) (1947).

[22] A more satisfactory procedure for this specific purpose is to examine mortality of actual cohorts of persons over time, where age and time can be observed while varying together, and their interaction can be taken into account. It is planned to examine this aspect of mortality change in Taiwan at some later date.

[23] Where S_x represents the number of survivors to exact age x, and D_x the number of them who died in age x, q_x (the probability of dying at that age) can be expressed directly as D_x/S_x. The arbitrary conversion of an observed central death-rate, m_x, such as by assuming $q_x=2m_x/(2+m_x)$, then becomes superfluous and can be by-passed.

[24] See Knibbs, G. H. (1917), pp. 86-88.

ably, do not relish the thought that their work consists merely of manipulating errors of observation.[25]

Taiwan's data throw some light on the relative magnitude of the random and the error components of irregularity in age-specific mortality rates. For example, one life table has been prepared for the period 1909-1911, in order to illustrate the risks of death at a time when they were still high. The mortality rates of this table (see Fig. 22) represent a small number of deaths, as do those of the succeeding tables, and have not been subjected to any graduation.[26]

The people in the lowest to the highest ages of any life table represent groups born over a long period of time, each of which might be expected to exhibit peculiarities of its own previous exposure to mortality. Nevertheless, the risks of death shown in Fig. 22 deviate only slightly from a smooth progression with age. The persons exposed to death at each age were few; in view of their number, much larger variability would appear reasonable. Even if we were to assume a complete lack of error in the data (throwing the whole burden of all deviations from continuity to the element of chance), the random component of these fluctuations is very small. A strong case for the notion of continuity can be made from this life table. But by the same token it appears that the *error* component of deviation from continuity in ordinary data is the major portion. Perhaps not much general significance for the variability of "true" mortality rates by age can be drawn from these data. Very likely, however, smoothing devices as commonly used have as their major function the adjustment for errors of observation. Aside from errors of omission, these presumably arise because information by age is incorrect and because deaths as usually registered do not belong to the people to whom they are assigned.[27]

Taiwan's mortality data have not been widely known. Two official

[25] There is in addition a possible third influence—the cohort effect, or effect of the date of birth. This is generally ignored.

[26] Strictly speaking, they represent the weighted averages of three cohorts of persons entering each year of age, in 1909, 1910, and 1911 respectively. The mortality rates are in the simple form $(D_1+D_2+D_3)/(S_1+S_2+S_3)$ in each year of age. This averaging has the effect of reducing the variability of single-year values as compared with the life tables to be presented later. The effect of different weighting for different cohorts is ignored.

[27] All this is not meant to imply that actuarial procedures are misguided or that smoothing is unwarranted when dealing with inferior data. The actual errors introduced in most instances by graduation of mortality rates are probably not very great. It does seem important, however, to know how close an approximation to continuity accurate data can give, as a basis for inferring that the error component of deviations is not inconsiderable.

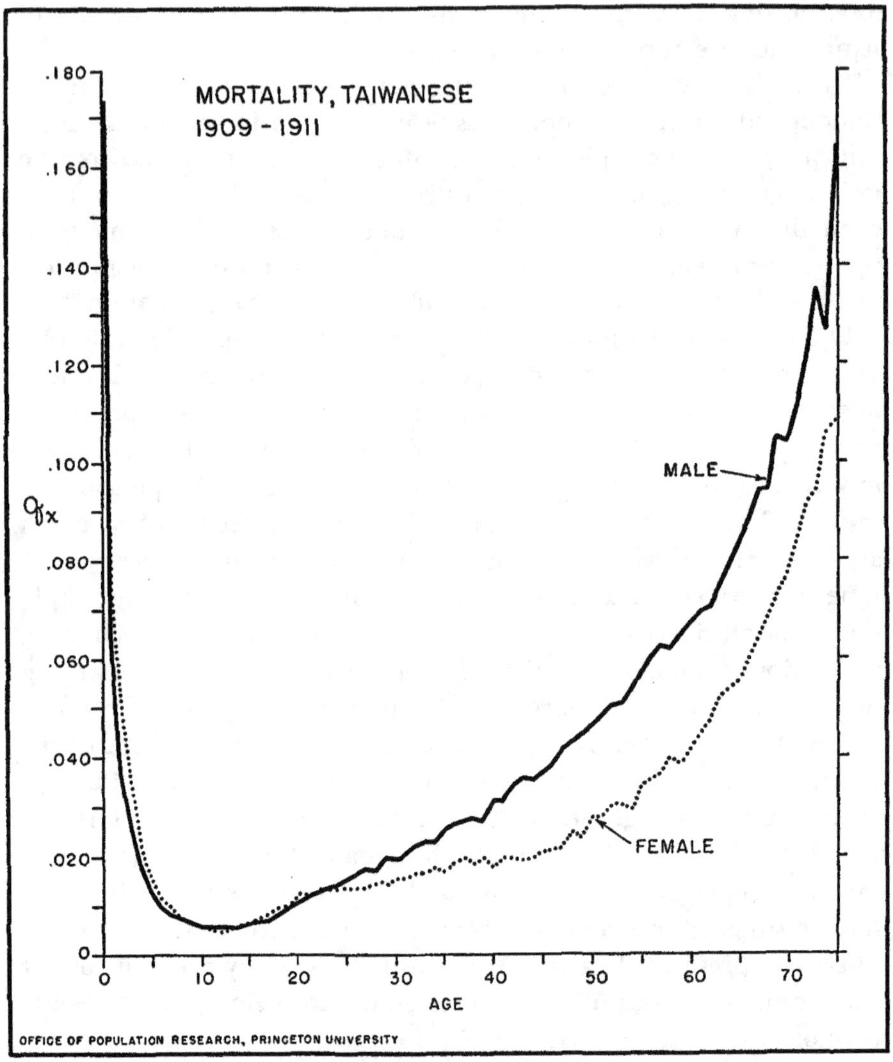

Fig. 22. Mortality of Taiwanese, Life Table of 1910-1911. Values of q_x, by Age, Male and Female.

life tables were compiled and published from them,[28] which have likewise not become well known to Western demographers. Consequently it is desirable to compare the conditions in Taiwan with

[28] These two official tables were constructed by conventional procedures. The 1926-1930 life table, the earlier of the two, covered a period when the information on year of birth had been temporarily dropped from publication of vital statistics. The second table, for 1936-1940, covered a span when the census population could no longer be matched to registered deaths. Hence, the more precise procedure used here was denied to both of them.

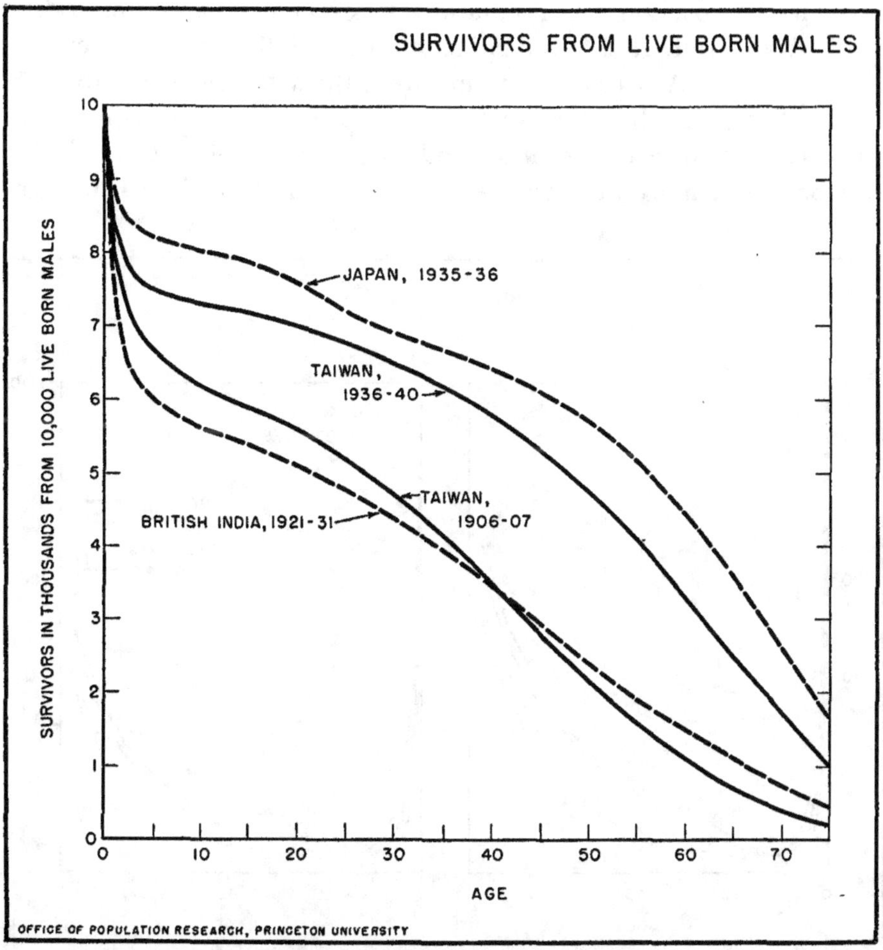

Fig. 23. Life Table Survivors of 10,000 Live Male Births, by Age (l_x). Taiwan and Selected Other Countries.

other examples that are more familiar. This is done in Fig. 23, where life-table survivors of an arbitrary 10,000 male births have been plotted for Taiwan in 1906 and 1936-1940, Japan in 1926-1930, and British India in 1921-1931. Even near the turn of the century, to take the year 1906 as an example, mortality in Taiwan was no higher than that of British India many years later. The gross effects of mortality in Taiwan had by 1940 come to a point closer to Japan during the 1920's than to the previous situation in Taiwan. The median age at death (the age at which mortality rates of the given period would have reduced a starting cohort by one-half) was nearly doubled between these two dates.

Such a comparison does not, however, reveal much about mortality in Taiwan itself. It shows next to nothing of the nature or extent of the decline. A better way to examine the shifts by age is to look at the changes in the risks of death. The probabilities of dying show these changes in each age independently of other ages. Graphically this profile of mortality appears for various dates in Fig. 24, plotted

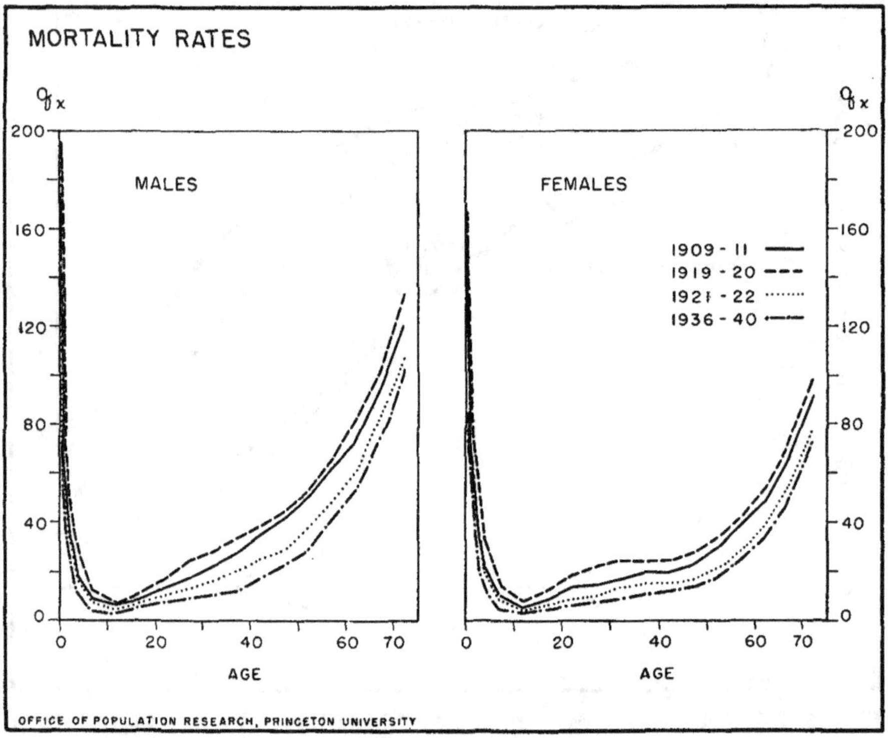

Fig. 24. Mortality of Taiwanese, by Age (q_x), Selected Life Tables. Males and Females.

on pivotal ages. The earliest point is the three-year period 1909-1911, expressing conditions that were greatly improved over those found in 1906.[29] It represents the effects of selective sanitation works (i.e., in the larger cities), and of mass disease controls of the crudest sort. Epidemics had been suppressed, but the full-scale attack on malaria,

[29] The procedures of preparing these life tables make them reflect the events of two calendar years. They are also based on the persons *entering* each age in the given year, some of whom did not die before the following year. The table for 1906, therefore, is composed mostly of deaths that occurred in 1906, plus some that did not take place until 1907. 1906 was the year of a severe earthquake in one Prefecture, and for this reason may have been less favorable than neighboring years.

for example, had not yet begun. Not long before, the Japanese had just succeeded in gaining undisputed control of the island outside of the central mountain region. By implication, the conditions in 1909-1911 thus give an indication of what is possible with the most rudimentary types of health measures. At that time most were still experimental, for the Japanese were just beginning to struggle with the problems of rationalizing agricultural practices, and had not had enough time to organize a concerted program against infection and disease.

If mortality had been reduced easily and quickly, the gain was not a very secure one. The reversals in 1915, 1918, and 1920 are shown in Fig. 24 in their incidence by age; they again restored temporarily the unhealthful state that had prevailed before. (Influenza in 1920 struck early in the year, and affected principally those who had not passed a birthday since 1919; the age cohorts of 1919 were the ones that absorbed the force of the disease.) By contrast, when the steady effects of economic and health policies gradually became felt, mortality risks (as exemplified by the period 1936-1940) were brought firmly down to much lower levels. Translated into figures for the mean expectation of life at various ages in each year, the risks of these years are summarized in Table 37.

The pattern of the decline appears only when the mortality rates themselves are viewed in detail. From age 15 to age 50, most people pass through the most active portion of their lives. Adults in a country of relatively high mortality move from ages when death is rare through a stage of steadily increasing risks. By age 50 in Taiwan at least half of the members of each cohort of births were no longer alive. Adulthood is usually associated with two chief hazards of death. In a society like Taiwan, the working activities undertaken by men and childbearing of women begin to bring people of both sexes into contact with greater risks of dying. The interval covers the entire normal childbearing period of women and most of the time of active employment of men.

Deaths occurred in different patterns for men and women in these ages. Mortality actually started at slightly lower levels for women who were approaching adulthood than for men. It also advanced less rapidly with age. In years of moderate mortality this progression with age was nearly continuous; when there were extraordinary hazards, they had the heaviest effect on women of younger ages and

TABLE 37

MEAN LIFE EXPECTANCY OF TAIWANESE AT DIFFERENT AGES

Selected Life Tables. Values of e_x, in Years

Age	*1906*	*1909-11*	*1919*	*1921*	*1926-30*	*1936-40*
			Males			
0	27.7	32.4	27.7	34.5	38.8	41.1
1	33.2	38.1	33.4	41.6	45.9	47.6
5	35.9	40.0	36.2	44.0	47.5	49.5
10	33.5	36.7	33.4	40.8	43.6	45.6
30	20.4	22.6	20.8	26.2	28.1	29.7
50	12.0	13.2	12.5	15.0	16.0	16.5
			Females			
0	29.0	35.6	29.6	38.6	43.1	45.7
1	34.0	40.7	34.4	45.0	49.4	51.5
5	38.8	44.7	38.9	49.2	52.5	54.6
10	27.2	41.9	36.9	46.4	48.8	50.8
30	25.5	29.0	25.8	31.9	33.5	34.8
50	15.5	17.4	16.4	19.6	20.3	20.6

Sources: Life tables of 1906, 1909-11, 1919 and 1921 were computed from the assembled data of Taiwan's censuses and vital registration. The table of 1926-30 is from Taiwan, Government-General (1936); that of 1936-40 is from Taiwan, Provincial Government (1947).

altered the entire pattern that usually prevailed (see Fig. 25).[30] Thus enlarged from the mortality rates given in Fig. 24, the disparity between male and female age structure of adult mortality also appears more strongly.

In spite of the differences in structure, male and female risks of death have both given the appearance of reacting in the same way to the changes in general conditions of health in the population. And this is very nearly true as far as secular decline in mortality was concerned. But the exceptional risks (as in 1915, 1918, and 1920) affected women very differently from men. Their age incidence remained unchanged for men. For women, these risks were heavily concentrated at some of the later years of the childbearing period.

The most typical pattern of sex selection of age-specific mortality is illustrated in the period 1936-1940 (see Fig. 26). The values are

[30] Fig. 25 is based on age-specific death rates rather than on life-table probabilities. It makes no difference in the pattern of the results. Death rates are adopted for this illustration because they show the events of the exact calendar years that are most appropriate for this comparison.

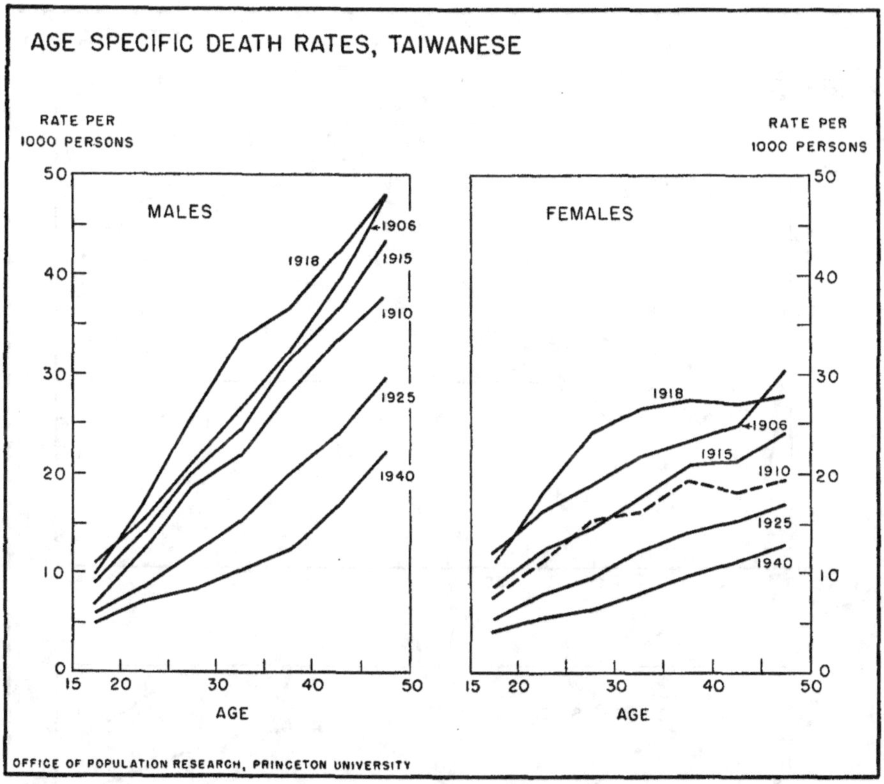

Fig. 25. Age-Specific Death Rates of Adults in Selected Years. Taiwanese Males and Females.

sex ratios of deaths at each age to an equal number of males and females beginning that age during the year in question.[31] The usual sex balance of mortality risks in Taiwan was different from what prevailed in other recorded Asian populations—e.g., Japan and India. It is, of course, not surprising to see that it was not the same as the United States. But the nature of the difference also runs contrary to what might be expected. In particular, it is startling to find that females were normally less likely to die than males at all ages over 15 years. This critical age span, when women of a high-fertility society are entering a period of frequent pregnancy and childbirth, is commonly thought to be likewise a stage of high mortality for them. The evidence as to fertility, which will appear in the following chapter, shows that Taiwanese women did not avoid these risks by avoid-

[31] Above age 4, the actual values plotted are sex ratios of $_5q_x$, or mortality rates over age intervals of 5 years each.

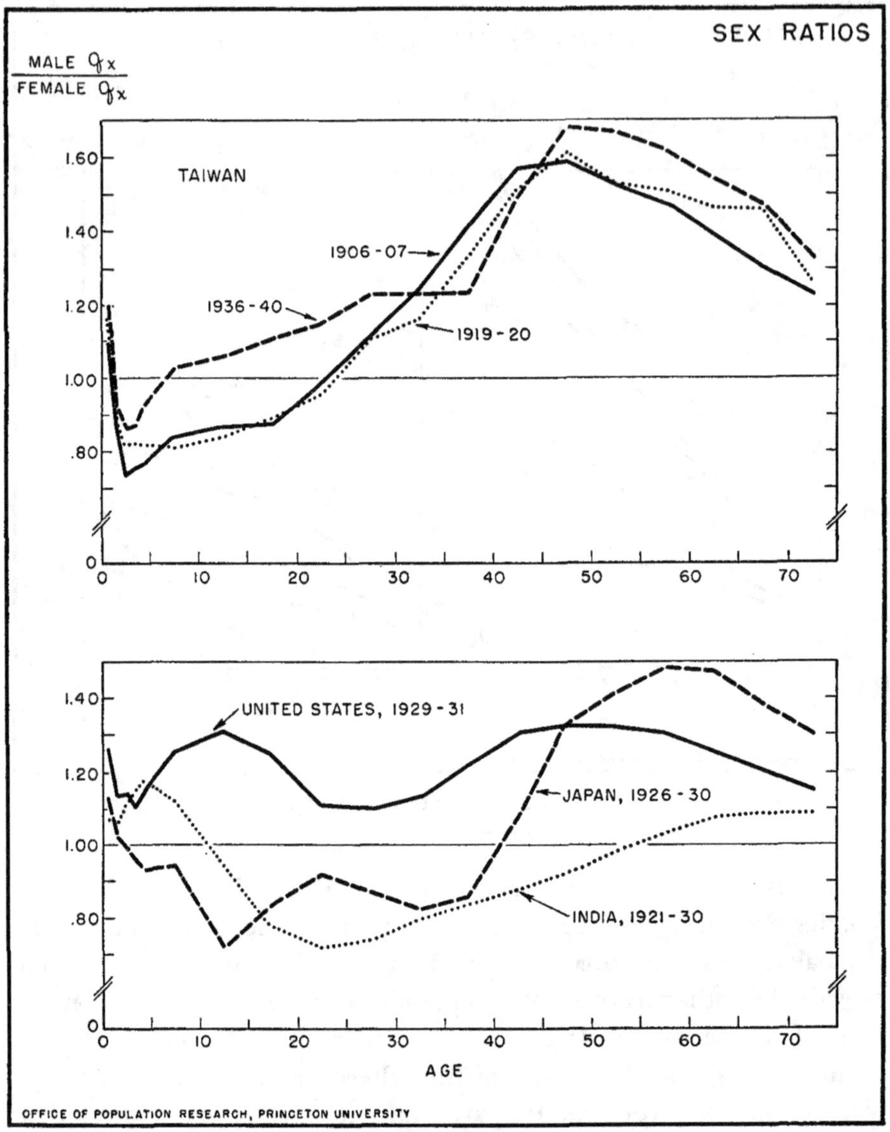

Fig. 26. Sex Selectivity of Mortality in Taiwan and Other Countries. Number of Male Deaths for Every Female Death, Among an Equal Number of Each Sex Entering Each Age.

ing childbirth. Fertility in Taiwan was consistently higher than for all of Japan, and yet in Japan women in childbearing ages were put at considerable disadvantage with men in their chances of survival.[32]

[32] In both societies, the cessation of childbearing is marked, for example at age 40 and above, by a decided improvement in likelihood of survival of women in relation to

Though Taiwanese women in most years succeeded in warding off more risks of death than men in early adulthood, they did not fare so well during times of greatest sickness or near-epidemic. In both 1906 and 1920 the situation was reversed. In all ages other than infancy up to mid-adulthood, females experienced higher risks than males. Their greater susceptibility in these times is as puzzling as their comparative robustness in other years. It did not move them much closer to the position of Japanese females in relation to males, for the pattern of selectivity was still distinct from that of Japan.

Regardless of the year of observation, young girls consistently suffered greater risks than boys. In the first year of life, as is usually the case, males invariably had inferior average chances of surviving to their first birthday. For the next nine or more years they more than made up for this initial disadvantage. Without fail, there were more male than female survivors to age ten from an equal number of each who managed to enter the second year of life (see Table 38). This was the case for all cohorts of which the record is available from the first birthday to the tenth—26 cohorts in all. Because of this, a higher proportion of boys than girls survived from birth to age ten.

It is easier to reconcile lower rates of survival for young girls with known features of Chinese society than it is the advantage held by women over men at all higher ages. With a few exceptions, the difference in risks was consistent in every year of age. It often extended to age 12 or beyond, after which males generally remained at greater risk for the rest of life. Sex ratios of even numbers of one-year-olds surviving to age ten show a steady movement toward equalizing the risks of death in this interval with the passage of time. It is well known that male offspring are especially cherished in Chinese families, for they provide the basis for family continuity over several generations. The resulting preferential treatment in childhood for boys rather than girls is borne out by the evidence of Table 38, since survival of young girls elsewhere in the world is usually found to be superior to that of boys.[33]

men. So it is barely conceivable that unhealthful activities of men simply over-balanced these special risks of women. (Due to tuberculosis in Japan, male mortality almost outweighed that of females for a short span between age 20 and age 30, despite the fact that mortality for women was high.) It seems unlikely, however, on comparison with the pattern for India (Fig. 26). India was similarly an unhealthful place for men, but placed women at an even greater disadvantage.

[33] A trace of this same phenomenon can be found in the early life tables for Japan. These are based, of course, on a particular period and not on actual cohorts. In the 1947 table for all Japan, however, mortality of males was higher at every age.

TABLE 38

TAIWANESE SURVIVORS THROUGH EARLY CHILDHOOD
(After Infancy)

Actual Survivors to Exact Age 10 of Each Thousand Males and Females Who Passed their First Birthday, by Year of First Birthday

Year	*Males*	*Females*	*Male Survivors per 100 Females*
1907	812	769	106
1908	822	781	105
1909	819	785	104
1910	825	792	104
1911	826	790	104
1912	820	784	105
1913	819	777	105
1914	813	777	105
1915	807	773	104
1916	812	780	104
1917	810	778	104
1918	814	787	103
1919	825	801	103
1920	843	822	102
1921	853	834	102
1922	865	846	102
1923	856	840	102
1924	852	834	102
1925	862	841	102
1926	863	846	102
1927	870	854	102
1928	870	854	102
1929	874	858	102
1930	870	855	102
1931	866	848	102
1932	873	861	101
1933	870	858	101
1934	870	858	101

Source: Based on Vital Statistics of each year.

In most of the world, more deaths occur in infancy than at any other year of age. This is especially true of Asia. Deaths before completing the first year of life used to eliminate close to one-fifth of all births in Taiwan. In many countries this figure is believed to be higher; cases of 25 per cent wastage of births in infancy have been known. Infant mortality is important for life tables also because it is difficult to measure. Most countries with high risks of death have been unable to keep adequate records of births, and infants who die after a few days or weeks in the world may not be accounted for either as births or deaths. The tests of completeness in registration and enumeration have demonstrated that in Taiwan nearly all children whose births were registered were also either enumerated in subsequent censuses or recorded as deaths if they did not survive.

The system of regulation that kept the local registers was severe as well as thorough. An entire community was held responsible, through its *pao-chia* organization, for failures to keep the registers in order. Some kinds of oversight might be successfully concealed, but if a child survived, its legal status as a person depended on having a record with the police, which was initiated by entering the event of birth. Pressure brought to bear by neighbors, if not prudence on the part of the family itself, tended to promote compliance with these rules. Consequently, a child could not easily remain alive very long and escape being entered in the official records.[34]

There remains, however, a problem of unregistered non-survivors, who might have died so young that no official cognizance was ever taken of their existence or decease. There are three kinds of evidence that some non-conformity of this sort existed early in the registration period. First, birth rates (Fig. 21) appear to have risen slightly, which though possible seems unlikely. Second, the rates of infant mortality that one can derive from unadjusted registration figures seem lower than they must have actually been, in view of the decline in mortality at other ages.[35] Finally, the sex ratio of registered live births was somewhat more masculine at the beginning than in later years. There is reason to suspect that some female infants might have been destroyed and not registered.[36]

[34] The government made provision for late registrations; there were very few, from which one can infer that almost all registrations that were made occurred soon after birth.

[35] All figures for infant mortality before 1916 that are shown here have been adjusted slightly, by a procedure that is described below. Unadjusted, the data make infant mortality appear to have *increased* over the first several years of record. One is led to believe that the opposite was true, in view of the fall of mortality at other ages.

[36] It is not easy to determine the extent or even the general existence of early infanticide in Taiwan. Missionaries and Western travellers often expressed indignation at the practice (see Pickering, Campbell, Davidson). Writings on both China and Taiwan have many references to it, mostly only gossip. Japanese officials took a strongly hostile attitude toward this disposal of infants, and apparently succeeded after a few years in

This idiosyncrasy of the registration system did not prevent our tests from demonstrating almost perfect correspondence among registered births, deaths, and children counted in the census. In other words, the omissions were exactly the same for births as for deaths. Internal evidence indicates that they were not permitted to continue very long. Infant deaths were also tabulated for small intervals within a year, from which probabilities of survival by month can be estimated. The probabilities for the first month of life form a reasonably close regression on those for the second and third combined, for all years *except 1915 and earlier.* Between 1906 and 1915, the probabilities as recorded in the first month were higher than the values that the regression would imply. If we assume the regression of yearly observations after 1915 to be correct, and the probabilities in the second and third months of life to be accurate throughout, then the values for the first month reflect omissions before 1916 of babies who did not survive to one month of age. Following this assumption, all figures for births and infant deaths before 1916 that are used here have been adjusted upward slightly from their registered number to fit what regression values of these probabilities imply for infant mortality and births.[37]

Two procedures are often employed to measure infant mortality. The more appropriate one is to compile it as the proportion born who died in the first year of life, based on births occurring in a calendar year and the deaths to this cohort of births before their first birthday. This is the measure that corresponds to the concept of life-table mortality, and that will be used here except where otherwise specified. Ordinarily, however, deaths are not known by the year of birth of the decedents, but only by the calendar year of occurrence and by age. In this case it is customary to compute what we shall here call infant death rates, using simply the ratio of calendar-year births and calendar-year infant deaths.

---

stamping it out. By 1906, when the vital statistics records can be relied upon in most matters, there was scarcely any trace of infanticide among Taiwanese.

To set limits on the extent of the practice, we may assume that all male births were registered, that infanticide occurred only to females, and that the true sex ratio of live births was 105. Then (the sex ratio of registered births in early years being 109), in the first five years not more than 2 per cent of female babies could have been disposed of in this way. In any case, the sex ratio of registered births soon fell to 105, and stayed between 105 and 106 thereafter.

[37] This is a conservative correction, since it entails the further assumption that these were the only omissions. The number of survivors to the end of the first year of life remains the same as before the adjustment.

TABLE 39

INFANT MORTALITY OF TAIWANESE*

Deaths Per 1,000 Live Births in Each Year

	Males		*Females*	
Year	*Death Rate (Calendar-Year Deaths)*	*Mortality Rate (Actual Deaths)*	*Death Rate (Calendar-Year Deaths)*	*Mortality Rate (Actual Deaths)*
1906	192	182	173	165
1907	174	175	161	162
1908	190	188	173	172
1909	182	183	162	163
1910	167	168	144	144
1911	176	171	144	141
1912	164	169	139	143
1913	177	178	149	152
1914	180	187	161	167
1915	203	202	183	180
1916	193	179	161	150
1917	173	182	148	155
1918	202	199	172	173
1919	186	196	160	167
1920	190	178	161	149
1921	173	175	144	147
1922	184	180	155	150
1923	164	171	133	141
1924	190	196	159	164
1925	186	177	158	150
1926	171	—	139	—
1927	175	—	145	—
1928	181	—	152	—
1929	171	—	141	—
1930	163	—	139	—
1931	177	—	146	—
1932	167	—	140	—
1933	161	169	137	143
1934	167	163	143	139
1935	160	163	133	133
1936	159	159	131	133
1937	157	159	132	134
1938	159	155	132	128

TABLE 39 (continued)

	Males		*Females*	
Year	*Death Rate (Calendar-Year Deaths)*	*Mortality Rate (Actual Deaths)*	*Death Rate (Calendar-Year Deaths)*	*Mortality Rate (Actual Deaths)*
1939	152	156	126	129
1940	148	136	122	114
1941	131	133	114	116
1942	136	—	116	—
1943	134	—	116	—

* Registered deaths have been adjusted slightly before 1916, based on a regression of mortality in the first month of life on mortality in the second and third months of life in 1916 and all subsequent years. Births have been adjusted accordingly. Data for actual mortality rates were not published for certain years.

Sources: Vital Statistics, individual years; *Statistical Summary*, Tables 64 and 89.

We must rely on death rates of this latter sort to examine the internal composition of infant mortality, for deaths by month-of-age were published only in this form. This approximation measures infant mortality with nearly the same yearly values as did the actual rates (see Table 39). It is worth while to tolerate some disagreement between the two in order to divide mortality of the first year into smaller intervals.

The progression of these death rates through time is plotted in Fig. 27. Infant mortality on the whole did not decline very sharply. (There will be occasion shortly to compare it with other ages.) If our guess about the defect in registration is correct, then two conclusions necessarily follow. First, the risks of death after the first month of age are documented fully, without omissions. Second, and more important, mortality in this span—the so-called postneonatal mortality—dropped no more than all infant mortality. Neonatal mortality then changed just as sharply as that of infants who survived the first month.[38]

Such a pattern of decline in infant deaths is contrary to what is commonly taken for granted. The usual suppositions about infant mortality in the process of decline have been made *a priori*, for

[38] In addition, according to our guess above, if additional events (births and deaths) ought to be added to the earliest years to make the figures absolutely complete, they must be added to the neonatal period, making mortality in the first month still higher at the beginning. This could only have the effect of indicating a more pronounced drop in neonatal mortality. There is almost no way of allocating extra deaths that could reverse the pattern shown in Fig. 27.

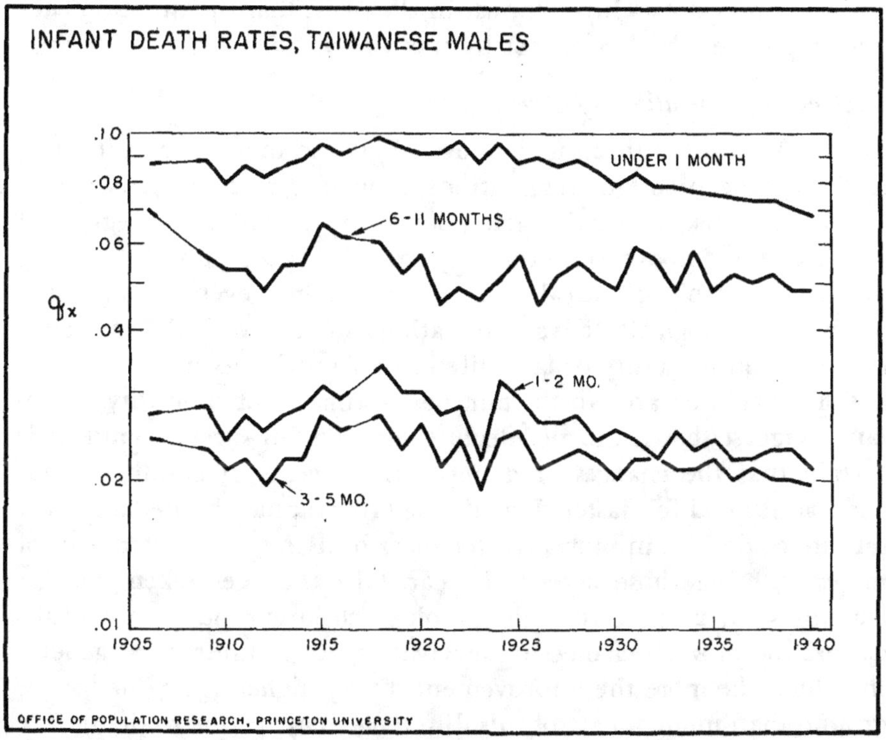

Fig. 27. Fall of Death Rates of Infants by Month of Age. Taiwanese Males, 1906-1940.

actual evidence is rare.[39] Neonatal mortality is thought to be resistant to measures that bring infant mortality under control and thus to most general health measures. Part of the reason may lie in particular environmental influences such as standards of nutrition in a population, the climatic conditions, and the customs governing childbirth and infant care. Part also may be linked with maternal health, which could exert a pre-natal as well as post-natal effect on the chances of live-born babies to survive. It is curious that the distinctive behavior of neonatal mortality in Taiwan (as compared with Europe and America) should coincide with the distinctive low mortality of adult women in childbearing ages. Whether or not one has influenced the other is impossible to say without actual information on the matter. The medical aspects of reproduction in such an Asian

[39] The evidence also has come from European and American countries. Unfortunately it has been subject to a large sampling bias, inasmuch as it represents those countries whose progress toward low mortality has occurred within a particular cultural order, of which the individual countries are but variants.

cultural order are so little known in the West that the question cannot be pursued further except by speculation.

Decline of Mortality by Age

The appearance that the data above give to infant mortality may lead us to keep certain reservations about their accuracy. No such doubt can exist about the general validity of mortality registered at age one and above. The tests reported in Table 34 and Table 35 present Taiwan's statistical system as a paragon even among those of the technologically advanced nations in the world. The trends they show in mortality of later life cannot but be accepted.

For what they are worth, our best estimates of mortality in infancy suggest that it did not decline sharply. On surer ground, it is certain that the chances of dying in later years of childhood and early adulthood fell faster. Fig. 28 displays graphically the basic data on rate of decline in mortality (chances of dying) at selected ages of males entering those ages each year.[40] In the ages taken here as examples—1, 2, 3, 4, 10 and 25—older children and young adults gained the most in chances of survival. Among children, in general the older, the more the improvement. Every higher age gained more ground than infants. Part of this difference may be due to the nature of changes made through colonial administration in the external risks confronting persons of each age. But doubtless a certain part is also due to the effect of carrying improved health from one age to the next by the same individuals—the "cohort effect." Yearly fluctuations are large enough, however, that no special patterns of either type are to be found without complicated manipulations of the data.

To find the risks declining more or less together at different ages does not imply that the number of years of life saved in the population was the same with advancing age. The saving of life in infancy was greater, despite the more moderate drop in the risks than at any other age. This fact holds true regardless of whether one adopts this period-by-period approach or follows the mortality of successive actual cohorts.

[40] The earlier values of the mortality rates at higher ages are connected with broken lines because the observations are not spaced at every year. Mortality rates for every year have been computed only for persons born after 1905.

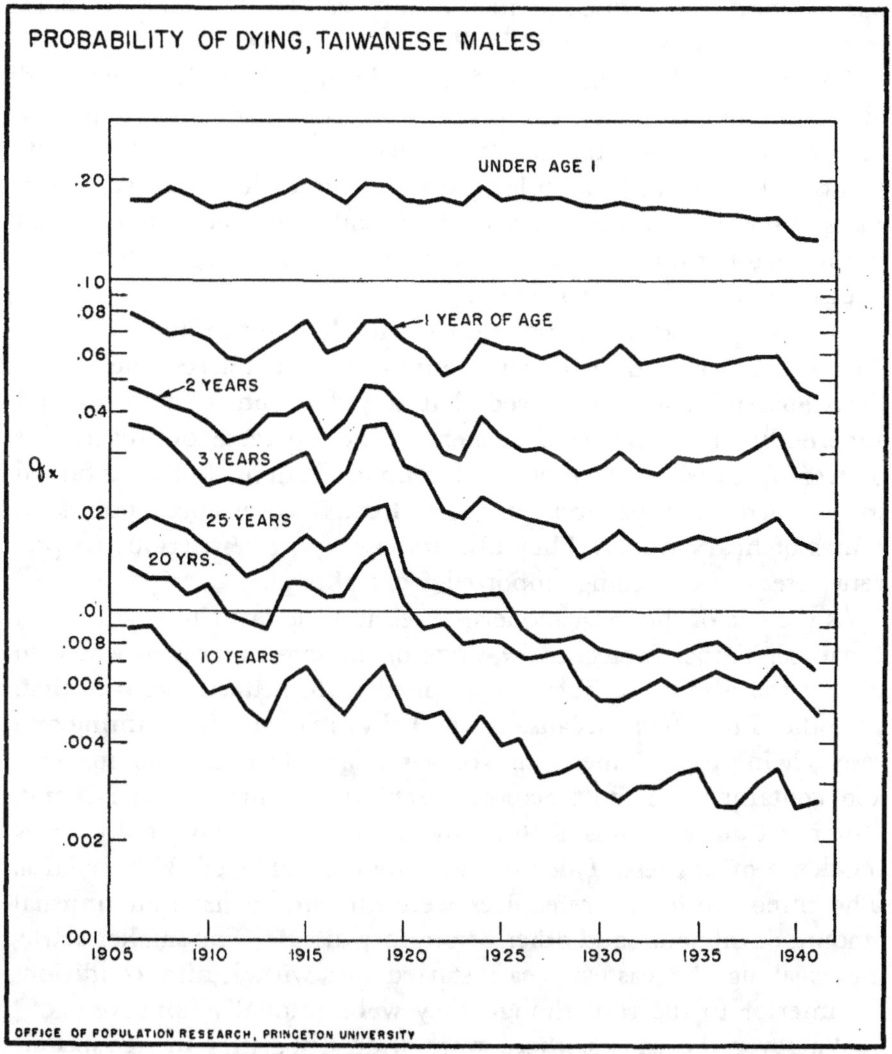

Fig. 28. Decline of Mortality by Age, 1906-1941. Taiwanese Males.

Sectional Differences in Mortality

It would be strange if for people of each age the risks of death were the same everywhere in Taiwan. It happens that most of our information can be obtained only for the island taken as a whole. The measures have been designed to take advantage of this and to present a detailed view of the total population at some sacrifice of knowledge about its parts. Moreover, with a total population that was so small, any reduction in the number of cases tends to make sensitive measurements unreliable.

The livelihood of Taiwanese farmers brought them into close and continual contact with their physical surroundings. Such a people cannot avoid some influence of climate and environment on its chances of survival. For a place so small there were marked differences in seasons and rainfall over the island. Whether or not related to this factor, from time to time local peculiarities in the incidence of disease have often been noted.

In pre-Japanese times, isolation of small localities kept much of the communicable disease from being transmitted across the island. Even epidemics were observed that stayed confined to towns and apparently did not become general. The Japanese destroyed this barrier by an efficient network of communications, but maintained special medical inspections on the railroads and at check points on routes of heavy travel. They also imposed port restrictions to prevent disease from being imported from abroad.

As the site of the most modern cities and the favorite residence of Japanese, Taipei Prefecture was one of the safest places in which to live. It was also more liberally supplied with medical facilities than any other Prefecture, because it was Taiwan's center for training and research in tropical medicine. It was relatively free from malaria, and contained the most elaborate sanitary facilities in the island. Other sections were less distinguished, unless by exceptionally heavy incidence of sickness. Taichung was the most afflicted with malaria. The three southern Prefectures were all said to have an unusual amount of influenza and other respiratory disease. The smaller settlements along the eastern coast started out with health conditions far inferior to the rest, though they were gradually improved.

Whatever the causes, there were wide disparities in age-specific mortality among the various Prefectures as late as 1925 (see Fig. 29, for males only). For some unknown reason Hsinchu was the most favored part of the island, followed by Taipei. The range from highest to lowest at this date was almost as great as between the beginning and the end of the Japanese period. It is interesting also that the differences were consistent at all ages, with almost no shifts in the standing of Prefectures at any age. At a time when there was very little migration between Prefectures, these life table values may be regarded as a good representation of actual differences.

Expressed as the mean expectation of life at selected ages (Table

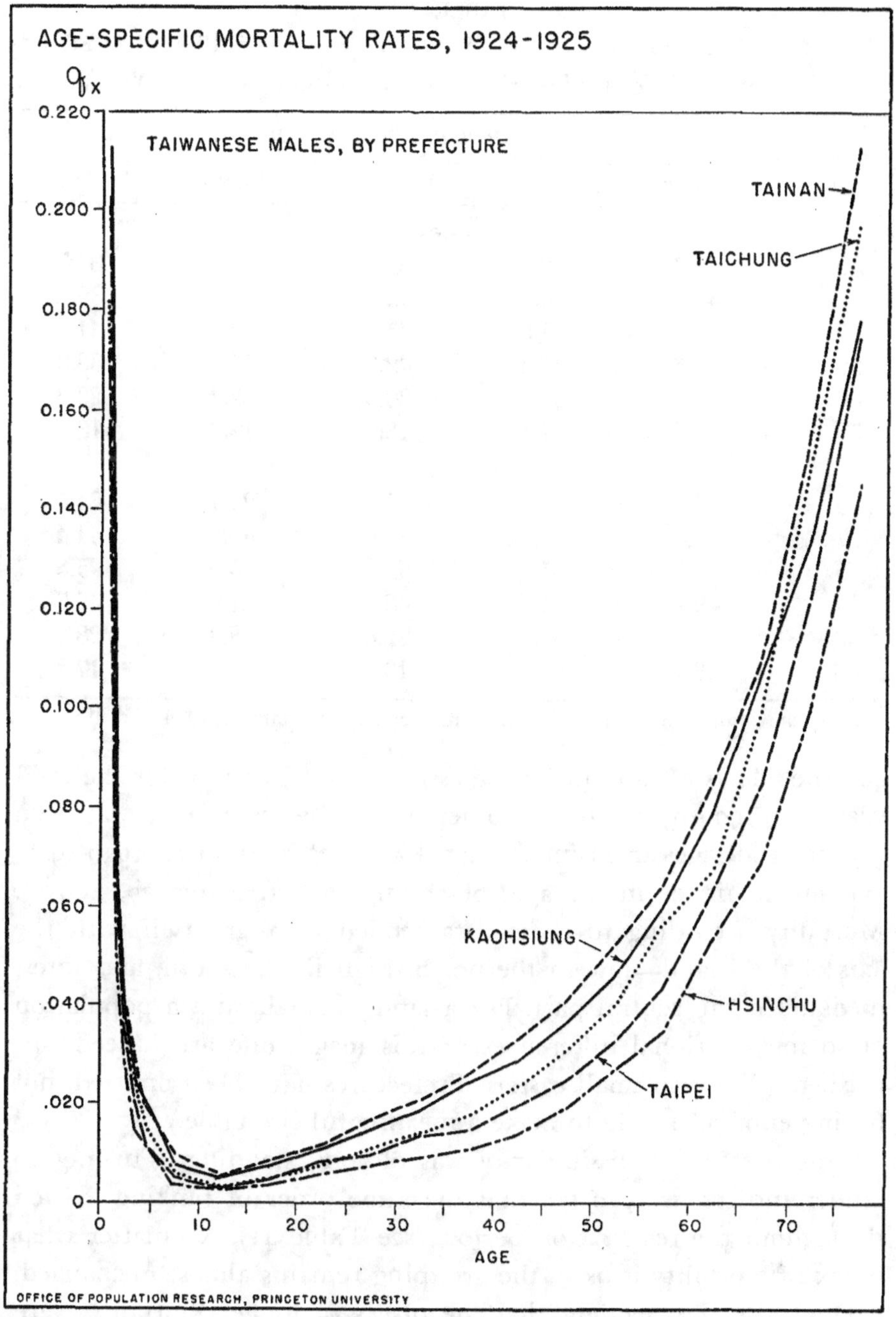

Fig. 29. Mortality of Taiwanese Males in Each Age, by Prefecture. Values of q_x, Life Tables of 1924-1925.

TABLE 40

MEAN LIFE EXPECTANCY OF TAIWANESE AT DIFFERENT AGES

Prefectural Life Tables of 1924-1925. Values of e_x, in Years

	PREFECTURE				
Age	*Taipei*	*Hsinchu*	*Taichung*	*Tainan*	*Kaohsiung*
			Males		
0	38.3	43.1	35.9	30.4	31.7
1	45.2	50.2	42.8	37.1	39.2
5	47.5	51.5	45.7	39.7	41.8
10	43.6	47.4	42.0	36.5	38.3
30	28.0	31.1	26.0	22.3	23.8
50	15.4	17.1	13.9	12.4	13.2
			Females		
0	42.2	46.6	40.7	34.7	34.5
1	48.3	52.3	46.9	40.8	41.4
5	52.8	55.1	52.0	45.0	45.8
10	49.2	51.4	48.5	41.9	42.7
30	33.7	35.4	32.6	28.3	28.8
50	20.1	20.4	19.1	17.0	17.2

Sources: Computed from census and vital registration data of 1924 and 1925.

40), the effects of mortality were as heavy in Tainan as for the total island in 1909-1911. On the other hand, the expectancy was even higher at all ages in Hsinchu than for all of Taiwan in 1936-1940, and much higher in the ages of childhood (cf. Table 37, above). Mortality according to these data tended to align itself with the axis of the island—low in the north, high in the south, and intermediate in the central part. For a land so small, and a population of so few, sectional differences of this magnitude are indeed surprising. (The two small eastern Prefectures have been omitted, not having enough people to make a meaningful life table.)

This pattern of dissimilarity was of long standing. Turning to cruder indices, we can see that the same order of ranking existed throughout the registration period (see Table 41). No matter what index of mortality is used, the grouping remains almost unchanged.

Here also it is evident that the places of higher mortality were making the faster progress toward control over death than the ones that were already low. This appears as well in the fact that the rela-

TABLE 41

TAIWAN. DIFFERENCES IN MORTALITY BY PREFECTURE, IN SELECTED YEARS

Crude Death Rates, Infant Death Rates, and Deaths Per Thousand Females Aged 15 to 49†

	PREFECTURES*							
Year	*Taipei*	*Hsinchu*	*Taichung*	*Tainan*	*Kaohsiung*	*Taitung & Hualien*	*P'enghu Islands*	*Total Island*
				Crude Death Rates				
1906	28	22	37	42	41	35	37	35
1915	25	20	30	36	34	30	26	29
1925	23	19	24	29	29	31	26	25
1930	22	17	21	23	24	21	22	21
1935	22	19	21	21	21	21	19	21
				Infant Death Rates				
1906	—	—	—	—	—	—	—	192
1915	162	138	176	192	191	148	204	174
1925	157	139	164	180	191	149	—‡	167
1930	157	130	153	161	179	152	172	156
1935	154	139	146	151	155	160	131	149
				Deaths per Thousand Women Aged 15-49				
1906	13	10	15	29	26	24	15	20
1915	11	9	13	20	20	16	12	15
1925	9	7	9	14	14	15	—‡	11
1930	8	6	7	9	10	8	9	8
1935	8	7	8	8	9	9	5	8

† All rates are averaged over three years around the census year. Those for 1906 represent one year only. Infant death rates have been omitted for 1906, as being unreliable.

* Prefectural divisions before 1920 have been matched approximately to the subsequent boundaries.

‡ Included in Kaohsiung Prefecture.

tive dispersion of death rates was continually being reduced along with the death rates themselves.

As expressed in terms of the *relative* variation among Prefectures in Table 42, the gains in survival were being spread more evenly over the various portions of the island as time went on. And part of the reduction in mortality for the total must have taken the form merely of levelling some of the initial inequities in health

TABLE 42

RELATIVE VARIATION OF MORTALITY AMONG PREFECTURES IN SELECTED YEARS

Coefficients of Variation for the Death Rates of Each Year in Table 41

Year	*Crude Death Rates*	*Infant Death Rates*	*Deaths/ Women 15-49*
1906	19.2	—	36.0
1915	17.7	13.2	27.9
1925	15.2	10.8	27.3
1930	9.6	9.3	15.2
1935	5.1	6.3	16.6

Source: Computed from data of Table 41.

conditions. Much headway was made in this process after 1925, when the life tables above revealed such large gaps in the degree of control over sickness and death. It must be kept in mind when studying mortality here and in other areas of rapid decline that initial achievement is likely not to extend to many in the population, and that later progress may be no more than bringing more types of people nearer to the same point as the ones who were privileged in the beginning.

Taiwan formerly had a well-earned reputation as a spot of capricious and unchecked risks to life among its inhabitants. Its position athwart trading routes of the last century made it a likely place to introduce epidemic disease from the rest of Asia. As it became drawn into contact with the outside world and its wider sources of infection, the state of medical knowledge among its people did not keep pace. The former government lacked the capacity and the incentive to adopt measures that might alleviate or forestall such sickness. Taiwanese were therefore often subjected to intense attacks of these diseases, some of them becoming general over the island.

In fifty years of administration the Japanese quickly eliminated epidemics. They succeeded in gradually making the other sources of fatal illness and ill health less prevalent, and thus postponed the prospect of death for Taiwanese. While some characteristics of the decline in mortality that they induced followed familiar patterns, it also carried certain distinctive traits of the society in which it occurred. Special features like the apparent vitality of adult women and the importance of neonatal mortality in the decline of total infant mortality we have established with repeated observations. As far as present knowledge is equipped to deal with them, these peculiarities must remain inexplicable.

The means to this accomplishment were inexpensive and rudimentary. Aside from probably raising levels of living, the Japanese developed a concerted program against an important group of dangers to health. They attacked those pestilent conditions that can be reached through sanitation and slight reorganizations on a mass scale of practices that were deeply rooted in custom. More thorough measures, which were also more burdensome, were avoided. Their health program relied on administrative efficiency and energy in execution to make up for what it lacked in elegance of equipment and technique.

It is significant to find that such an approach could achieve the results that it did. In many other areas of high mortality the desire to reduce the risks of death is prompting steps in the same direction, and Taiwan's experience ought to prove instructive for such efforts. It is only a modest sample of what might be done in a "backward" region with effective administration—without necessarily incurring the great expense often thought to be associated with high standards of public health. Recent progress in research and development of drugs can make success more certain than before. Future strides in medical knowledge can enhance it still further.

The greatest limitation is that health promotion among people with high mortality requires constant vigilance. Default threatens such a program with collapse, for medical procedures now known are still not automatic, nor are they foolproof. Japanese measures to control disease were primarily suppressive. They did not eradicate malaria or remove the potential sources of cholera infection. Failure to appreciate these latent dangers led to severe outbreaks of cholera and malaria after the island was taken over by forces from the mainland in 1945. Since then the standards of administration, which had been allowed to deteriorate, have been raised again; with the improved technical knowledge at its disposal, the Nationalist government may be able to keep mortality at levels even below those of the Japanese period. The example of Japanese health policies, however, remains a useful lesson in what energetic measures can accomplish without the benefit of these superior medical facilities.

CHAPTER VI. APPENDIX

TAIWANESE LIFE TABLES

Number of Survivors to 10,000 Live Births (l_x), Selected Years, by Year in Which Persons Entered Each Age

Age	1906		1909-1911		1915		1919		1921		1926-1930		1936-1940		Age
	Males	*Females*	*Males*	*Females*	*Males*	*Females*	*Males*	*Females*	*Males*	*Females*	*Males*	*Females*	*Males*	*Females*	
0	10,000	10,000	10,000	10,000	10,000	10,000	10,000	10,000	10,000	10,000	10,000	10,000	10,000	10,000	0
1	8,078	8,270	8,261	8,510	7,980	8,200	8,037	8,328	8,080	8,377	8,257	8,546	8,444	8,706	1
2	7,458	7,552	7,728	7,892	7,363	7,472	7,422	7,611	7,590	7,811	7,775	8,004	7,959	8,169	2
3	7,100	7,061	7,446	7,491	7,045	7,033	7,061	7,158	7,290	7,450	7,551	7,705	7,713	7,876	3
4	6,841	6,721	7,253	7,232	6,829	6,750	6,802	6,838	7,097	7,209	7,420	7,541	7,578	7,717	4
5	6,668	6,498	7,125	7,072	6,683	6,562	6,613	6,607	6,974	7,062	7,337	7,445	7,495	7,627	5
10	6,189	5,945	6,811	6,717	6,337	6,159	6,217	6,121	6,694	6,745	7,154	7,258	7,319	7,453	10
15	5,949	5,680	6,624	6,543	6,139	5,980	6,009	5,876	6,554	6,612	7,038	7,150	7,216	7,354	15
20	5,646	5,353	6,379	6,273	5,872	5,704	5,691	5,528	6,329	6,419	6,860	6,975	7,048	7,199	20
25	5,222	4,948	5,986	5,886	5,477	5,344	5,212	5,043	6,020	6,122	6,592	6,724	6,809	6,988	25
30	4,707	4,514	5,491	5,486	4,954	4,938	4,617	4,524	5,634	5,816	6,268	6,440	6,530	6,754	30
35	4,123	4,061	4,924	5,058	4,355	4,511	4,015	4,014	5,194	5,446	5,884	6,114	6,201	6,479	35
40	3,479	3,615	4,301	4,605	3,725	4,061	3,398	3,550	4,705	5,074	5,423	5,749	5,820	6,156	40
45	2,841	3,193	3,625	4,183	3,063	3,620	2,805	3,140	4,154	4,696	4,892	5,377	5,234	5,816	45
50	2,217	2,753	2,944	3,739	2,413	3,201	2,236	2,744	3,590	4,305	4,290	4,986	4,766	5,443	50
55	1,642	2,285	2,278	3,227	1,812	2,696	1,712	2,324	2,957	3,884	3,637	4,534	4,101	4,990	55
60	1,153	1,819	1,658	2,674	1,260	2,150	1,224	1,884	2,311	3,366	2,938	3,988	3,347	4,424	60
65	735	1,344	1,139	2,092	812	1,586	798	1,434	1,689	2,766	2,192	3,315	2,546	3,734	65
70	414	892	697	1,498	456	1,056	443	996	1,087	2,107	1,472	2,553	1,738	2,926	70
75	191	502	368	931	212	573	217	595	616	1,413	845	1,750	1,010	2,005	75
80	73	232	137	477	80	244	80	281	288	745	387	1,007	465	1,126	80
85	24	103	45	212	26	108	26	125	95	330	128	446	153	461	85
90	5	31	9	64	5	32	5	38	19	99	26	134	30	114	90

Sources: Life tables of 1906, 1909-11, 1915, 1919 and 1921 were computed from the assembled data of Taiwan's censuses and vital registration. The table of 1926-30 is from Taiwan, Government-General (1936); that of 1936-40 is from Taiwan, Provincial Government (1947).

CHAPTER VII

The Setting for Family Life

No matter what part of Taiwanese life we have investigated, it has not been possible to proceed very far without encountering evidences of familial pressures and sentiments. This has been true of the organization of farming, the "inheritance" of skills, the reluctance to migrate, certain special patterns of mortality, and the attainment of peace and order by the Japanese. Yet kinship is something that people usually consider as a private matter (and moreover take for granted without inquiry as it exists among themselves), and so it is not easy to increase our knowledge of it.

The aspect of kinship that makes it so important is the framework of obligations and expectations that it imposes on people's activities in related spheres.[1] Like many forces affecting behavior, the Chinese family system is an intangible thing, and must be approached by indirection—for example, by construing some of the basic moral precepts that the society has received from the past, which is the usual procedure, or, as we shall essay in this chapter, by examining some of the patterns that people display in their familial roles. The former of these devices has been singularly appropriate, for Chinese have one of the richest accumulations of expressions about their sentiments in family matters that ever existed; but it has left us with a one-sided and sometimes unclear view of the subject, largely because it has been followed with little reference to the latter. While neither of these alternatives gives a perfect representation of the family system in actual operation, the advantage here lies in using Taiwan's census data to illuminate a few points on which accurate information has previously been lacking.

The Size of Household Units

Japanese authorities showed that they were aware of the family's practical significance to the people, for in Taiwan they made it the basis of their census and vital registration statistics as well as of their regular civil administration. In each census the blank forms that were distributed to be filled in with personal information were all made out with the *household* as the unit of enumeration. The head

[1] For thorough discussion of the family's role in Chinese social organization, see Lang, O. (1946) and Levy, M. J., Jr. (1950).

of a household was the one responsible for entering the correct facts regarding each member. The Japanese owed much of their creditable success in census enumeration in Taiwan to the way they were able to secure conformity to these standards by household heads. Once they were in possession of authority to do this, the family system did the rest.[2]

The household is not identical with a family unit. It includes some persons living with a family group who are not related by birth or marriage to the others, and it leaves out all who are temporarily or permanently absent at the date of the census. But the household, properly defined, is the unit that counts in Chinese society. It is the concrete group in which joint decisions are made, and in which the obligations of the family system operate most directly. Also, it is the foremost, for some people the only, unit of participation in the society at large.[3] Provided that sufficient information is given about its members, the household is probably a more useful basis for enumeration than kinship, strictly defined.

[2] The high caliber of their census system did not owe everything to this expedient, however. It had been a common feature of the ancient registrations of people in China, where in pre-modern times it had not given such gratifying results. Japanese adapted the lessons of experience in these matters by Western nations, and added some innovations of their own. They worked out sets of definitions which provided meaningful categories and consistent groupings of the population (as well, of course, as some that did not), and they developed an effective administration to carry out the work of enumeration.

In such a society the most modern innovations in census technique are useless by themselves. Similarly, the family system *without* special statistical standards may be a poor instrument for recording information about its members—there is every encouragement to evasion unless this is forestalled. Systematic omissions might be more serious in household statistics than in any other type of tabulation, for they would probably be concentrated in certain types of household members whom there was some incentive to conceal—the biases would be strongest in a table that showed household membership.

In order to control the responses in these household schedules, the census rules defined an ordinary household as those persons actually present who had residence, family budget, or both, in common. People, or branches of a family, who did not meet these simple but effective requirements were enumerated as separate households; special types of living arrangements ("quasi-households," q.v. below) were assigned to another category. These and other rules of procedure were maintained with only minor changes of wording in all of the seven censuses of Taiwan. They were reported fully in the explanatory section or appendix of the main descriptive volumes for 1905, 1915, 1920 and 1930.

[3] In Taiwan there was another basis for organizing family solidarity, the so-called "clan" or *tsu*. It was very prominent, especially in pre-Japanese times when it was the basis for setting in motion insurrections and often the means for restoring peace and order. But the clan was never a *family* in the sense of a common unit of participation in the society. It was a loose alliance of affiliated families rather than the unit in which everyday matters were conducted. For the distinction between the two, and a discussion of the *tsu* as it appeared in South China, see Hu Hsien-chin (1948).

Chinese cultural norms set no limit to the number of family relatives that it is desirable to maintain in a single household, but attach great merit to holding together many branches of a family in one unit. Though Chinese are thus inclined to feel that the bigger the family the better—there seem to be no general class or status differences in the ideal size that they should strive for—so many degrees of relationship are eligible for inclusion that other considerations usually enter and help to settle the question. In practice, the real limitations tend to be how strongly a particular family feels it can enhance its prestige through adherence to tradition, and how well it can afford financially to do so.

TABLE 43

SIZE OF HOUSEHOLDS IN TAIWAN IN SUCCESSIVE CENSUSES

Average Persons per Household, All Types of Household, All Ethnic Groups, 1905 to 1940

1905	5.2
1915	5.3
1920	5.3
1925	5.5
1930	5.7
1935	5.8
1940	6.0

Sources: *1935 Census, Statistical Tables*, Descriptive Section, p. 30.
1940 Census, Summary Returns, published in the Gazette of the Government-General of Taiwan, April 22, 1941.

Despite the considerable emphasis on their size and cohesion, these family units actually are not exceptionally large. From the total numbers of households and of people, published with the regular report of each census of Taiwan, we can first establish a few main features of the case to guide the more detailed discussion that is to follow. Expressed as the average number of persons to a household, these figures show that the size of households (for everyone, mixing together all nationality groups and all types of household arrangements) started out in 1905 at 5.2, and rose steadily during the census period (see Table 43). The increase was not especially rapid, but it was unbroken and marked by acceleration with the passage of time. Correlated with what is already known about the growth of population in Taiwan, this steady movement implies that households were not keeping up with the increase of people, and that family groups were therefore undergoing some change in their composition. Though some aspects of this change can be shown more satisfactorily below, the process is most easily seen in these figures, since they cover the complete span of the census administration.

As usual, the published results of these census materials did not do justice to the care that went into their collection. Household tables were not always shown in useful form, and the figures of Table 43 do not convey very much even about the size of families in Taiwan. Obviously in order to draw reliable conclusions about families of Taiwanese it must be possible to separate them as a group in the statistics, and to make sure that the statistics employed are a fair representation of family groups. For exactly this purpose, the Japanese treated one kind of household as standard, the so-called "ordinary" household, to cover the "normal" types of living arrangements. People in certain special categories were excluded; residents of these non-family households, or "quasi-households," will be omitted from most of the tables that follow.[4]

Information about quasi-households is sketchy and hard to find. The size of these establishments is unknown for separate nationality groups, perhaps through a deliberate effort to conceal the military forces (though they would nearly all have been classified as Japanese anyway, according to the status of the person in charge). The figures can be pieced together for the entire population, and appear in Tables 44 and 45. Quasi-households were a very small part of the total, but accounted for a much larger portion of non-Taiwanese. Only one person in a hundred of all nationality groups lived in such circumstances; 6.6 per cent of Japanese and 20 per cent of Mainland Chinese lived in quasi-households in 1930, but relatively few of the Taiwanese were found outside of ordinary households. Since Taiwanese are the main source of interest in the problem, the few living in quasi-households are unimportant, and for the remainder of this chapter the term "household" will be used to refer to "ordinary" households only.

On the average, ordinary households of Taiwanese contained be-

[4] They comprise people counted in hospitals, prisons, schools, military barracks, police and other special dormitories, and hotels. Although they must be removed before the household data can be said to represent patterns of familial life, the line drawn between the two types of household is not entirely rigorous. Many of these people, especially the ones in hotels and schools, were only temporarily absent from their homes, and their family affiliations may have continued undiminished.

TABLE 44

PER CENT OF TAIWAN'S POPULATION LIVING IN "ORDINARY" HOUSEHOLDS, 1905-1930

Both Sexes

Year	*Persons Living in Ordinary Households*	*Persons Living in "Quasi-Households"*	*Per Cent Living in Ordinary Households*
	All Nationality Groups		
1905	3,021,260	18,491	99.4
1915	3,461,282	18,640	99.5
1920	3,624,403	30,905	99.2
1930	4,546,970	45,567	99.0
	Taiwanese		
1920	3,454,956	11,551	99.7
1930	4,293,234	20,447	99.5
	Japanese		
1920	151,862	12,404	92.4
1930	213,314	14,967	93.4
	Other Nationalities*		
1920	17,585	6,950	71.7
1930	40,422	10,153	79.9

* "Other nationalities" consists almost entirely of Mainland Chinese.

Sources: *Census of 1905, General Volume of Statistical Tables,* Table 114.
Census of 1915, Statistical Tables, Table 109 and 116.
Census of 1920, Descriptive Report with Appendix, Appendix Table 149, 164, 165 and 169.
Census of 1930, Statistical Tables, Total Island, Table 5.

tween five and six persons during that portion of the census period when they can be observed separately. Because Taiwanese made up almost the entire population and because most of them lived in family groups, the initial approximation of Table 43 was fairly close to the actual size of their households. Differences begin to emerge when other nationality groups are listed by themselves; the households of both Japanese and Mainland Chinese on the average were smaller by a considerable margin than those of the Taiwanese, and remained that way (see Table 45).

Not only did Taiwanese follow the ideal of large households more closely than the other population groups in Taiwan, but they displayed a different pattern in approaching it. Distributed according to the number of persons in each, only the households of Taiwanese

TABLE 45

SIZE OF HOUSEHOLDS, BY TYPE AND NATIONALITY OF HEAD

Average Persons Per Household, "Ordinary" Households and "Quasi-Households"

All Nationality Groups, Taiwanese, Japanese and Other Nationalities

1905 to 1930

Year	*Ordinary Households*	*Quasi-Households*
	All Nationality Groups	
1905	5.19	6.2
1915	5.31	12.4
1920	5.30	20.6
1930	5.64	17.1
	Taiwanese	
1920	5.45	
1930	5.82	
	Japanese	
1920	3.37	
1930	3.74	
	Other Nationalities*	
1920	3.79	
1930	3.84	

* "Other nationalities" consists almost entirely of Mainland Chinese.

Source: From data of preceding table. Certain army and navy barracks were included as quasi-households in the Census of 1920 for the first time, accounting for much of the increase over 1915 and 1905 in the average size of quasi-households shown above.

were in a pattern that reveals a predominance of families with two or more generations, families of the sort that must be required to maintain a high rate of natural increase. Their households were found most commonly with four and five members, more rarely of smaller sizes. The process by which the average size of Taiwanese households rose from 1905 on was not a completely general shift toward larger units, but rather one of forming relatively fewer small households (with the exception of people living alone) and raising the proportion of very large ones (see Fig. 30). The sizes most often achieved remained very nearly the same as before, and the distribution simply became more skewed. (Expressed in terms of the numbers of persons involved, the effect of this change would, of course,

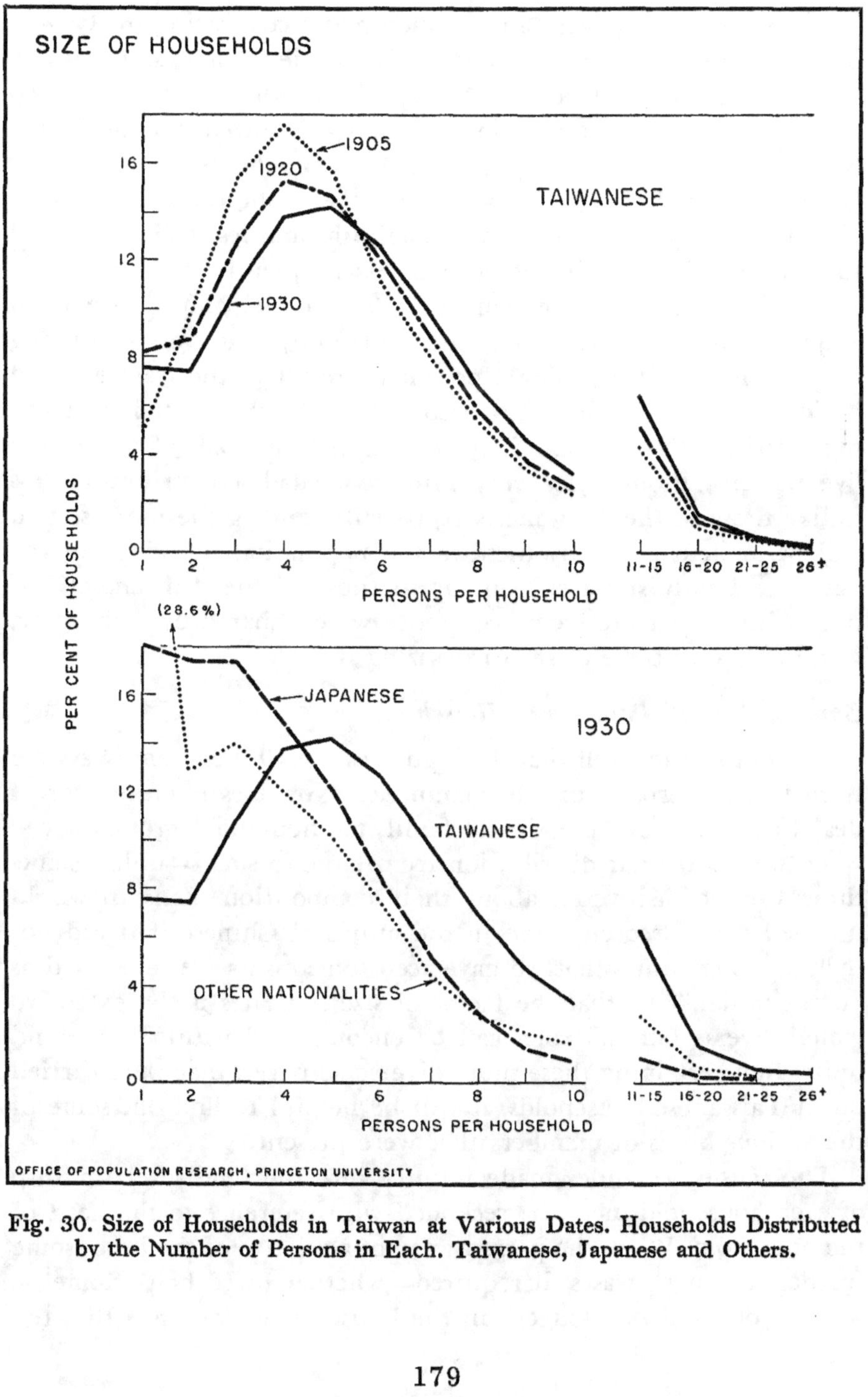

Fig. 30. Size of Households in Taiwan at Various Dates. Households Distributed by the Number of Persons in Each. Taiwanese, Japanese and Others.

be multiplied in households of larger size, since they were larger by virtue of containing many people.)

A great many Japanese and Chinese nationals staying in Taiwan obviously were separated from close family ties—for example, those who lived alone, and perhaps some of those in households of two or three persons, not to mention the ones who stayed in quasi-households. Few in either group maintained households in Taiwan as large as those that were usual among their countrymen at home. The Japanese gradually began to establish families in Taiwan, and to take up solitary living somewhat less frequently than at the beginning of their rule. In contrast, an extremely high proportion (29 per cent) of Chinese from the mainland by 1930 were still living alone in households of single persons, a result of the transient and impermanent status that they occupied in the island. It is interesting that in both of these minority groups, households of more than five persons, though not very numerous, had a distribution less unlike those of the Taiwanese. Apparently among the more settled and permanent non-Taiwanese in the population the ideals of the desirable family size were similar to those of the Taiwanese; but this attitude seems to have been more widely shared by Taiwanese, who as a group came closer to realizing it.

Composition of Taiwanese Households

It is not size in itself that distinguishes the Chinese family system from its counterparts in other countries. Nor does it mean a great deal to know about the size of family or household groups—even when we know their distribution from large to small—unless something can be discovered about their composition. Kinship would not be such a preoccupation in the minds of Chinese if it did not include other things that we have accustomed ourselves to regard as "non-familial." All that the factor of size indicates is the extent to which diverse familial roles can be encompassed within household units. In ascertaining these more diverse activities that were carried on in Taiwanese households, it will be helpful to find out some of the various kinds of members that were present.

The census schedules made inquiry into the family relationship of each household member, reckoned with reference to the head of the household. When the person was not a relative of the head, some further statement was still required—whether hired help, domestic servant, or simply a "lodger" in the house. The trouble is that the greatest part of this information was discarded by the time the census reached the stage of publication. The work of tabulating and publishing the wealth of material that was collected on people's family affiliations—which would have entailed tremendous cost—was apparently never carried out. With the 200-odd different positions of kinship that are recognized in the language, and the nine proverbial generations through which they might be counted, probably most of the population of Taiwan would prove to be mutually related if their full genealogies were known. Consequently, the tables that resulted from these censuses indicate relationship only in the indefinite sense of "family members," without giving any clear idea of what this term actually meant.[5]

Only two censuses, those of 1920 and 1930, published information on household composition that can stand comparison in detail.[6] The membership of "ordinary" households at both dates is shown in Table 46, in terms of the average number of persons per household, in each census category. The totals, 5.45 and 5.81 respectively, correspond to those given in Table 45 above. Taiwan's households were made up mostly of "family members," or relatives of the household heads; the entire group of related persons is represented by *both* of these two categories combined. Non-related occupants were rare—averaged over all households, they were so few that for most purposes they may be thrown together into one group, "Other."

One member of each household was expected to be entered as the "head" in the census enumeration. This designation meant the person who actually represented the household with the outside world and who held authority in making joint decisions that affected the group as a whole. The category was well adapted to the situation, for the same person would as a matter of course assume responsibility to fill out the household's census report. Almost all of the heads were men; but in view of the strong ideal that this should be

[5] The directions for filling out the forms in the census of 1920 stated that it should be interpreted to mean "lineal relatives," and we know from the general features of the family system that kinship in this sense would ordinarily be restricted to relatives on the male side only. But no more definite instructions were given on this point by the census regulations. See *Census of 1920, Descriptive Report with Appendix*, p. 15 of descriptive section.

The meaning of "lodger" (or "guest," or "visitor," as the term might also be translated), is still unclear; apparently it was a catch-all for all people who did not fit into the other categories.

[6] The census of 1915 contained some similar household tables, but these have not been available for this study. Those published for 1920 are the most complete and detailed of all, and will be drawn upon most heavily.

TABLE 46

COMPOSITION OF TAIWANESE HOUSEHOLDS, 1920 AND 1930

Average Number of Persons per Household, by Status in the Household, and Sex

	1920			*1930*			*Change 1920 to 1930 (1930/1920 x 100)*
	Total	*Males*	*Females*	*Total*	*Males*	*Females*	*Both Sexes*
All Household Residents	5.45	2.79	2.66	5.81	2.95	2.87	107
Heads	0.99	0.87	0.12	0.99	0.86	0.12	100
Family Members	4.36	1.85	2.51	4.71	2.01	2.71	108
Occupied							
a. In Household } b. Outside	1.48	0.85	0.63	0.96	0.57	0.38	89
b. Outside				0.35	0.27	0.08	
No Occupation	2.88	1.00	1.88	3.41	1.17	2.24	118
Employees	0.05	0.05	*	0.05	0.05	0.01	110
Domestics	0.01	*	*	*	*	*	
"Lodgers"	0.04	0.02	0.01	0.06	0.03	0.03	

* Indicates less than 0.005. Due to rounding of figures, sub-totals occasionally do not add to the correct totals.

Source: From *Census of 1920, Detailed Tables,* Table 36 and *Census of 1930, Statistical Tables, Total Island,* Table 5.

the general rule, there is significance in the fact that more than ten per cent of all households were managed by women. Several signs, which can be discussed somewhat later, suggest that it is not always looked upon as out of the way for women to attain this position.

At the moment of enumeration, Taiwanese had more households than heads of households, or not enough heads (regardless of sex) to go around. In this detail Taiwan was different from both Korea and Japan, where there was an inflexible requirement that each household must have one of its members counted in this role. The difference apparently came from a peculiarity of administration, because for some reason the Japanese did not apply the same regulation in Taiwan. This is not to say, however, that certain households were "headless"—the excess of households over heads meant either that some heads maintained more than one establishment (which might be possible through concubinage), or that the person in this position was in certain instances temporarily absent from home (in which case he would be counted merely as a member of some other household, wherever he might be).[7] This discrepancy is present in all the tables that follow, but is usually very small and can be ignored.

Of the remaining family members in both 1920 and 1930, those who had an occupation were outnumbered by those who had none. There is nothing unusual in this, for the family nearly everywhere is conspicuous for the amount of dependency that it regularly supports. The generality of this fact is partly due to nothing but the generality of relying on families to bring forth and nurture new generations of adults, which all known societies have done in greater or lesser degree. But dependency is especially prominent in Taiwan and similar countries: children there are very numerous, and they are joined by the aged in partaking of the family's resources on a non-productive basis. The support of each person above as well as below the limits of the working life falls completely on his kinsmen—this is an expectation enforced throughout the society, and it concentrates practically the entire burden on the resources of individual households.[8]

Excluding the heads of households (who in almost all cases were employed), nearly three-fourths of all other family members had no recognized occupation in 1930—the fraction being less than this for males, somewhat higher for females. Non-producing members took up a large part of family groups in more than just a static sense; people with no occupation also accounted for the major part of enlargements in household size that accompanied population increase. Even though the period of comparison here is short (the decade between 1920 and 1930), it is clear that on the average the largest gain per household was in this large category (see the final column in Table 46). In other words, the institutional system translated the growth of population into an increase of dependent family members as well as an increase of families, and turned the greater lon-

[7] This second possibility is more plausible, since the excess was greatest where heads were most likely to be absent—in Prefectures with most emigration, outside of agriculture (as compared with agricultural households), and in those households with larger numbers of non-relatives. The same was true of Japanese living in Taiwan.

[8] Even though this burden may be mitigated by the fact that old people are *not* very numerous, and that children *are* put to work, high mortality usually ensures that a high proportion of infants will survive only long enough to claim their full share of dependency, and will die before contributing any large measure of productive effort. Moreover, countries that are faced with this problem also lack the extra-familial provisions (schools, labor-saving equipment) that many industrial countries have utilized to offset this burden.

gevity discussed in the previous chapter into additional old and young members of non-working ages.[9]

Family Membership in Households

Not all households had the variety in their membership shown by the average of all of them in Table 46. In fact, it was not common for households to contain non-family members at all, and the internal affairs of most households did not involve persons other than near relatives. Owing to the indefinite criterion of family relationship in the census data, no more than a crude approach can be made to discovering what special or unusual features were present in those families that incorporated "outsiders" into their households.

The traditions that shape Chinese familial life are explicit as to why large families are desirable and how they should be achieved. Their foremost concern is that of descent, of preserving the continuity of a particular family indefinitely into the future. The most emphatic rule of descent is that it should be patrilineal, that a family line may be perpetuated only through its male side. There are no notable exceptions to this rule; in cases where it cannot be followed to the letter, its purpose is observed by means of adoption, changing of surnames, or even reversing some of the usual procedures in marriage, as we shall see in the next chapter.

Since the exact relationships are not shown, it is never possible to be certain just *which* family relatives were included in a household of a given size. But the nuclear group might be described as husband, wife, and unmarried children, for the kinship system does not customarily provide these people (or such of them who remain alive and present) any alternative place of residence. With this group alone, much of which was usually made up of dependent children, the actual size of most households was not large enough to leave room for either additional relatives or "outsiders." (See Fig. 30, above.)

The goal of still larger families, which was realized by a restricted though substantial part of the population, could not have been attained without encountering special difficulties imposed by the family system itself.[10] But any further enlargements of a family could be

[9] There was some change in the standard of what constituted employment for women between these two censuses, and this accentuated slightly what otherwise would be the pattern of change in Table 46. The same pattern results, perhaps less strongly, if only males are used in the comparison.

[10] Of course, the parents of the husband or other relatives of the father's (or higher)

made in only one way—by retaining in it two or more brothers, with *their* nuclear family groups, if any. In achieving the extended families that have been cherished in Chinese tradition this is the crucial step, for there are counter-pressures that tend to discourage it. Collateral ties are known to be relatively weak among Chinese—sons do not have bonds of the same strength with each other that they have with their fathers. These ties are especially difficult to maintain after the death of a father, for sons may exercise individual claims to shares in the family property. These claims sometimes lead to division of the family and its property even before the father dies; they are intensified as soon as the brothers are married. Extending the family unit to any considerable size implies some ability to coordinate these conflicting interests and requires leisure for devoting attention to managing its collective affairs, not to mention special resources to support its existence on a more elaborate scale. Obviously it was unusual to succeed in preventing family division along such lines as these. If everyone had succeeded, the number of households in Taiwan would have remained about the same, and the entire increase of population would have gone toward enlarging those that were already there. Although this is not what actually happened, the fact that larger households in Taiwan increased in proportion after 1905 (see Fig. 30) may be a sign that the opportunities for staving off the division of families were improving.

Changes in the size distribution of households are probably an accurate indicator of the rise and fall of family fortunes, if not a very illuminating one. For in reality, when one speaks of ordinary households among Taiwanese, it is practically the same thing as speaking of family groups and nothing else. Nearly everyone who lived in a household of more than one member was a blood relative of the head. In these "co-resident" households, excluding for the moment those Taiwanese who lived alone, over 98 per cent of all Taiwanese in 1920 were related to the household head (if the head

---

generation might be added, for they had claims of support that could not be disregarded—one of them might even be the head of the household. But Taiwanese did not live long enough to allow more than three lineal generations to be represented for very long at the same time in the same family.

On the other hand, daughters ordinarily ceased to be included in a family after marriage, since the rule of male descent worked in reverse for them—they were expected to enter the families of their husbands, where in most cases they were found in census enumerations. Though the actual practice in these matters was less uniform than has usually been supposed, it remains true that the expected and preferred arrangement is that outlined here.

TABLE 47

EXTENT OF FAMILY RELATIONSHIP IN TAIWANESE HOUSEHOLDS, 1920

Persons in All (Ordinary) Households, Those Living Alone, Those Living in Households with Others ("Co-Residents"), Co-Residents Who Were Mutually Related, and the Per Cent Who Were Related. By Type of Household

	All Household Residents	*Persons Living Alone*	*Co-Residents (1)–(2)*	*Mutually Related Co-Residents (Including Head of Household)*	*Per Cent of Co-Residents Mutually Related*
All Households					
a. All Types	3,454,956	51,694	3,403,262	3,343,175	98.2
b. Purely family			3,093,000	3,093,000	100.0
c. Mixed			310,262	250,175	80.6
Households with Head Occupied					
a. All types	3,111,558	44,417	3,067,141	3,012,945	98.2
b. Purely family			2,788,813	2,788,813	100.0
c. Mixed			278,328	224,132	80.5
Households with Head Not Occupied					
a. All Types	343,398	7,277	336,121	330,230	98.2
b. Purely family			304,187	304,187	100.0
c. Mixed			31,934	26,043	81.6
Head Occupied in Agriculture*					
a. All Types	2,230,098	14,929	2,215,169	2,189,415	98.8
b. Purely family			2,033,653	2,033,653	100.0
c. Mixed			181,516	155,762	85.8
Head Occupied Outside Agriculture					
a. All Types	881,460	29,488	851,972	823,530	96.7
b. Purely family			755,160	755,160	100.0
c. Mixed			96,812	68,370	70.6
Head Occupied in Manufacturing					
a. All Types	212,380	7,547	204,833	194,852	95.1
b. Purely family			173,210	173,210	100.0
c. Mixed			31,623	21,642	68.4
Head Occupied in Commerce					
a. All Types	242,048	6,991	235,057	223,124	94.9
b. Purely family			192,816	192,816	100.0
c. Mixed			42,241	30,308	71.8
Head Occupied Elsewhere Outside Agriculture					
a. All Types	427,032	14,950	412,082	405,554	98.4
b. Purely family			389,134	389,134	100.0
c. Mixed			22,948	16,420	71.6

* Includes Forestry.

Source: From *Census of 1920, Detailed Tables,* Table 36.

is also counted in the figure). This held true in almost the same degree throughout some of the major portions of the society—whether or not the head had a regular occupation, and on the average regardless of the particular occupation of the head (see Table 47).

Closer inspection reveals that the apparent similarity in membership existed chiefly through a preponderance of households made up exclusively of family members, with no outsiders ("purely family households" in Table 47). Of all "co-residents," over nine-tenths lived together in households of this kind, and the case was the same in all the major occupational groups. Whatever differences arose in each occupational group as a whole, therefore, stemmed from a minority of households containing families together with non-relatives—the "mixed households." It is only within *this* segment that the principal characteristics distinguishing various groups in the population can be found. While four-fifths of all people in even these "mixed" units consisted of family relatives, the proportion was larger in those households dependent on agriculture, and considerably smaller where the head was employed elsewhere (especially in manufacturing and commerce) (see Table 47).

There were different ways of becoming a member of a household, according to the kind of member one was to be, and some of these differences are reflected in the balance between male and female in households of various sizes (see Table 48). Relatives entered a family unit through circumstances well covered by institutional rules or procedures—most commonly by birth or by marriage. Neither of these channels permits much latitude of choice to the parties most directly involved—birth is non-voluntary for those being born, and marriage is usually an alliance arranged by persons other than the partners being married. Hence marked sex disparities should not be expected in households that are formed on the basis of kinship alone. However, these "normal" paths of entry were not the only ones, though the predominance of purely family households very nearly made them so. Men obviously had moved out of many family units, especially the smaller ones, and into mixed households of various sizes—*not* conspicuously into the larger ones. A considerable share of these men must have been single, for departure accompanied by a wife would not have altered the sex balance as between larger and smaller households.

Although very few households contained any outsiders, the larger the unit the less likely it was to consist solely of related persons. It

TABLE 48

FAMILY RELATEDNESS AND SEX COMPOSITION OF HOUSEHOLD RESIDENTS

By Size of Household, 1920

Persons per Household	Total Taiwanese Residents (in Ordinary Households)*	Per Cent in Mixed Households, Each Size	Males per 100 Females†		
			All Households	Purely Family Households	Mixed Households
1	51,694	—	421	—	—
2	110,618	4.2	122	116	407
3	242,469	3.4	100	98	186
4	385,756	3.8	99	97	144
5	465,810	4.6	100	99	132
6	461,430	5.9	103	102	123
7	394,282	7.6	106	104	122
8	298,984	8.4	107	106	123
9	219,402	10.8	107	105	121
10	162,460	13.1	106	104	121
11–15	409,643	16.4	106	103	120
16–20	142,703	22.5	105	102	112
21–25	59,615	26.9	105	104	109
26–30	24,760	33.2	106	105	107
31 and above	25,306	41.6	111	104	121

* This column was computed by multiplication, and its total is 24 persons less than the totals published in other tables.

† These sex ratios were computed from figures for the entire population, Taiwanese and other groups together. Taiwanese, however, preponderate.

Source: *Census of 1920, Detailed Tables*, Tables 33 and 35.

might seem inevitable that households that had added outsiders would be larger than others, but the circumstance is less obvious than at first appears: as we shall see shortly, the households of greater size were not larger by this fact alone, for they also had more family members as well, implying that their familial structure must likewise have been distinctive in some respect. Only in households of more usual size, say of less than eight or nine persons, was the purely family type nearly universal. Yet it should be noted that more than half of all Taiwanese in households of more than 25 persons were also living in units made up exclusively of their family relatives—incorporating outsiders was not essential in order to achieve large size.

Persons Living Alone

For a people who take family matters as seriously as they do, Taiwanese appeared to forego to a remarkable extent the relationships that grow out of residing together in some kind of household group. The proportion who lived alone does not look especially large—1.5 per cent in 1920 and 1.3 per cent in 1930 (though these people formed a much larger figure when counted as households, as in Fig. 30). But this meant that more than 50 thousand Taiwanese in 1920, and 56 thousand in 1930 were out of immediate contact with a family group at the time of the census (see Table 49).

TABLE 49

TAIWANESE PERSONS LIVING ALONE, 1920

("Single-Person Households.") By Occupation

	Persons Living Alone	*Per Cent of Total*	*Per Cent Female*
Total	51,694	100.0	21.5
Occupied	44,417	85.9	13.9
Not Occupied	7,277	14.1	68.1
By Occupation:			
Agriculture	14,929	28.9	15.7
Outside Agriculture	29,488	57.0	13.0
a. Manufacturing	7,547	14.6	23.1
b. Commerce	6,991	13.5	7.7
c. Other	14,950	28.9	10.3

Source: *Census of 1920, Detailed Tables,* Table 36.

It should not be supposed that for this reason they were out of touch with the kinship system. Fourteen per cent were listed as "not occupied" in 1920, most of whom were probably retired parents without sons or living apart from them. The remainder may have included people temporarily absent from home, perhaps even some of the household heads who were not enumerated with their families. By their livelihood they do not appear to have been a very representative group, for most were spread through miscellaneous occupations outside of agriculture, but were rarely found among farmers. Only one-fifth were women, still fewer among those who were self-supporting.

Without more knowledge about these people there is little that can be done except to remark on their numbers, and perhaps to entertain suspicions that many of them were counted apart from familial households due to arbitrary application of census rules, when they actually were more closely affiliated with some group of relatives. Having the information in Table 49, however, we can separate these relatively isolated individuals from those who *were* living in constant association with other household members, and thereby gain a better picture of the patterns that arose from this association. This is the meaning that will be given to "co-resident" households in the subsequent discussion.

The Composition of Co-Resident Households

The average number of persons living together in all "co-resident" households was larger than the figures in Table 46 above.[11] The average size of purely family households was almost the same—"outsiders" were so few that their total number was scarcely noticeable in the figures for households of all types together (see Table 50). But the composition of all households resembled that of purely family households only because nearly all were of the latter type. Mixed households, considered by themselves, were distinguished by more than simply the presence of "outsiders." On the average they also had more members who were family relatives (see the last column in Table 50). Being larger in both categories brought their average total size up to 8.1 persons, as compared with 5.7 in purely family households. Outsiders thus were not incorporated into families of the usual sort, but into families that were already exceptional for their large size. In addition, these non-relatives were actually more of a group to be reckoned with than it first appeared; they were distributed so unevenly that they formed a considerable part of the households where they were found.[12]

The picture of membership for all households was dominated in a similar manner by those households with the head actively employed. Since most fell into this category, the figures for all households in Table 46 or Table 50 are little more than a representation of those whose heads had some occupation. The case was the same

[11] The 1920 census was the only one that allows this distinction to be made. Therefore, when comparisons are to be drawn between 1920 and 1930, these "single-person households" must be restored.

[12] Some "outsiders" formed households that were nothing but business enterprises, usually small handicraft establishments, with no nucleus of family members. Most, however, were incorporated into households already organized as family units.

TABLE 50

COMPOSITION OF TAIWANESE HOUSEHOLDS—TOTAL, HEAD OCCUPIED AND HEAD NOT OCCUPIED, 1920

Average Persons per Household, by Position in Household, Type of Household, and Sex. (Persons Living Alone Are Excluded)*

	Households of All types			*Purely Family Households*			*Mixed Households*		
	Both Sexes	*Males*	*Females*	*Both Sexes*	*Males*	*Females*	*Both Sexes*	*Males*	*Females*
1. All Households									
All Members	5.8	3.0	2.9	5.7	2.9	2.8	8.1	4.5	3.7
Head	1.0	0.9	0.1	1.0	0.9	0.1	1.0	0.9	0.1
Relatives	4.7	2.0	2.7	4.7	2.0	2.7	5.6	2.4	3.2
Others	0.1	0.1	0.0	–	–	–	1.6	1.2	0.4
2. Households with Head Occupied									
All Members	5.9	3.0	2.9	5.8	2.9	2.8	8.1	4.5	3.6
Head	1.0	0.9	0.1	1.0	0.9	0.1	1.0	0.9	0.1
Relatives	4.8	2.0	2.8	4.8	2.0	2.7	5.6	2.4	3.2
Others	0.1	0.1	0.0	–	–	–	1.6	1.2	0.4
3. Households with Head Not Occupied									
All Members	5.3	2.4	2.9	5.1	2.3	2.8	8.1	3.9	4.3
Head	1.0	0.5	0.4	1.0	0.5	0.4	1.0	0.5	0.5
Relatives	4.2	1.8	2.4	4.1	1.8	2.3	5.6	2.4	3.3
Others	0.1	0.1	0.0	–	–	–	1.5	1.0	0.5

* Rounding makes some figures fail to add up to the totals that are shown.
Source: From *Census of 1920, Detailed Tables*, Table 36.

for both the purely family and the mixed units. Where the head was *not* occupied, however, there were certain differences. For one thing, these had more females and fewer males. In purely family households, this shortage of males made the average total size smaller than in those where the head was employed (see Table 51). Mixed households with the head not occupied, which also had higher proportions of females, were as large as they were elsewhere; but here the deficiency of males for some reason was made up by non-family members. For example, almost half of the domestic servants (male and female) found in all Taiwanese households appeared in those whose heads were not occupied—they averaged more than one for every three households.

TABLE 51

COMPOSITION OF TAIWANESE HOUSEHOLDS, BY OCCUPATION OF HEAD, 1920

Average Persons per Household, According to Position in Household, Taiwanese Households Only. Persons Living Alone Are Excluded. Total, Both Sexes*

	Households of All Types	*Purely Family Households*	*Mixed Households*
1. Head Occupied in Agriculture			
All Members	6.3	6.1	9.3
Head	1.0	1.0	1.0
Relatives	5.3	5.1	7.0
Others	0.1	—	1.3
2. Head Occupied Outside Agriculture			
All Members	5.1	4.9	6.6
Head	1.0	1.0	1.0
Relatives	3.9	3.9	3.7
Others	0.2	—	1.9
3. Head Occupied in Manufacturing			
All Members	4.9	4.7	6.5
Head	1.0	1.0	1.0
Relatives	3.7	3.7	3.5
Others	0.2	—	2.1
4. Head Occupied in Commerce			
All Members	5.6	5.3	7.0
Head	1.0	1.0	1.0
Relatives	4.3	4.3	4.0
Others	0.3	—	2.0
5. Head Occupied Elsewhere Outside Agriculture			
All Members	4.9	4.8	6.0
Head	1.0	1.0	1.0
Relatives	3.8	3.8	3.3
Others	0.1	—	1.7

* Rounding makes some figures fail to add up to the totals that are shown.
Source: From *Census of 1920, Detailed Tables,* Table 36.

Just as in many other instances, the greatest contrast among those with head occupied was that between farming and non-farming households. Those directly dependent on agriculture averaged over six persons each, larger than the rest. The greater part of farming households, however, were purely family establishments (cf. Table 47, above), which did not exceed other familial households in size by any large margin. Many of the largest families, therefore, must have been concentrated in that portion of farming households in which outsiders were mixed with family members, which reached an average size of 9.3 persons each. Agriculture thus provided the most favorable setting for realizing the goal of extended and joint families, although one suspects that large farming households may have been partly due to lack of employment opportunities elsewhere.

But though large families and the presence of non-family members tended to go together in Taiwanese agriculture, the opposite was true in most other parts of the society. Mixed households outside of agriculture were actually *smaller* as family groups than their counterparts consisting of family members only. At the same time, mixed households outside agriculture had substantially more outsiders than mixed farming households. While the mixed households in agriculture were large by virtue of the cohesion provided by family ties, they were larger outside of agriculture in spite of it.

Whatever weakening of one's own familial connections was associated with working or living in the household of someone else, it was not equally available to persons of both sexes. The Chinese family system makes little provision for women to live away from the family of either their parents or their husbands, and in Taiwan hardly any of them did so.[13] There were few women anywhere in Taiwan living in households where they were unrelated to the head—less than one per cent of all those counted in 1920 (see Table 52). The fraction that lived in quasi-households was negligible. Though men were also limited in their opportunities for individual achievement unencumbered by family obligations, such restrictions were nearly unavoidable in the case of women. Even in those households shown in Table 50 and in Table 51 that did contain some outsiders —i.e., the mixed households—less than one-fifth of the women were

[13] Many of these women must have been merely the wives of men who were staying in the households of others. Most of the non-related women in mixed households were in the ambiguous category of "lodgers," which leaves us without any clear indication of the circumstances of their position.

TABLE 52

"OUTSIDERS" IN TAIWANESE HOUSEHOLDS, 1920

Per Cent of All Members Who Were Not Relatives of the Head, by Sex, and by Occupation of Head.
(Heads of Households Are Included, Persons Living Alone Excluded)

	Males	*Females*
A. Households of All Types		
All Households	2.6	0.9
Households with Head Occupied	2.7	0.8
Households with Head Not Occupied	2.5	1.1
Head Occupied in Agriculture	1.8	0.5
Head Occupied Outside Agriculture	4.8	1.7
Manufacturing	7.4	2.2
Commerce	7.3	2.7
Other	2.1	1.1
B. Mixed Households		
All Households	26.8	10.3
Households with Head Occupied	27.0	10.0
Households with Head Not Occupied	25.2	12.3
Head Occupied in Agriculture	21.0	6.2
Head Occupied Outside Agriculture	37.1	18.1
Manufacturing	40.5	17.4
Commerce	36.0	17.3
Other	34.2	20.4

Source: From *Census of 1920, Detailed Tables*, Table 36.

not family members, whereas outsiders usually were at least twice as frequent among the men.

Participation by Women in Household Roles

The Chinese are notable in not allotting to women a status of any particular prominence or responsibility in the society at large. As a result, their participation in non-familial activities is very restricted, and the evidence of previous chapters has not often shown them to be engaged in affairs outside of their family groups. Since they are not found anywhere else, it is of some interest to discover what is possible about the position of women in the household.

Significantly, in the households of various types shown here, women were distributed almost everywhere in about the same pro-

TABLE 53

PROPORTIONS OF FEMALES IN TAIWANESE HOUSEHOLDS, 1920

By Type of Household and Occupation of Head

	Households of All Types	*Purely Family Households*	*Mixed Households*
A. Per Cent Female:			
Family Members*			
All Households	49.6	49.6	50.1
Households with Head Occupied	49.0	49.0	49.3
Households with Head Not Occupied	54.7	54.6	56.4
Head Occupied in Agriculture†	49.0	48.9	50.2
Head Occupied Outside Agriculture	49.1	49.3	47.3
a. Manufacturing	50.0	50.4	46.9
b. Commerce	49.4	49.6	47.9
c. Other	48.5	48.6	46.6
B. Per Cent Female:			
Head of Household			
All Households	11.2	11.3	10.6
Households with Head Occupied	7.1	7.2	6.5
Households with Head Not Occupied	45.1	45.1	45.7
Head Occupied in Agriculture†	7.4	7.3	7.3
Head Occupied Outside Agriculture	6.4	6.5	5.5
a. Manufacturing	12.8	13.5	7.5
b. Commerce	3.8	3.7	4.3
c. Other	4.6	4.6	4.8

* The head of the household is included as a family member.
† Includes Forestry.
Source: From *Census of 1920, Detailed Tables,* Table 36.

portion to men (see Table 53). Slightly less than half of the membership of most households was female, and it made almost no difference what was the family's source of support.[14] Despite the association between sex composition and household size found in Table 48, the degree of subordination of women apparently did not vary as between any of the principal lines of employment—women did not gain their positions in Taiwanese households through independent achievement, but chiefly through their attachment to men.

[14] The proportions of *all* household residents who were women is not shown in Table 55. Since women were nearly all members of the family, their percentages among *family* members is practically the same thing, except in mixed households.

This uniformity was due in large measure to the fact that almost all women were members of their households by virtue of kinship, and hardly any of them stayed as non-relatives in the families of others. True, slightly over 20 per cent of all persons who were counted as outsiders were women; but this still did not amount to a large *number*, and it has already been pointed out that many must have been wives or children of men in this status.

Though on the average they were found in nearly equal numbers with men, there is no chance that women occupied the same positions in their families. Chinese ideas of propriety in behavior are never more consistent than in creating a distinction in familial roles based on a person's sex. The patriarchal ideal of authority in Taiwanese families is illustrated by the infrequency with which women became heads of households. Among those of the household heads who were employed (that is, practically all of them), men exceeded women by nine to one; in all but seven per cent of these households it was reported that the affairs were managed by men. In the minority of families where the head was not employed, this responsibility fell almost as often on women as on men—45 per cent of these households were managed by women. The only way for most women to accede to this position was through the death of their husbands. Therefore the concentration of female heads of households among the households with no apparent source of family support most likely represents those widows who were not taken in by their husbands' relatives.

Family Membership and Employment

Questions of livelihood, which are important to all peoples, are treated with a particular seriousness by Chinese. They are usually regarded as questions of household management, and thereby become closely interlocked with the ideas and values of the family system itself. When this happens, a large part of a society's economic life is likely to be sealed up in self-sufficient family units, and to lack the aspect of inter-dependence that characterizes the activities of individuals in the industrial regions of the world.

The households of Taiwan were the scene of most of the effort that went into providing support for the population, and hence are the most appropriate place to look for traces of its organization. A good indication of the contribution to household support in different classes of households is given by the extent of regular work by male residents. The work of women may have been equally important; but the indices for assessing it have the same shortcomings in making such comparisons that they had in measurement of the labor force—female labor was almost entirely contained within household units, and the census statistics do not represent it accurately at all, but only the willingness to acknowledge and report it as such.

Work by men was looked upon more readily as maintaining the household in relation to the external society, despite a similar tendency for it to be in actuality an internal matter. Male family members seemed to have regular employment in almost the same proportion regardless of the occupation of the head of the household. Slightly over 60 per cent of them reported some occupation in 1920 if the head is counted. This, of course, is only what is implied by the findings in earlier chapters, for the figure is close to that fraction of the entire male population in working ages. Although the average size of family varied among different groups, the share of family members' services taken by full-time work did not. The one exception to this rule large enough to appear in Table 54 occurred in families engaged in commerce, which for some reason held more non-employed men than families in any other non-agricultural type of work.[15] But if leisure was supported to any appreciable extent in Taiwanese families, there is little sign that it was concentrated in any particular field of livelihood.

It will make the comparison more complete if we also adopt an alternative view of dependency. Since in households with head occupied the head by definition cannot be a dependent, it is only fair to compare family members in commercial and other households after the family heads are excluded. The remaining males are the ones whose conduct is subordinate to the authority of the head, and who represent the part of the population most likely to have leisure status where a family's wealth will permit. It would appear that farming families, which had more of these subordinate members to support, put their services to much greater use. Only 35.5 per cent of subordinate males in commercial households reported employment in 1920 (35.9 per cent in purely family households). Other families tended to be distributed in between (see the columns "Excluding Head" in Section B, Table 54).

[15] Whatever the explanation for this peculiarity, it stemmed from an unusually *large* number of non-occupied men rather than abnormally *few* who had an occupation, since commercial families were uncommonly large in every respect as compared with other non-agricultural households.

Families with unoccupied heads, which in several respects formed a class by themselves, were not so distinct when it came to employing their subordinate male family members. When the head is included in the computation, the fact that he (or she) was not occupied gives an appearance of dependency far greater than that found anywhere else in the population. Excluding the head (in Table 54) reveals that more of the remaining family members were employed than in any other field of livelihood except agriculture. Unfortunately there is no way of knowing what sorts of work they did; if

TABLE 54

EMPLOYMENT AND DEPENDENCY IN TAIWANESE HOUSEHOLDS, 1920

Male Family Members Who Reported a Regular Occupation, and Those Who Reported None, by Type of Household

A. *Average Male Family Members Per Household, Occupied and Dependent*†	*Households of All Types*	*Purely Family Households*	*Mixed Households*
All Households			
a. Occupied	1.74*	1.74*	1.84*
b. Dependent	1.15	1.13	1.43
Households with Head Occupied			
a. Occupied	1.85	1.84	1.96
b. Dependent	1.11	1.09	1.36
Households with Head Not Occupied			
a. Occupied	0.86	0.86	0.85
b. Dependent	1.49	1.46	2.04
Head Occupied in Agriculture‡			
a. Occupied	2.01	1.99	2.32
b. Dependent	1.18	1.15	1.66
Head Occupied Outside Agriculture			
a. Occupied	1.52	1.53	1.48
b. Dependent	0.97	0.97	0.97
Head Occupied in Manufacturing			
a. Occupied	1.46	1.45	1.47
b. Dependent	0.89	0.89	0.90
Head Occupied in Commerce			
a. Occupied	1.56	1.57	1.49
b. Dependent	1.11	1.11	1.13
Head Occupied in Other Non-Agricultural Occupation			
a. Occupied	1.54	1.54	1.47
b. Dependent	0.93	0.94	0.81

TABLE 54 (continued)

B. Per Cent of Male Family Members Occupied	*Households of All Types* Including Head	*Households of All Types* Excluding Head	*Purely Family Households* Including Head	*Purely Family Households* Excluding Head	*Mixed Households* Including Head	*Mixed Households* Excluding Head
All Households	60.2	45.8	60.6	46.1	56.3	42.4
Households with Head Occupied	62.5	45.6	62.8	45.8	59.0	43.1
Households with Head Not Occupied	36.6	47.7	37.2	48.7	29.5	36.2
Head Occupied in Agriculture	63.0	48.0	63.4	48.2	58.3	45.7
Head Occupied Outside Agr.	61.2	38.4	61.3	38.6	60.4	36.4
Manufacturing	62.0	40.0	62.0	40.2	61.9	38.4
Commerce	58.4	35.5	58.7	35.9	57.0	33.0
Other	62.3	39.3	62.2	39.3	64.5	40.3

* Household heads with no occupation are of course not included. All figures of average persons per household have been rounded, and sometimes will not add to the totals that are shown in other tables; they also will not always produce the exact percentages shown in the lower section of this table.

† "Dependent" refers to persons reporting no occupation in the census.

‡ "Agriculture" includes Forestry.

Source: From *Census of 1920, Detailed Tables*, Table 36.

many of the unoccupied heads were widows who had not re-married, it may be surmised that these households probably had representatives in most occupational groups.

But the most pervasive distinction in engaging in work or leisure within families appeared in those that incorporated outsiders to assist in the work of the household—the mixed households—which made less use of labor by family members than households consisting of family members only. In all but one of the occupational classes of Table 54, employment was less common among members of the families living in mixed households, whether the heads are counted or not. Households with heads not occupied were no exception. Even their subordinate male family members were put to work less often—when not dependent solely on their own resources of manpower, such families supported the greatest amount of leisure that can be found in any of these groups.

Differences of Occupational Status

The variation that these data show in the composition of family groups was recorded at a date before any strong force of Japanese government policy could have been felt in this sphere, and so it must have been a pattern of long standing among the Taiwanese. Though there is no way of knowing how much the variation amounted to between individual families, between various sources of livelihood it was of a very restricted nature. One of the principal features of the Chinese social order, however, is that there has been very little variation in the general notions that people in different stations hold about what forms of conduct are *desirable*—the standards of behavior within one's family, or with members of related families, have been remarkably similar from group to group, whether or not these ideals are completely fulfilled in fact. It has also been characteristic of this system through many historic periods that it has not given rise to rigid status and class distinctions that became hereditary and remained fixed over time. The commonest sources of prestige have been associated with symbols that leave some room for personal achievements, and not simply privileged birth, in their attainment—the adoption of genteel as apart from vulgar pursuits, a highly esteemed and arduous classical education, and observance of traditional forms of ritual that are inappropriate to commonplace affairs. Wealth, in almost any form of livelihood, has conferred a capacity (e.g., through leisure) to practice these ideals, in many ways that poverty denied to the greatest part of the society.

Status distinctions of this sort are lines that cut across most if not all of the occupational divisions recognized in Japanese census practice, though they obviously were present in some more than others (commerce or government service, for example, more than agriculture or fishing). There are further resources, however, to use in finding out the extent of variation within occupations. In the one master table published with the census of 1920, households were also classified by three additional categories of "occupational status"—"Owners" or "Independent Workers," "Officials," and "Laborers."[16] Each household, if the head was occupied, was assigned to one of these groups as well as to a regular occupation, so as to specify more fully the nature of the head's position. The classification is limited in value, for it is not certain that the terms signify anything that is

[16] The English terms are only approximations of the meaning in Japanese. The sense of "Independents" (*Yeh-chu* in the Chinese reading of the term) really is closer to the notion of "master" of an enterprise, somewhat like the term "self-employed" in Western census practice. "Officials" (*Yi-yüan* in Chinese, where it means a lowly and subordinate position) has an honorific connotation in Japanese. "Laborer" (read *Lao-wu* in Chinese) is relatively unambiguous, though it is not clear what line divides it from the others.

consistent from one occupation to another. In agriculture, a person *apparently was "independent" if he actually operated* a farm (without distinction between landlords and others), and "laborer" if simply working for another. Agricultural occupations had hardly any positions that could be designated as "officials"; practically all of these were found as government officials or professionals of some kind. These terms are so vague that it is useless to be distressed over what they do not reveal. The service they *do* perform is to separate, within each broad occupational class, the more from the less successful families ("independent" as opposed to "laborers," based on the fortunes of the household head), and to distinguish a few of the cases that do not easily fall in either of these (the "officials," wherever they occurred).

The households of "laborers," in each of the main classes of occupations, were on the average smaller than those in the same occupations that were more prosperous, and smaller even than those of "officials" (see Table 55). The more prosperous ("independent") households were consistently larger than either of the others, whether they were composed solely of family members or included outsiders.[17] Mixed households of "independent" heads were the largest of all, and had smaller proportions of outsiders than mixed households of the two other "status" groups. In other words, the wealthier mixed households exceeded the lesser ones in the same manner that had marked the difference between mixed households and those composed of family relatives only—chiefly through the extension of their families rather than the incorporation of outsiders. Not merely in the families of farmers, but within any occupational category, the households of the well-to-do were larger than those of the poorer portions of the population, and in this same pattern.

Households whose heads were "independently" employed had the smallest proportions of their male family members engaged in full-time work. But while leisure, as measured by this standard, was especially common in "independent" households whether outsiders were present or not, it was greater in mixed households of this group

17 Here, as before, persons living alone ("single-person households") have been excluded, and Table 55 represents co-resident households only. Therefore the actual number of persons per household is less important (e.g., for comparison with later dates in Taiwan or with other data), than the pattern of variation from group to group in Table 55. It happens in this case that most of the single-person households were of the "laborer" group, and so would make the contrast between the two more pronounced if included, by giving the "laborers" a still smaller figure for average household size.

TABLE 55

AVERAGE SIZE OF HOUSEHOLD AND EXTENT OF MALE EMPLOYMENT IN FAMILIES CLASSIFIED BY "OCCUPATIONAL STATUS," 1920

By Occupation of Head and Type of Household

	Number of Households	*House-holds of All Types*	*Purely Family House-holds*	*Mixed House-holds*
A. Average Persons per Household, both Sexes, by Occupation of Head.				
All Occupations				
a. Independents*	388,635	6.4	6.2	8.7
b. Laborers	128,768	4.4	4.4	5.4
c. Officials	1,462	4.9	4.6	5.8
Agriculture				
a. Independents	309,158	6.6	6.4	9.5
b. Laborers	41,314	4.2	4.2	5.5
Outside Agriculture				
a. Independents	79,477	5.7	5.5	7.1
b. Laborers	87,454	4.5	4.5	5.3
B. Per Cent of Male Family Members Who Reported an Occupation				
All Occupations				
a. Independents		62.0	62.3	57.9
b. Laborers		65.1	65.0	69.2
c. Officials		54.0	52.5	60.9
Agriculture				
a. Independents		62.6	63.0	58.1
b. Laborers		67.6	67.6	65.2
Outside Agriculture				
a. Independents		58.8	59.0	57.3
b. Laborers		64.0	63.7	70.0

* For an explanation of the meaning of these terms, see text.
Source: From *Census of 1920, Detailed Tables*, Table 36.

than anywhere else (see Table 55, Section B). Apparently these more prosperous households also took in outsiders for different purposes. Though not shown in Table 55, the non-relatives in "laborers' " households were chiefly "lodgers" (whatever might be included under this term); the ones in "independent" households were mostly listed as employees, who allowed family members to be released from regular work.

Changes Between 1920 and 1930

The decade between 1920 and 1930 produced little change in household or family structure as far as size or other observable features were concerned (see Table 46, above). Families on the average became slightly larger than before, but chiefly by additions to their dependent children and possibly older relatives. When the data for 1920 are put back into terms appropriate for comparison with 1930 (that is, by replacing the single-person households in the computation of averages), it appears that the growth of households was distributed almost uniformly in different portions of the population—it is necessary merely to add the figure of about 4/10 to the average size of households in each major occupational group in 1920 to approximate the size found in that group in 1930. The tables showing household composition were much abridged in 1930, and permit only restricted comparison. In many of the features already used to describe their structure in 1920, however, households in 1930 were practically the same. They were made up almost entirely of family relatives; and presumably the contrasts between mixed and purely family households were unaltered. The same uniformity in sex composition prevailed among the various classes of occupations, with the same exception in the case of households with non-occupied heads. Since these data contribute nothing to the discussion, they have not been reproduced here.

There is more to be gained by comparing economic activities of family members. The burden of dependency was on the average slightly increased between 1920 and 1930, as we have seen (Table 46, above). By 1930, households representing all the main sources of support (i.e., occupations of heads) had smaller proportions of male family members occupied than 10 years before.[18]

Agricultural households seemed to share less in this rise of family dependency than others (see Table 56). In part the divergence may be because peasant agriculture is better able to provide a secure livelihood for many who could not find steady employment elsewhere—especially young boys and older men. We have found, in

[18] How the added burden was shared between households of only family and mixed households cannot be ascertained, though the similarity of other patterns leads one to presume that this one remained nearly the same as in 1920. This was one of the items of detail omitted in publication of the 1930 census.

TABLE 56

CHANGES IN THE EXTENT OF MALE EMPLOYMENT IN TAIWANESE FAMILIES 1920 TO 1930

(Persons Living Alone Are Included)

	Per Cent of Male Family Members Occupied, Including Head	
	1920	*1930*
All Households	61.0	56.9
Households with Head Occupied	63.4	59.6
Households with Head Not Occupied	36.6	36.6
Head Occupied in Agriculture*	63.4	60.0
Head Occupied Outside Agriculture*	63.4	58.5

* The remaining occupational groups are not shown for comparison here, because the tables published in 1930 followed a different scheme of classification for households—according to the "*industry*" of the heads. The category "Agriculture" has been made comparable in 1930 by taking those engaged in "Cultivation" only. (A special table published in 1930 shows that almost everyone in this category was also classified as having an agricultural "occupation"; workers in "Forestry," of course, are not included.) The group with head "Not Occupied" is the same in both occupational and industrial classifications.

Source: From *Census of 1930, Statistical Tables, Total Island,* Table 5. Data for 1920 from preceding tables.

Chapter IV, that agriculture in Taiwan exerted its greatest attraction compared with other occupations for men of these ages. Thus men of these borderline ages probably were reported as employed in agriculture, and as dependents elsewhere, and some of this divergence may be simply a difference of standards rather than of work that was performed. But farming families had more use for the services of these people (and of those with physical disabilities); it is possible that the greater readiness to recognize these services—of women as well as of men—reflects their actual importance in contributing to the support of their households.

This apparent trend toward creating a gap between agriculture and other parts of the society was not a very impressive one. It is worthy of attention chiefly because it stands alone; there are no other new patterns of dependency to be found between 1920 and 1930, since the other occupational categories cannot be matched at both dates. And, more important, insofar as there was a leisured group or class among Taiwanese, it was still not to any marked extent occupationally aligned.

Work Within the Household

People's working activities play a part in familial life that is larger than merely the support that they provide. Since they are ordinarily not carried on in isolation, these activities supply one of the connections between the family and the remainder of the society. In industrial countries they sometimes appear to dominate this connection, and have become one of the criteria that fix a person's station in society. In agrarian countries it tends to be the other way around; the working roles of most adults are carried on as adjuncts to their other familial roles, and depend on kinship obligations for coordination. This, for example, is almost completely the case in household enterprises, and holds true in varying degrees for such wider market transactions that exist.

In Taiwan, the productive effort of most people was in fact confined to work pursued in cooperation with other family members and organized as household duties. This has already been demonstrated in a negative way as far as women were concerned—the occupational statistics, in failing to show very much about the work of women, do confirm that they were scarcely ever employed outside of their households. In household enterprises—and practically all farming was conducted on this basis—the head of the household was almost automatically the chief participant. However, since the statistics give no positive answer in the case of women or household heads, it is in the activities of subordinate male family members who were employed that we have the best indication of the concentration of work within households, and of its variation in different sections of the society.

Except for the minority counted as "employees," these remaining men were the ones with most opportunity to find work unrestricted (or unaided) by their kinship affiliations—i.e., in something that might approach a "labor market." Yet as late as 1930, over two-thirds of the Taiwanese men in this group still pursued their occupations in the households of their own families (see Table 57). In reality their labor was even more family-centered than this. In the large majority of households the head had some occupation, and there 76.1 per cent of all occupied male family members worked in the same enterprise. The remaining household heads had no occupation themselves, and hence did not operate family enterprises that could claim the services of men in their families. Most of the men in these fam-

TABLE 57

CONCENTRATION OF EMPLOYMENT WITHIN HOUSEHOLDS, 1930

Per Cent of "Subordinate" Male Family Members (i.e., Excluding the Household Head) Who Were Employed Within Their Households

(Taiwanese Households Only, Including Persons Living Alone)

	Per Cent of Employed "Subordinate" Male Family Members Whose Employment Was Inside Their Household
All Households	68.2
Households with Head Occupied	76.1
Households with Head Not Occupied	21.6
Head Occupied in Agriculture*	87.3
Head Occupied Outside Agriculture	34.2
Manufacturing	33.1
Commerce	42.2
Other	26.3

* See note to preceding table.
Source: From *Census of 1930, Statistical Tables, Total Island*, Table 5.

ilies who were occupied found employment outside—only 21.6 per cent of them carried on their work in the family.[19]

Among those households with heads occupied, there were differences just as great between the fields of livelihood that provided support for the households. Farming families kept 87.3 per cent of their subordinate working males occupied at home. It was their numerical weight in the population that made the figure for all occupations so high—in non-agricultural households it was only one-third (see Table 57). The influence of the more modern parts of the economy is indicated by the fact that families engaged in these fields had the greatest proportion of working-out among their eligible men.[20] Of the non-agricultural categories of occupation shown in Table 57, the commercial households came the closest to conforming to the norm exemplified in agriculture.

[19] Literally, the data of Table 57 refer to those working in the "same occupation or same enterprise" as the head of the household. The meaning is not so broad as the literal translation might suggest, because "same occupation" did not mean merely "also in agriculture" or "also in commerce" or some other large category. It means the same type of work in considerable detail—"also a butcher" or "also a bean-curd maker," for example. In nearly every case it probably meant work in the same family enterprise.

[20] Of course, many who worked out may have gone to work for relatives, and still did not enter the labor market.

Of interest for the sake of comparison are the corresponding data illustrating the variation between different parts of the island (Table 58). In most of the individual Prefectures there were only minor differences in the extent to which employed men in all families (excluding the heads) performed their work at home. The most populous sections seemed uniform in the proportion that were so engaged; the deviations in the two Prefectures on the East Coast (where hardly anyone worked outside of his household), and in P'enghu Islands, did not affect many people. Taipei Prefecture was the significant exception to the rule, for it was the only place with considerable numbers of male workers occupied in extra-familial pursuits.

TABLE 58

CONCENTRATION OF EMPLOYMENT WITHIN HOUSEHOLDS: VARIATION BETWEEN PREFECTURES OF TAIWAN, 1930

Per Cent of Employed "Subordinate" Male Family Members Whose Employment Was Inside Their Households

Name of Prefecture	*All Households*	*Households With Head Occupied*	*Head Occupied in Agriculture**	*Head Occupied Outside Agriculture*	*Head Reporting No Occupation*
Taipei	50.4	59.6	81.8	21.4	10.5
Hsinchu	72.3	79.5	88.5	34.3	19.7
Taichung	71.0	79.1	88.3	36.5	25.6
Tainan	71.6	79.5	88.6	41.6	25.7
Kaohsiung	72.2	78.4	85.7	45.9	26.5
Taitung	95.1	95.8	97.6	52.0	69.9
Hualien	82.5	85.0	91.8	30.5	34.1
P'enghu	64.5	64.5	75.1	54.8	30.7
Total Island	68.2	76.1	87.3	34.2	21.6

* See footnote for Table 56.

Source: From *Census of 1930, Statistical Tables,* by Prefecture (respective Prefectural volumes), Table 5.

The more detailed columns of Table 58 help to clarify the source of the variation. As the site of the capital city and administrative center of the island, and the portion in which Japanese concentrated their efforts in developing modern conveniences and comforts, Taipei had even before 1930 gained many features of distinction over the rest of the island. It was at this time the transportation hub (built around shipping from the port of Chilung, which later declined), the home of one-third of all Japanese, the location of the better educational facilities, the commercial area of most importance for trade in other than farm products, and of course the center of most large government and business offices. Taipei Prefecture, therefore, had proceeded farthest in the spread of non-agricultural activities in its population. Even though a substantial group in this population does not appear in these tables because they were Japanese, the effect of their presence is evident in the way that non-farming occupations were conducted by Taiwanese—all but 21 per cent of the men in such work (excepting the heads of households and people staying in the households of others) were employed away from their families, a proportion less than any other Prefecture and only half the figure in some. Agriculture was much less affected by the unusual character of other pursuits, but it did not go untouched. Though most farmers in Taipei did their work in their own households, they fell somewhat below the mark set by the rest of the agricultural population.[21]

Significantly, in all of the other Prefectures (except P'enghu, which was not of much account in size), agricultural households were nearly uniform in the degree to which they retained the use of services by subordinate men in their families—close to 90 per cent of the men in this category who lived with their families.[22] The principal differences from one Prefecture to another when all households are considered at once, therefore, must have arisen from the prevalence and the mode of organization in activities *outside* of agriculture, for they practically disappear when farming households alone are compared.

There can be little doubt that the family system, through its weight in the conduct of household affairs, has furnished the most important social setting for behavior of the Taiwanese. We have not only the testimony of Chinese tradition to support this conclusion, but the corroboration of statistical evidence as well. Practically everyone was a member of some familial household—most were related by

[21] Taipei was the site of tea plantations, which, through a greater use of wage labor, may have been responsible for the deviation from the pattern elsewhere in the island. A plantation might employ men (and actually did employ many women) on a more or less regular basis from several farming households, and leave their services free at some seasons of the year for work in their own fields.

[22] Naturally this does not include those who had left home to enter some other occupation; these would appear as outsiders in some other households or as persons living alone, perhaps in some cases as separate families.

kinship, and those who were not, the "outsiders," generally owed their membership to the work that they performed in the families of others. In addition, many strong obligations were observed among people who were related but not living together in the same household. So in reality the significance of the family system was wider than can be adequately conveyed by the facts of this chapter; it extended beyond the bounds of kinship, in its application to nonrelated household residents, and beyond the limits of individual households, in governing the intercourse between related families.

As for those Taiwanese who lived in their own familial households, the best-documented of all their activities is the work that they performed. The extent of male employment in these family groups showed no large differences as between the major classes of occupations. But leisure, as judged by the abstention from regular work, was apparently more widespread in families of greater affluence, regardless of their particular source of support. And their households were also the ones that made the most use of services of non-family members, which was one of the ways of making leisure possible.

It is significant that the work of most men was carried on in household enterprises inside their own families. In a sense this was a fulfillment of traditional exhortations that families should be self-sufficient, but a great deal more was involved at the same time. A society which is family-centered in most respects cannot afford to make very far-reaching exceptions in the case of economic activities: since employment, if it occurs outside of the household, is a possible avenue for a person to advance in social position independently of family influence, it also is potentially a competing source of loyalty. In this and various other ways, the stability of the social order was buttressed by the force of its own organization as well as through the support of its moral precepts, by making it difficult for people to by-pass the family system in pursuit of their self-interest.

Though the span of observation is short and confined to a relatively early period in Taiwan, the facts betray no remarkable sign of yielding in this household structure. And changes that did not alter this fundamental pattern could not amount to very much. The failure of "colonial development" to be a clearcut departure from the past among Taiwanese should be attributed very largely to the stability of their familial institutions.

CHAPTER VIII

Patterns of Marriage and Divorce

UP TO THIS POINT, it has been possible to describe the manifestations of the Chinese family system in Taiwan only through an abbreviated view of the families existing at a particular moment—the view which is afforded by enumeration of households in the census. This approach suffers from several shortcomings. The delineation of what should comprise a family, inherently arbitrary, was one that took account of only those family members who resided together, and thus understated the influence of kinship in the society. Also, the data give but a sketchy indication of family members' characteristics from which we might deduce more satisfactorily their familial roles (items like age, marital status, and their degrees of relationship to each other). In short, our knowledge of what occurs in Taiwanese families is not so well documented as the behavior of their members outside of the family units, and comes largely by inference from this second kind of information.

Part of this gap may be filled in two ways from other sorts of data. The conclusions about family composition will be supplemented in this chapter by a discussion of *marriage*, on which depended the formation of new family units and the continuation of old ones. The next chapter will be devoted to measuring the fertility of Taiwanese, through which their families replenished the population with new members.

Like people in other countries, most Taiwanese marry sooner or later. The differences between Taiwan and many Western countries are superficially those of degree—for most Taiwanese men and women marriage comes early and is nearly universal. It ranks as one of the most significant events that can happen in a family, and is attended by attitudes and customs that reflect the importance ascribed to it. The wedding itself is ordinarily solemnized by the most elaborate and festive ceremony that a family can afford.[1] The idea of marriage is so endowed with importance and virtuous purpose that for a person to remain celibate is usually a mark of unexampled mis-

[1] There are many descriptions of the conduct of Chinese on these occasions and the ways in which this fits in with other familial life. Cf. Lang, O. (1946), and Levy, M. J., Jr. (1949).

fortune. In contrast to the West, Chinese culture entertains no alternatives that offer serious competition to the "normal" family roles.

TABLE 59

PROPORTIONS OF TAIWANESE EVER-MARRIED, BY AGE AND SEX, 1905 TO 1935

Males and Females

Age	*1905*	*1915*	*1920*	*1925*	*1930*	*1935*
			Males			
10–14	0.1	0.0	0.2	0.1	0.1	0.1
15–19	10.2	5.7	6.3	5.3	7.3	5.7
20–24	45.7	40.1	42.8	44.7	51.6	49.8
25–29	77.4	72.9	76.5	78.2	82.9	83.1
30–34	89.4	88.1	88.6	89.7	91.3	91.9
35 and over	95.3	95.4	95.5	95.8	96.2	96.0
			Females			
10–14	2.3	0.7	0.6	0.4	0.5	0.4
15–19	47.3	34.7	32.8	29.4	32.6	28.1
20–24	91.6	87.4	86.6	84.4	86.3	83.0
25–29	98.2	96.6	96.9	96.2	96.1	95.9
30–34	99.2	98.5	98.5	98.3	98.0	97.7
35 and over	99.7	99.5	99.4	99.3	99.3	99.0

Source: Tables of the Taiwanese population by age, sex and marital status in the reports of each census. The "Informally Married," who in 1920 were shown as a subtotal of "Unmarried," have been reinstated here as "Married," in conformity with the census procedure at other dates.

There has been no indication from related spheres of activity already discussed that these pressures to marry were anything but constant and unyielding during Japanese rule in Taiwan. The percentages of Taiwanese over age 30 who eventually married remained about the same—all but one or two per cent of women, and all but nine or ten per cent of men. Yet the proportions of Taiwanese who had ever been married did not remain constant at all ages. The younger people of both sexes displayed some signs of altering the time when their marriage took place (see Table 59).

So far as this evidence is germane, however, it offers conflicting testimony: the pressures would appear to have been weakened for women under age 30 and to have grown stronger for men. Faced with this apparent inconsistency, we naturally cannot vouch for the inner motives of people about to marry. Nor can we adopt the usual course in demography and merely say that there was a trend for people in Taiwan to "marry earlier" or "marry later," for this is to say nothing about why men and women apparently were of different minds in the matter. But thanks to the assiduity of the Japanese in maintaining Taiwan's population statistics, the problem is open to closer examination with the help of additional data.

TABLE 60

SEX BALANCE OF TAIWANESE IN MARRIAGEABLE AGES

Males per 100 Females Enumerated in Ages 15–49 in Successive Censuses, 1905 to 1940

Age	*1905*	*1915*	*1920*	*1925*	*1930*	*1935*	*1940*
10–14	122	113	109	107	105	103	104
15–19	126	116	112	109	106	104	100
20–24	123	121	115	112	108	106	102
25–29	122	123	120	114	111	108	104
30–34	119	119	120	118	114	110	107
35–39	116	114	114	118	116	112	109
40–44	112	107	108	110	114	114	110
45–49	100	100	99	101	105	109	108
Total, 15–49	119	115	112	111	109	107	104

Source: Tables of the Taiwanese population by age, sex and marital status in the reports of each census.

It is worth while first to consider the conditions of the marriage market in Taiwan, in terms of the relative supply of men and women available to marry. Since, practically speaking, the Taiwanese were a "closed population," this is one instance where demographic trends in births and deaths may be observed very simply in their bearing on the more complex aspects of behavior. We have already seen that the chances of surviving through infancy and childhood had been extremely poor for girls born before 1895, and that this handicap disappeared only gradually in later years. As a result, by the time they were nearing age 20—the range when most of them married—there were not enough women to furnish wives for the eligible men.

In 1905, for example, there were more than 20 "surplus" males for every 100 females in the age group 15-19, who could not find wives from the same age group, and would have difficulty in finding them from any younger groups of girls which had suffered similar high mortality (see Table 60). Apparently, as girls began to catch up with the boys in the chances of surviving in earlier life, they lost some of this advantage relative to men in marrying; and, as the scarcity of marriageable women became less of a factor conditioning the marriage opportunities for men and women, the result was that the chances of marrying at each age (under, say, 30) improved for men and declined for women.

TABLE 61
EXCESS OF MARRIED WOMEN IN TAIWAN, 1905-1935

	Married Men	*Married Women*	*Difference (2) – (1)*	*Males per 100 Females*
1905				
Taiwanese	594,827	598,556	3,729	99.4
Japanese	12,302	8,246	–4,056	149.2
Other	3,487	220	–3,267	1,585.0
Total	610,616	607,022	–3,594	100.6
1920				
Taiwanese	641,746	648,764	7,018	98.9
Japanese	37,377	32,946	–4,431	113.4
Other	7,427	2,270	–5,157	327.2
Total	686,550	683,980	–2,570	100.4
1935				
Taiwanese	913,655	924,963	11,308	98.8
Japanese	56,562	52,663	–3,899	107.4
Other	15,342	8,132	–7,210	188.7
Total	985,559	985,758	199	100.0

Sources: *Census of 1905, Detailed Tables*, Table 5; *Census of 1920, Descriptive Report with Appendix*, Appendix Table 26; *Census of 1935, Statistical Tables*, Table 7. The category of "Married" as published in 1920 has been reconstituted so as to make it the same as that shown in the other censuses.

All this would be strictly true only if the Taiwanese population had been "closed" against marriage with other groups as completely as it was against migration. There were barriers to intermarriage, but in fact they were less effective. To some extent women enjoyed their felicitous marriage prospects because their nuptial horizons were not entirely restricted to Taiwanese men. Some of them married Mainland Chinese or even Japanese, which helped to enhance their scarcity. These mixed unions probably had a dubious legal status, for many of the male Japanese and Chinese nationals in Taiwan were little more than transients, and some who reported themselves as married may have done so because of a wife at home. It is unknown how many supplemental unions of this sort with Taiwanese women there were. They were not legally registered as marriages where Japanese were involved, for prior to 1932 such marriages were prohibited by law.

The legal status of a union, however, did not make so much difference in the census figures on married persons, since the census was designed to record unregistered as well as "legal" marriages. In this it seems to have been successful, even for those that were not fully legitimized by law, and the census reports are therefore a fairly good source to detect whether or not mixed unions existed.[2] A brief summary of this information is given in Table 61. With monogamous mating and without intermarriage, there should have been equal numbers of Taiwanese married men and married women at any one moment.[3] Actually, every census showed an excess of women over men who were married: a proportion in the neighborhood of one per cent of Taiwanese women were "unmatched" in this sense.

But although some of these had undoubtedly become wives of Japanese or Chinese nationals, from the census materials there is no way of determining how widespread this intermarriage was. In the first place, Taiwanese men of wealth were said to take concubines, after the fashion of old-style Chinese gentry, and thereby may have accounted for some of the extra married women.[4] Also, from the Japanese (and Chinese) side, there is no way of knowing how many of these men were reported as married because of wives in Japan (or China), and how many because of wives among the Taiwanese.

Finally, a small though unknown number of Taiwanese men had found wives from women in the other nationality groups in the island, and these have the effect of cancelling some of the "excess" of married Taiwanese women.

These factors make the situation more complicated than it would

[2] The first census (1905) was an exception. Liaisons with Japanese men and Taiwanese women were explicitly not recognized, though such unions involving Mainland Chinese were. In all other censuses, the "informally married"—i.e., those whose marriages were not legally registered—were always shown separately, though sometimes included as a subtotal of "married" and sometimes as a subtotal of "single."

[3] Some Taiwanese men, by the time of the later censuses, were absent in Japan and elsewhere in the Empire, but they were too few to have any noticeable effect in these tabulations.

[4] By the same token, the sex imbalance of married Taiwanese cannot be said to be a measure of concubinage, because of the unknown amount of intermarriage. Neither of these two questions, both important, can be clarified beyond this indeterminate state of information.

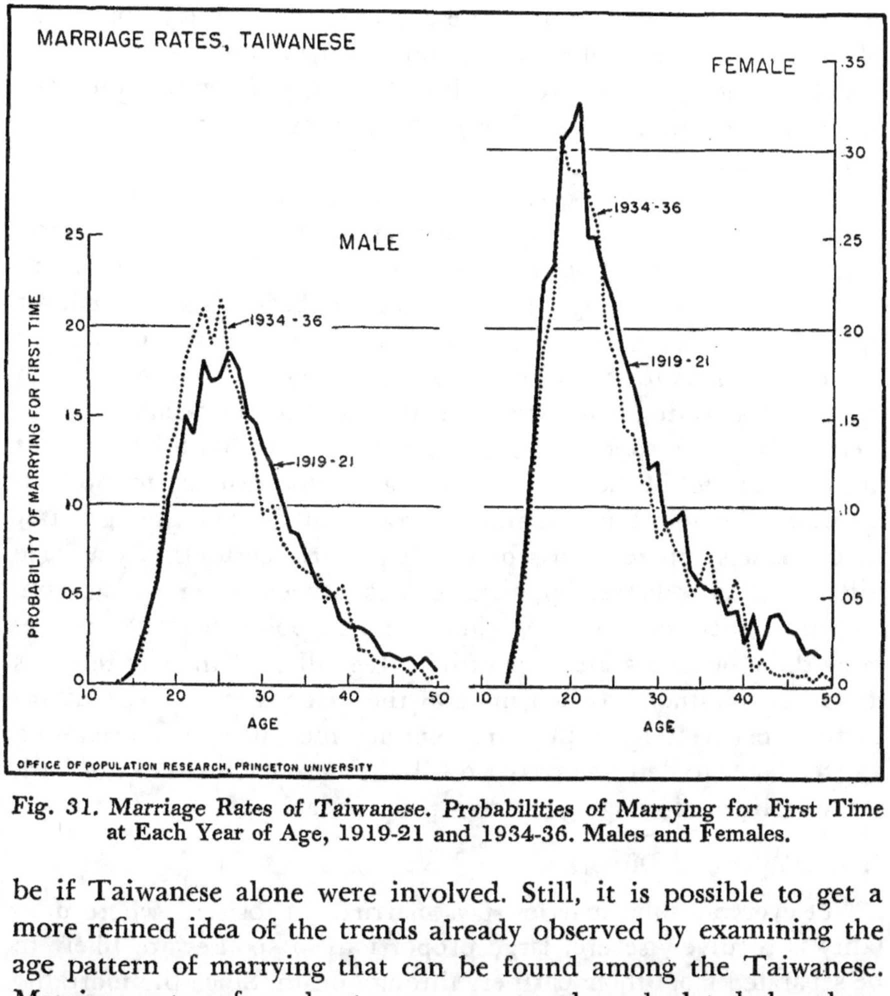

Fig. 31. Marriage Rates of Taiwanese. Probabilities of Marrying for First Time at Each Year of Age, 1919-21 and 1934-36. Males and Females.

be if Taiwanese alone were involved. Still, it is possible to get a more refined idea of the trends already observed by examining the age pattern of marrying that can be found among the Taiwanese. Marriage rates of moderate accuracy can be calculated, based on registered marriages with adjustments for those which were not registered.[5] But because the data on marital status were not published

[5] Marriage rates in this sense have been computed in the form of a "gross nuptiality table." In this form they are often termed "probabilities of marrying," which must first be computed as "probabilities of remaining single." They are exactly analogous to the "probabilities of dying" in a life table, in that they represent the proportion of persons entering each year of age who would have married during that age if none had died, according to the age pattern of the particular calendar year in question.

The rates given by such a table in its raw form are deficient; registered marriages in Taiwan were enough only to produce the number of "legally" married couples that were recorded in each census, but insufficient to have supplied all those whom the census found to be "actually" married (i.e., living together in socially recognized unions). This first set of marriage rates was therefore *adjusted* to bring it more nearly into accord with the facts as shown by the census. The adjustment was arrived at by calculating separately, from the census alone, a nuptiality table for "actually" married and

in full detail at each census, there are just two occasions for which satisfactory marriage rates can be found—1920 and 1935. Marriage rates for these two dates are shown in Fig. 31, representing the marriages of three years averaged around the census year (i.e., 1919-21 and 1934-36).

The data of Fig. 31 pertain only to those being married for the first time, since the first marriage removes a person permanently from the unmarried. They show something less than the full extent of the changes in marriages that have already been demonstrated, for the shifting that appears in Fig. 31 is confined to half of the total period of observation. Already by 1920 women's extremely high chances of marrying before age 25 had begun to subside and those of men to rise. Even so, the persistence of this change is clearly evident in the latter half of the period. Marriage rates continued to move in opposite directions for men and for women after 1920 (though after 1920 it is less apparent for women). Taiwanese customs of marriage still allotted the better opportunities to women when young, concentrating these near age 20, while the high point in men's chances came three or four years later in life. Regardless of their differences in earlier adulthood (when most of the first marriages actually occurred), between 1920 and 1935 neither men nor women showed any tendency to defer marrying until after age 25—the rates of both sexes declined after age 30 and in the later 20's.

Widowhood and Divorce

Not everyone who marries stays married. In societies where mortality is relatively severe, large proportions of spouses are likely to be separated from their partners through death. Since the mortality of Taiwanese was higher for men than for women, wives were more likely to be bereaved than husbands, and there were more widows than widowers. While every census found substantial portions of people of both sexes who had once been married but whose husbands

"legally" married persons; the ratio of the one to the other was used for "correcting" the rates based on registered (legal) marriages. This procedure leaves something to be desired; the most that can be said in its favor is that it converts into useful form data that would otherwise be useless.

The procedures of estimating nuptiality from census data were an adaptation of those discussed in Mortara, G. (1949). These figures might be suitable to use in place of the data that actually appear in the text, but for the fact that they reflect unduly the events of the census year, and thus give a poor indication of trend. The age pattern of unregistered marriages has no significance as such, for there was nothing to prevent unregistered marriages from being subsequently registered.

or wives had died, the proportions at nearly every age were two to three times as great for women as for men (see Table 62).

TABLE 62

WIDOWS AND WIDOWERS IN TAIWAN

Per Cent of Taiwanese Men and Women Who Were Counted as Widows or Widowers in Each Census, 1905 to 1935, by Age

Age	*1905*	*1915*	*1920*	*1925*	*1930*	*1935*
			Males			
20–24	1.0	0.7	0.8	0.5	0.5	0.4
25–29	2.5	2.1	2.4	1.4	1.2	1.1
30–34	4.3	4.1	4.2	2.9	2.3	1.9
35–39	6.8	6.1	6.6	4.9	4.0	3.4
40–44	10.1	8.8	9.2	7.7	6.5	5.7
45–49	14.0	12.1	12.4	10.7	10.1	8.9
50 and over	28.6	26.3	29.3	23.1	22.2	21.3
			Females			
20–24	2.1	1.7	1.9	1.2	1.0	1.0
25–29	4.8	3.7	4.0	2.7	2.3	2.2
30–34	9.4	6.9	7.4	5.3	4.7	4.4
35–39	17.6	13.2	13.2	10.2	9.3	8.2
40–44	30.2	23.7	22.5	18.7	16.5	15.0
45–49	43.4	37.9	35.2	29.9	27.2	24.1
50 and over	72.2	71.2	69.2	65.1	61.6	57.9

Source: Tables of the Taiwanese population by age, sex and marital status in the reports of each census.

By 1935, the proportions of adult women who were widows had gradually fallen at all ages, until they were no more than half as high as they had been in 1905. The decrease in proportions of widowed men was similar, though less pronounced. Most of this decline probably arose from the fact that spouses of both sexes became less likely to die during early adulthood, thanks to improved mortality. Not all, however, can be definitely attributed to an actual decrease in widowhood, for the census recorded as widowed only those who remained in the status of widows.

Just as death of a husband or wife is a way to end a marriage, remarriage is a way out of widowhood. In the case of women it is one that is not highly regarded by Chinese tradition. A wife leaves her original family and enters that of her husband, where her status at first is uncertain and tends to be the target of considerable hostility.[6] But if she bears a child, especially a son, during the husband's lifetime, her membership in his family is made relatively secure, for she becomes the means for continuation of the family line. If the family has enough wealth and enough adult family members to prevail in the matter, it is to be preferred that the wife remain a widow rather than remarry. The attitudes generated by the family system, which manage to induce nearly everyone to marry once, act to some extent as a restraint on the number of years that may be spent in married life. Depending on the circumstances, widowhood therefore may be permanent and have the effect of preventing many women from being mothers of additional children.

But the prohibition against remarrying is often given lax observance. In Taiwan special arrangements were sometimes made to ease the practical difficulties.[7] Many women must have lost their husbands before providing a male heir, and a childless widow might have very little claim to standing in her husband's family. Because the remarriage of widows was not looked upon with favor, they were not likely to enjoy the prospects of so good a match as those of unmarried women. It is commonly known that a cheap wedding can be arranged with widows, and so they probably became wives of poorer men. With the shortage of marriageable women that existed in early Taiwan, the abundance of widows doubtless was a factor in finding wives for many men who otherwise might not have married at all.

Remarriage is not regarded so austerely for widowed men; the same circumstances affect them, but all work in the other direction. A man has compelling reasons to remarry after the death of his wife, and these are even stronger if he has become the head of a household and the father of children. A widower's incentive was equal to that of a widow, and he had fewer obstacles.

Like widowhood, *divorce* also removes some men and women from married life and helps to reduce still further the efficiency of mar-

[6] See Levy, M. J., Jr. (1949), Chapters III and IV.

[7] Since the Chinese conception of marriage and descent is patrilineal, the "normal" course for a widow who remarries would be to enter the family of the second husband. The presence of children born to her as a wife, however, complicates the situation, for they are regarded as descendants in the male line—i.e., members of the first husband's family—and would not ordinarily be relinquished. Among poorer Taiwanese there existed a special form of marriage in situations of this sort, observed also in many parts of China, which provides that the second husband marries *into* the family of the widow's children. Marriage of this kind is deprecated and probably occurs chiefly when a widow is left without able-bodied members of her husband's family.

riage in cementing marital unions. Divorces are different, however, in that most of them occur early, rather than increasing with the length of married life. They leave (at least initially) an equal number of ex-partners of either sex who can remarry if the institutional system permits. They also leave a lesser total residue of persons in a non-married status. The divorced enumerated in the censuses were very small proportions of Taiwanese adults, and showed no trend with the passage of time save reduction to still smaller sizes at the younger ages (see Table 63).

TABLE 63
DIVORCED MEN AND WOMEN IN TAIWAN
Per Cent of Taiwanese Who Were Counted as Divorced from a Previous Marriage, 1905 to 1935, by Age

Age	*1905*	*1915*	*1920*	*1925*	*1930*	*1935*
			Males			
15–19	0.3	0.1	0.1	0.1	0.1	0.0
20–24	1.2	0.8	0.8	0.7	0.7	0.6
25–29	1.9	1.8	1.8	1.6	1.4	1.3
30–34	2.1	2.3	2.3	2.0	1.8	1.6
35–39	1.8	2.1	2.4	2.2	1.9	1.7
40 and over	1.3	1.5	1.8	1.8	1.8	1.8
			Females			
15–19	0.7	0.4	0.4	0.3	0.3	0.2
20–24	1.2	0.9	1.2	0.9	0.9	0.7
25–29	0.9	1.0	1.3	1.0	1.0	0.9
30–34	0.8	0.9	1.2	1.0	1.0	1.0
35–39	0.7	0.8	1.1	1.0	1.0	0.9
40 and over	0.4	0.6	0.8	0.8	0.7	0.8

Source: Tables of the Taiwanese population by age, sex and marital status in the reports of each census.

A paucity of divorced people has led observers from time to time to conclude that divorce itself is all but unknown among Chinese. On similar grounds, the abundance of widows is often taken as a rough measurement of how great are the proportions of people who have been widowed. The reasoning behind both types of inference is that the chances of remarriage are poor (especially for women), and therefore the number of observed survivors of divorce and widowhood are a gauge of their frequency.

But neither divorce nor widowhood has been seriously investigated in an agrarian society. Though one must admit that reliable data have been rare, scholars have usually fallen back on stereotypes drawn from the folklore and value statements of the societies themselves. This approach has its pitfalls, especially when these statements are accepted literally without much attention to the social situations in which they have their effect.

Divorce, we are told, happens at the whim of the husband or his family; a wife may be sent back to her original home if her behavior fails to satisfy them on any of several grounds, all very explicitly stated. The divorced woman must return disgraced to her family, nevermore to be sought in marriage. The harshness of this procedure is tempered, mercifully, by prospective loss of the dowry to the husband's family, by recognized conditions that call forth forbearance on their part, and by "local sentiment" which may be offended by the arbitrariness of the whole affair.

In short, the prescriptions of archaic Chinese moral codes leave one with just about as much insight as to what to expect as if he knew nothing of them. In reality not a great deal can be said about the reasons for divorce with the assurance that it is generally accurate. It differs from widowhood in being the outcome of decision rather than death, decision affecting the two families between which the original marriage had been arranged. If a dispute is involved, which is likely, the focal point will probably be the relations of the wife with her husband's family, but only if the marriage was patrilocal. The grounds may be anything rising from these relations, which are known to be difficult. Grievances may exist on either side, though it is easy to see that they originate more readily from that of the husband's family.

Luckily there is a way of checking on the frequency of divorce in Taiwan, as there is not in the case of widowhood. Its legal significance was judged by Japanese to be sufficient to warrant keeping records of divorce as it occurred. Divorces were registered each year, according to the time elapsed since marriage (in single years of duration up to five, and thence in broader intervals). These data have been slightly rearranged, assuming (with some error) that all of those which occurred less than one year after marriage belonged to marriages made in the same calendar year, that those occurring between the first and the second year of the marriages' duration belonged to marriages of the previous year, and so on. It is then possible to calculate approximately the number of marriages of any particular year that ended in divorce within five years[8] (see Table 64).

TABLE 64

MARRIAGES ENDED IN DIVORCE, 1906-1940

Per Cent of Registered Marriages of Each Year That Were Dissolved by Divorce within 5 Years' Duration Taiwanese Only

Year	*A. Assuming That* All *Taiwanese Marriages Could End in Divorce*	*B. Assuming That Divorce Occurred Only to* First *Marriages*
1906	14.4	22.3
1910	9.4	13.8
1915	10.5	14.0
1920	7.9	10.6
1925	7.7	9.4
1930	5.8	6.8
1935	4.7	5.2
1939	3.6	3.9

Source: *Statistical Summary*, Table 77.

It makes some difference whether we include those persons who were marrying for the second (or subsequent) time or whether we assume that only first-married couples were divorced. Since the truth probably lies somewhere between these alternatives, Table 64 has a column of figures for each, based of course on the same number of divorces in both cases. Close to 10 per cent of Taiwanese marriages before 1920, nearly 15 per cent if first marriages alone are considered, were regularly being dissolved within five years. The outcome of marriages in 1906 may suggest that divorce had an even higher

[8] For example, it is assumed that first-year divorces in 1910 belonged to marriages of 1910, and that divorces in the second year of marriages to these people all took place in 1911, in the third year 1912, etc. This procedure makes no allowance for those marriages that might have been broken by death, but it will be seen that this omission merely makes the evidence of trend more conservative, and does not exaggerate it.

In most years, between 60 and 70 per cent of registered divorces happened within the first five years of married life. Table 64 must be confined to this period for each annual crop of marriages, because the published data show only the first five years' divorces by single year of duration. The result is that the "divorce rates" of Table 64 represent only two-thirds to three-quarters of the divorces that eventually occurred. This fraction fell slightly during the period of registration, leading to some exaggeration of the decline in divorce shown in Table 64.

incidence before the registration system was established, but also may have been nothing more than a peculiarity of the early operation of the registration system itself. Whatever its initial level, the divorce rate fell steadily throughout the Japanese occupation. Somewhat under four per cent of marriages registered in 1939 failed to last for five years.

The Prevalence of Remarriage

It is beyond the capacity of these resources to reveal the percentages of any year's marriages that ever ended in divorce. Our disregard of divorces if they occurred more than five years after marriage and the omission of many marriages from registration make it not worth while to strive for more than this approximation. More pressing is the question of what happened to all the people whose marriages suffered this adverse outcome. Even at its lowest stage in Taiwan, divorce was still not uncommon, and produced far more divorced people than the census enumerations were able to detect. Yet experience with these census materials has justified a high respect for their accuracy; there is no reason to doubt that they are the most dependable of all public records in Taiwan. It follows, then, that a large share of those who had been divorced, amounting to most of all those divorced before age 25 or 30, must have remarried. Moreover, they must have remarried without delay, for as a group they spent too little time out of wedlock for more than a small fraction to be counted as divorced in any census.

By way of illustrating the grounds for these conclusions, Table 65 shows the numbers of Taiwanese recorded as divorced in the census of 1920. In adjacent columns are the numbers of remarriages that were registered to divorced persons during that year. In the second portion of Table 65 the same information is given for widows and widowers. Unfortunately the case cannot be made more rigorously. Since there is no way of knowing how many people of each age became divorced or widowed during the year, the total time spent in either status cannot be estimated, and we cannot construct "remarriage rates" by the same procedures applied to people marrying for the first time. In Table 65 it is nonetheless evident that the turnover in divorced and widowed spouses was remarkably high.[9] Remarriages

[9] The turnover may well have been higher than that suggested by Table 65: some remarriages were probably not registered, and some may have been registered incorrectly as first marriages.

TABLE 65

REMARRIAGES OF WIDOWED AND DIVORCED PERSONS, 1920

(Taiwanese Only)

Age	*Males*		*Females*	
	Divorced Men Counted on October 1	*Remarriages Registered During 1920*	*Divorced Women Counted on October 1*	*Remarriages Registered During 1920*
A. Divorced*				
10–14	3	1	20	16
15–19	155	66	622	586
20–24	1,303	506	1,389	1,193
25–29	2,362	825	1,185	738
30–34	2,771	727	999	412
35–39	2,756	434	929	236
40–44	2,081	211	786	115
45–49	1,377	100	711	45
50 and over	1,943	53	1,097	20
Total, All Ages	14,751	2,923	7,738	3,361

Age	*Males*		*Females*	
	Widowers Counted on October 1	*Remarriages Registered During 1920*	*Widows Counted on October 1*	*Remarriages Registered During 1920*
B. Widowed*				
10–14	17	1	22	8
15–19	154	48	607	412
20–24	1,278	445	2,504	1,269
25–29	3,191	923	4,224	1,560
30–34	5,058	1,254	7,263	1,455
35–39	7,743	1,364	13,457	1,081
40–44	8,548	930	20,061	624
45–49	9,214	595	27,215	284
50 and over	35,819	503	137,752	133
Total, All Ages	71,022	6,063	213,105	6,826

* The categories of "Widowed" and "Divorced" in this table are restricted to the persons whose original marriages had been registered. Those widowed or divorced men and women whose marriages were not registered have been excluded, for if they remarried they would probably register the event as their first marriage. Accordingly, the numbers in this table are slightly lower than those shown in most census tables for 1920.

Sources: *Census of 1920, Detailed Tables, Total Island*, Table 2; *Vital Statistics of the Population, 1920*, Table 12.

at some ages were almost as numerous as those who were found to be eligible at the census date.

In 1920, divorced women were favored over men in remarriage, but widows apparently were not. One cannot help noticing that more widows were remarrying in 1920 than widowers—6,826 as against 6,063, taking all ages together. This could happen only because there were many more of them to seek remarriage. The actual likelihood of marrying again was almost certainly poorer for widows than for widowed men, partly for the reasons already mentioned. While the experience of divorced persons was superficially about the same—3,361 remarriages of women, compared with 2,923 of men—the real situation was almost reversed. Since divorce withdraws an equal number of men and of women from marriage, any later sex disparity among the divorced (aside from some loss of men through heavier mortality) must be the result of unequal chances of remarrying. It turns out, therefore, that divorced women enjoyed better chances than divorced men to marry again. Even during the earlier years when divorce was exceptionally widespread in Taiwan, it probably interfered less with future childbearing among the women affected than did widowhood among widows.[10]

Though these facts do not advance us very far toward explaining the reasons for the wide incidence of divorce in Taiwan and its fall, it helps to know that entering divorce (or widowhood) was not an irrevocable step, provided that the people involved were young enough.[11] Some of the advantage that divorced women maintained over widows was simply that they were younger (though it was more than this, since they also remarried more readily at the same ages). But in order to get a more complete answer one must look for the consequences of the high divorce rates among those who were marrying. For this answer it is necessary to put one additional question: Whom did people find to marry in their second attempt?

Under conditions in Taiwan after 1895, and probably also under those that were current before, a remarkably small proportion of all marriages were introducing people into matrimony for the first time. Only 717 of every thousand marriages in 1906 had this effect for men, still fewer—644—for women. A mere 585, less than 60 per cent,

[10] Of course, divorced women were younger, and this made remarriage more likely. But men and women at the same ages also showed the same disparity.

[11] This is, of course, only another way of saying that part of the handicaps often associated with divorce and widowhood arise because many people in these categories are older than the ages at which it is customary to marry.

TABLE 66

THE SHIFT TOWARD FIRST MARRIAGES IN TAIWAN

Persons Marrying for the First Time, Per 1,000 Total Marriages between Taiwanese, 1906-1943

Year	*Husbands*	*Wives*	*Both Husband and Wife Marrying for First Time*
1906	717	644	585
1910	754	685	629
1915	791	746	691
1920	776	746	684
1925	835	825	766
1930	858	854	797
1935	887	893	836
1940	896	907	851
1943	901	921	864

Source: *Statistical Summary*, Table 70.

united *both* partners for the first time. The remainder went toward restoring to married life the widowed and divorced, who were very numerous. Because so many people dropped out, marriage had become surprisingly inefficient as a way of perpetuating family lines, and a large-scale duplication of effort was regularly incurred by those who tried again.

As time went on, however, we have seen that the shortage of women of marriageable age began to disappear, death separated husbands and wives less frequently, and divorce gradually declined in its incidence. By 1940, marriages had become more lasting and less recidivous for both men and women. The margin by which the proportion of women marrying for the first time lagged behind that of men almost vanished, and as high as 85 per cent of all registered matches were first marriages for both husband and wife.

There were further implications of this shift away from remarriage. Other things being equal (such as the prestige or importance of the particular family connection), a match in which the opposite partner was being married for the first time would be preferred, by the family of either the bride or the groom, over one in which the partner had been divorced or widowed from a previous marriage. The Chinese do not impose on relatives of the deceased the obligation (which is binding in some societies) of marrying a widowed husband or wife; far less do they have any preference for divorced

TABLE 67

RELATIVE RESTRICTION OF CHOICE IN MATES BY MEN AND WOMEN MARRYING FOR THE FIRST TIME

Per Cent of First Marriages in Each Year That Occurred with Divorced or Widowed Partners of the Opposite Sex. Taiwanese Only

Year	*Unmarried Men. Per Cent Marrying Divorced Wives or Widows*	*Unmarried Women. Per Cent Marrying Divorced Husbands or Widowers*
1906	18	9
1910	16	8
1915	13	7
1920	12	8
1925	8	7
1930	7	7
1935	6	6
1940	5	6
1943	4	6

Source: *Statistical Summary*, Table 70.

persons as candidates for marriage. When people marrying for the first time must take this less desirable latter alternative, it amounts to a restriction in marital choice, through circumstances of poverty or low prestige. We have already found that in their matrimonial position men in some ways were situated unfavorably, owing to the scarcity of eligible women. It is a reflection of this handicap that in the earlier years of registration a much larger proportion of Taiwanese men than women in their first marriage had to accept divorced wives or widows. In this matter of latitude of choice, the subsequent trends in marriage patterns can be summed up as a process of reducing the amount of restriction and equalizing this difference (see Table 67).

The prospects of widowed or divorced people in remarriage are of course the opposite sides of the same picture, since by Chinese cultural standards their position is expected to be unfavorable. Other things being equal, *their* most advantageous matches are with people previously unmarried. The situation being defined in this way, their chances are closely related to the trends in first marriages—so long as unmarried partners cannot be found for some persons marrying for the first time, these chances might be fairly high.

But it is also true that widowed and divorced people of both sexes declined as a portion of the population. For this reason, their chances on remarriage of finding partners not previously married were steadily improved, in spite of the fact that the first-married became less dependent on the widowed and divorced for their supply of

TABLE 68

RELATIVE ADVANTAGE OF MEN AND OF WOMEN IN REMARRIAGE

Per Cent of Registered Remarriages by Widowed and Divorced Persons with Previously Unmarried Partners of the Opposite Sex Taiwanese Only

	WIDOWED		*DIVORCED*	
Year	*Husbands. Per Cent Marrying Unmarried Women*	*Wives. Per Cent Marrying Unmarried Men*	*Husbands. Per Cent Marrying Unmarried Women*	*Wives. Per Cent Marrying Unmarried Men*
1906	15	30	32	49
1910	17	33	37	53
1915	20	35	39	48
1920	23	31	39	47
1925	29	34	48	48
1930	30	33	54	51
1935	44	40	60	55
1940	48	42	63	54
1943	52	43	68	52

Source: *Statistical Summary*, Table 70.

spouses (see Table 68). Let it be said, however, that these chances were never very poor. The scarcity of women helped to place widows and divorced women in a position that was surprisingly good, especially in view of the contrary impression given by the accepted notions about their low repute in China.

Men made much larger gains than women, and here they not only equalled but eventually surpassed women in the degree to which they succeeded in getting such terms on remarriage. Judged by this standard, divorced people of either sex were better off than the widowed. This was partly because they were younger and in that respect more marriageable; but in any case if their prospects were so bright, it is impossible to assert that a Chinese taboo against remarriage of divorced people is very strong.

So it is evident that the explanation for these trends in divorce rests upon answers to questions about other trends and patterns of marriage, and that these more significant answers are incomplete without some explanation of the peculiar role of divorce in early Taiwan. But there is a common thread running through both of these problems. The negotiation of marriages has been profoundly influenced by the supply of eligible women in relation to that of men—the marriage market formerly was one in which women of marriageable age were scarce. This situation conferred several advantages on the families containing eligible girls, as against those with young men seeking marriage: (1) an excellent chance to avoid permanent spinsterhood by eventually marrying, (2) a better chance to find a partner not previously married, (3) a better chance for them to remarry, if a widow or divorced, and (4) more favorable terms on remarriage.

The premium formerly enjoyed by marriageable women supplies the best clue not only to the favorable matches open to families with adult daughters, but also to the reasons why they might afford to suffer the supposed indignity of a divorce. It has been pointed out above that Chinese tradition views divorce one-sidedly—it is something to be initiated by the husband's family, since the wedding makes the wife a member of their household, and the household is where the well-known strains attending her presence arise. But the trends in divorce cannot be explained on this basis. It would imply that husbands, or their families, provoked a profusion of divorces when their own chances of remarriage were at low ebb, and that they became less desirous of divorce as these chances improved.

The wife's parental family does not actually suspend its attachments or obligations to her upon marriage, though commentaries on the Chinese family system commonly give this impression. Her relatives are ordinarily a party to the marriage itself, and may be very alert to the connection which it establishes between the two families. They can often choose whether to let a dispute develop into a break in this connection; sometimes they ensure this turn of events by upholding her interests, or by quarreling over unfulfilled terms of the marriage agreement, whereas they would show more restraint if her chance for remarriage were not good.

Nor is the position of the wife herself always so helpless as it is depicted. Over one-fifth of the earlier registered marriages between Taiwanese were not of the "ordinary" type at all, but were matrilocal. Though they did not all have the same standing in custom,[12]

[12] They include three recognized forms: adoption of a future son-in-law by a girl's parents, who may then be in charge of him from childhood on; simply marrying-in by the husband; and marrying-in with apparently some restriction to his rights of inheritance. The exact distinctions are left somewhat unclear, for the terms are Japanese, and the facts Chinese. It is also likely that there were variations in procedure from one place to another.

TABLE 69

PER CENT OF ALL REGISTERED MARRIAGES BETWEEN TAIWANESE THAT WERE MATRILOCAL, 1906-43

1906	21.8
1910	20.4
1915	18.4
1920	17.5
1925	16.1
1930	15.7
1935	9.8
1940	7.8
1943	6.2

Source: *Statistical Summary,* Table 65.

these marriages had in common the fact that the husbands entered the families of the wives, in the reverse of the pattern that was considered normal. These extraordinary marriages were a measure of necessity rather than a repudiation of tradition, for they diminished as a share of all marriages along with the major difficulties of men in finding brides. But matrilocal marriage signifies a considerable compromise with the dominance allotted to men by Chinese tradition. Where it occurs, it means that in order to maintain the rule of male descent, either the husband must be relegated to a less important position or the continuity of the wife's family must be broken. Chinese may on different occasions prefer one or the other of these alternatives, but when they resort to matrilocal marriage it is a sign that precedence has been given to continuation of the wife's family line. This solution makes the husband's status in the wife's family rest on sufferance, and cannot avoid undermining his dignity and authority.[13] The norms of patriarchal authority were not undermined, however, in the Taiwanese population as a whole: when men were no longer obliged to marry on these degrading terms, they began to shun this type of marriage (see Table 69). Because it was inconsistent with the rest of the family system, matrilocal marriage presented a special occasion for discord—men were led to expect one kind of familial role as husbands, but required to accept another one that was inferior.

[13] Further compromise is actually possible. Various devices are practiced in China, such as entering the husband on the registers of the wife's family, changing his surname to theirs, and perhaps admitting him to her inheritance, as ways to smooth over the departure from tradition in such marriages. How urgent these niceties are probably depends on the importance and wealth of the families involved—i.e., how urgently they feel the need to keep up conventional appearances.

Evidently it is mistaken to consider divorce simply as a prerogative of the husband or his family, just because the Chinese believe that it ought to be. Several sources of friction can be found in Chinese family structure that might lead to divorce, but by their manifestations in Taiwan they point to the wife's side, and not the husband's, as having been responsible for its exceptionally high incidence. A great many of the divorces that were recorded must have been precipitated by the wife's family (if not by the wife herself), and it seems inescapable that their willingness to do so was governed largely by the opportunities to find another match for her. The patterns of marriage as well as divorce lend support to this conclusion.

The Reproductive Span of Married Life

One reason for giving attention to marriage is that it is the principal step by which people pass into adult familial roles, and thus embodies many of their ideas about the significance of these roles. It is also a matter of great interest in connection with reproductive behavior, since in all known societies some form of marriage establishes the approved social setting for bringing children into the world. From the standpoint of replacement of members in a population, however, the important thing is not simply when people first become married, but how much time they actually spend in married life. But because a particular marriage almost never lasts through the lifetime of both its immediate partners, the duration of married life cannot be precisely determined for Taiwanese. People are arriving and departing continually, and not all of them leave a sufficient trace in the sorts of demographic statistics that are usually available.

The most practical expedient for estimating the amount of time spent in marriage is to consider only those women of reproductive ages who are currently married at some particular time.[14] In Table 70 they are arranged as proportions of all women at these ages at census dates, confirming what has already been implied above—that many years were spent without their husbands by women who had been married, because widowhood and divorce were too prevalent to be cancelled out by remarriage. As women became older more of them became widows, but the percentages of women who dropped

[14] From the standpoint of demographic concepts, there is nothing inherently "better" about narrowing attention to women instead of men. The main reason for doing so here is that we have ways of estimating the fertility of women in Taiwan according to age, but not that of men. The choice of 15-49 as the age interval to use is dictated by convention, but in other populations it has been found to include nearly all cases of maternity.

TABLE 70
PER CENT OF TAIWANESE WOMEN CURRENTLY MARRIED, BY AGE, AT VARIOUS CENSUS DATES

Age	*1905*	*1920*	*1935*
15–19	45.9	32.0	27.7
20–24	88.3	83.5	81.2
25–29	92.5	91.6	92.8
30–34	89.0	89.8	92.4
35–39	81.2	84.7	89.3
40–44	68.8	75.8	82.8
45–49	55.9	63.2	74.2
Total, 15–49	75.7	72.2	74.1

Source: Tables of the Taiwanese population by age, sex and marital status in the respective censuses. "Married" in 1920 includes women whose marriages were *not* registered.

out of married life in this way declined sharply with the fall in mortality among husbands and in the frequency of divorce. Hence some of the time lost to young wives through later marriage was made up by others through prolonged survival of their husbands. One cannot say with certainty that the *net* result was a lengthening of married life for the women of Table 70.[15] But even if it had been, this lengthening might not make much of a contribution to the fertility of women in reproductive ages. It had most of its effect over age 35, when many women had already completed their childbearing.

When it comes to patterns of difference in marriage between groups of Taiwanese, there is not much to find. Little information

[15] There is no simple answer to the question of whether the time spent in marriage increased or not. Other things equal, the fact that women lived longer would result automatically in a lengthening of married life—fewer wives at these ages would die before their husbands. Similarly with longer life for husbands (and less divorce)—women would spend a greater *proportion* of their time married.

The case becomes complicated as soon as new generations of women entering the reproductive ages are included. These new groups of women were becoming larger every year, making the extra time that they spent awaiting marriage still greater, and offsetting some of the increase of the married among older women.

The balance of these effects at census dates is shown by the proportions of women married in the entire age group 15-49, which fell after 1905 and partially recovered later. But these do not give the only answer to the question, for there is no doubt that those women *already* married would stay married longer than women had before, owing largely to the reduction of mortality in the population. It makes a difference whether the question about years spent in marriage is put in terms of a particular group (or "cohort") of women at different times or different groups of women at some particular time. Although the first of these alternatives is really more pertinent to the other problems of interest, even an approximate answer makes extravagant demands for data, and the second form is the one in which related questions (such as local differences, in this chapter, and of fertility, in the next) must be phrased.

exists to indicate the marrying habits of the people according to their occupations; and for the meager material that is available, the study of Taiwan's occupational data has shown that these can be relied upon only for men, whereas it is the women that interest us here.[16] A comparison can be made, in 1920, between the principal

TABLE 71

PER CENT OF TAIWANESE WOMEN MARRIED, 1920, BY AGE AND ANCESTRAL PLACE OF ORIGIN

Age	*Fukien Origin*	*Kwangtung Origin*	*Other Taiwanese**
15–19	31.9	31.1	37.3
20–24	84.2	81.1	76.2
25–29	92.0	91.3	83.6
30–34	89.9	90.8	84.1
35–39	84.5	86.5	82.6
40–44	75.0	80.0	75.7
45–49	61.8	70.4	66.9
Total, 15–49	72.1	72.9	70.8

* "Other Taiwanese" consisted almost entirely of non-Chinese members of aboriginal tribes in Taiwan.

Source: *Census of 1920, Detailed Tables,* Table 2.

"Married" includes women whose marriages were not registered.

groups of Taiwanese according to place of origin. Those married among Chinese who traced their ancestry from Fukien, and those from Kwangtung, are listed separately in Table 71. Both had almost equal proportions of all their women 15-49 married in 1920. The group from Fukien, which comprised most of the population in Taiwan, apparently married somewhat earlier, but were more widowed in the higher reproductive ages. The women from families of Kwangtung origin, most of whom are descendants from the "Hakka" group in Taiwan, were married to a lesser extent while young, but were able to avoid widowhood until later in life.

It is not possible to find out definitely whether Kwangtung widows were more likely to remarry, or whether they simply had hardier husbands and became widows less often. Their smaller quota of widows can be partly explained away, however, by two facts: their

[16] The later census reports did not show this information at all. In 1920 a long and complicated table was devoted to cross-tabulation of occupation and marital status by age, and similarly for the census of 1905. But for the reason noted in the text they are not of much value in answering the questions raised here. Figures for registered marriages were published according to the occupation of each spouse, but for these and additional reasons these tables are practically useless.

whole age pattern in marrying was a later one (and therefore probably made their husbands younger in relation to themselves); and most of them lived in Hsinchu Prefecture, which gave them and their husbands better chances of surviving. In view of these considerations, it seems that greater remarriage of widows probably was not very important in producing this difference.

The entry for "Other Taiwanese" in Table 71 gives some indication of the prevalence of marriage in those small groups of the island's aborigines who lived in the foothills and plains. Their women were distinguished from the Chinese by earlier marriage, and poorer chances both of marrying for the first time and of remarrying when widowed or divorced. They were a small group, however, and information about them probably tells nothing about the inhabitants of the interior, who were not enumerated in the census of 1920.

TABLE 72

PER CENT OF TAIWANESE WOMEN MARRIED

By Age, Inside and Outside Major Cities*

1925 and 1935

	1925		*1935*	
Age	*Inside Cities*	*Outside Cities*	*Inside Cities*	*Outside Cities*
15–19	24.4	29.4	23.9	28.3
20–24	73.3	83.5	73.8	82.4
25–29	85.9	93.5	87.3	93.7
30–34	87.2	92.7	87.6	93.1
35–39	83.4	88.3	84.6	90.1
40–44	74.8	80.1	78.6	83.5
45–49	63.0	68.9	69.1	75.0
Total, 15–49	67.0	73.0	69.4	74.9

* "Inside Cities" includes the nine cities of Municipal rank in 1935. The data for 1925 have been rearranged to conform to this rule.

Source: *Census of 1925, Statistical Tables,* Table 3; *Census of 1935, Statistical Tables,* Table 7.

Local conditions peculiar to different parts of Taiwan also produced a certain amount of variation in the extent of marriage by women. A clear-cut distinction of this sort is that which appears between the people in the major cities and those in the surrounding rural regions. When all the cities that were of Municipal rank in 1935 are grouped together, and then the remainder of the population collected in another group, the women in cities are found to have lagged behind the others by a considerable margin in getting married. The gap in proportions married was greatest for the young women in the age interval 20-24, narrowing with advancing age (see Table 72). The gap was similar and located at the same ages both in 1925 and 1935, suggesting that the cities probably shared with the rest of the island in the trend toward later marriage for women.

TABLE 73

VARIATION IN PROPORTIONS MARRIED

Per Cent of Women in the Ages 20–34 Currently Married
By Prefecture, Inside and Outside Major Cities, 1925 and 1935
Taiwanese Only

	1925		*1935*		
Name of Prefecture	*Inside Cities*	*Outside Cities*	*Inside Cities*	*Outside Cities*	*Name of City*
Taipei		88.4		88.3	
	76.2		76.1		(Taipei)
	79.0		84.0		(Chilung)
Hsinchu		87.3		87.2	
	84.7		84.0		(Hsinchu)
Taichung		90.2		89.8	
	86.8		86.1		(Taichung)
	85.5		87.1		(Changhua)
Tainan		92.2		92.1	
	80.2		78.6		(Tainan)
	86.1		87.5		(Chiayi)
Kaohsiung		87.6		85.8	
	87.9		87.1		(Kaohsiung)
	87.1		85.7		(P'ingtung)
Taitung		80.4		83.7	
Hualien		84.0		87.8	
P'enghu Islands		84.6		84.7	
Total Island	81.6	89.3	82.2	89.0	

Source: *Census of 1925, Statistical Tables,* Table 3; *Census of 1935, Statistical Tables,* Table 7.

One cannot deny that there were better incentives or opportunities outside than inside the major cities for women to marry while very young. The extent of marriage among women in these cities is one of the principal features that set them off from the rural sections. But the sharpness of the difference is misleading, and gives an impression of contrast between country and city that is unwarranted. The notion of "urban" as distinct from agrarian conditions does not accurately characterize cities that are so little urbanized as those in Taiwan. Some of the difference in Table 72 comes, not from their distinctness as cities, but from the characteristics of people in their surrounding areas. It turns out that cities were less unlike the rural sections of the island when they are compared with those parts from which they drew many of their people (see Table 73). One city actually had a *higher* proportion of its women 20-34 married than the rest of the Prefecture in which it was located.

The case is similar when variation in the individual rural Districts that make up the remainder of the Prefectures (outside of the major cities) is taken into account. Most of it falls in the ages 15-19, which are not shown in Table 73. Even in the ages dealt with here these smaller civil divisions exhibited considerable differences in their marriage customs, which make it impossible to discern patterns of any consequence in the proportions married, as far as cities are concerned, that might denote change. Those places where women had a relatively late start in marrying were sometimes among the *highest* in proportions married by age 30; some of the early-marrying ones were among the lowest in those still married of their older women. But insofar as these local peculiarities represent differences in the way that marriage was regarded by the people, one common factor stands out in all of them—the variation seems to have been in scheduling *when* the women should marry, and not in fixing the proportion who eventually were found to be married.[17] The percentages of women married over age 30 were similar in all smaller civil divisions, both Municipalities and rural Districts. And so the principal result of their diversity may have been to make localities gain or lose in the time that their younger women spent in married life.[18]

[17] The local peculiarities seem also to have been firmly rooted in custom and not patterns of accidental variation, for they were fairly stable through time. The differences in proportions married repeated themselves: they were correlated with nothing else more strongly than with the same proportions at a later date, even though the women involved of course were different each time. Some idea of this stability can be gained by comparing 1925 and 1935 in Table 73, though the case is more impressive when all rural Districts are compared separately. Although it might be expected that young women with lower incidence of marriage would also have lower fertility, there is no indication that this was so in Taiwan to any marked degree, as we shall see in the next chapter. Part of the explanation is doubtless that the differences followed this pattern of local custom more than one of change.

[18] Local variations cannot be said to be linked to the same factors that were discussed above for the entire island. For example, families of young men seeking marriage might, if confronted by a local shortage of young women, arrange a match in a neighboring place. Moreover, the shortage itself might not be one revealed in the statistics, but merely one of families having eligible *surnames* (or sufficiently distant relationships). Chinese regard marriage between persons of the same family name as incestuous, and the residents of small communities often are nearly all of the same

In order to understand fully the motives that lie behind attitudes and actions toward family life, one needs to pursue a comprehensive study of the many sides to the problem. This is especially true in analyzing the family system of the Chinese, which enters prominently into most of their everyday affairs. If one were concentrating on this task alone, it would be necessary to go thoroughly into (a) the sentiments that they hold and (b) the conduct that they display where kinship is concerned. Most study of the subject has dealt with the first of these two parts, for Chinese have in their literature provided convenient (though often unlikely) statements of their beliefs in these matters and there have been only casual records to check how closely their behavior conforms to these statements.

Patterns and trends in people's passage from one marital status to another, which can be discovered in demographic data, contribute most directly to the second part of the problem. They also increase our knowledge of the interconnections between the sentiments and actions, particularly with regard to some of the behavior that is often thought to issue from the internal structure of relationships in the family unit. This behavior apparently is subject to considerable variation in response to the circumstances that confront it in the external society—circumstances that may arise in turn through the conduct of others, perhaps in full conformity with the conventions of the society. The clearest example is the result of preferential treatment of boys during infancy and childhood: the girls who survived to adulthood were too few to furnish wives for eligible men, and there were far-reaching consequences of the shortage when it came to marriage.

It is also instructive to be able to determine the incidence of divorce, which Chinese do not sanction for resolution of ordinary family discord, and remarriage, which they disapprove when it can be avoided. Actual practice, as we have found, may depart widely from the stereotyped picture that is often entertained about the degree of abhorrence felt toward these expedients. There is an apparent discrepancy between the views that are overtly professed by some Chinese and those reflected in the conduct of others, which contains a hint that the moral pronouncements have not yet been examined sufficiently in relation to the functioning of familial groups.

Finally, the shifts that have been observed above in marriage and divorce have considerable significance. They cannot be traced to any substantial changes in the system of family values, but can be

surname. A local shortage of women from this cause is just as real in its consequences as an absolute shortage in numbers.

traced to differences in the framework of opportunities that existed for fulfilling these values. In spite of some similarity of appearance, these trends bear no real resemblance to the kinds of social change that have come to be regarded, often wishfully, as inalienable appurtenances of "economic development." In fact, some worked in the opposite direction. The desire to marry while young apparently did not slacken; young men actually succeeded in marrying earlier than before, and the fact that women did not seems due to reasons beyond their control. Divorces could scarcely have been a sign of "individualism" in marriage, because they were most frequent at a time when the force of tradition was at its strongest, and declined rather than mounted in incidence with the events that might have introduced change. The total time spent in married life did not fall—it certainly rose for men, since more of them married, and probably (through prolongation of life) for women too. If the only trends discernible in marriage and divorce had little or nothing to do with changes in the normative system—i.e., "social change" in the most usual sense of the term—then the total impact of Japanese colonial policies on people's motives in this sphere must have been negligible. Discussion of fertility patterns in the next chapter will reveal how minor this impact really was.

CHAPTER IX

The Fertility of the Taiwanese

JUDGED by appropriate standards, the Japanese made an impressive success of improving health in Taiwan. In less than 50 years they transformed the island from a turbulent and pestilential area into a place where the major hazards to existence in former times were removed. It was a place where the Japanese themselves could live more healthily on the average than their countrymen did in Japan.[1] Measured in any conventional way, mortality among the Taiwanese was sharply reduced. Its decline was as rapid as almost any other contemporary case for which there is a record.

Like the economic program of the Japanese, the health program was carefully designed to function through the society that existed in Taiwan, and not to reform it. Therefore, the policies that made deaths less prevalent in the population did substantially nothing to the incidence of births. The result was the growth of population described in Chapter I, which doubled the number of Taiwanese in less than half a century.

Improvement in mortality would not have had this consequence if it had not been for the high level of fertility among the Taiwanese. Birth rates, as illustrated in Fig. 21, remained about the same throughout this period, fluctuating from year to year, perhaps even rising slightly from the beginning.[2] Though the fertility of Taiwanese was not the highest that has been recorded, and their mortality was far from the lowest, in conjunction these two factors created a natural increase that became as rapid as any yet known.

Steady high fertility produced more than a steady flow of births. While death rates fell and birth rates persisted at former levels, the total annual deaths stayed at almost the same number and the births that occurred each year mounted sharply (Fig. 21). Many people remained living who previously would have died, and thus had opportunity to give birth to children who otherwise would never have entered the world.

1 See Taiwan, Government-General, Research Bureau. *Life Tables of Taiwan, 1926-1930* (First Issue) (1936). The health of Japanese in Taiwan may appear better than it actually was, for their deaths were not always registered in Taiwan. Many were recorded back at the legal residence of their families in Japan.

2 The trend takes on a slightly different appearance when measured in different terms, as we shall presently see.

Regrettably there is very little actual knowledge of the early demographic situation in Taiwan that preceded this development. Poor records are most often characteristic of such conditions, for the same factors that stand in the way of promoting longevity also inhibit modernization in other respects. But ignorance of the details need not prevent us from ascertaining broadly what was the state of affairs that formerly prevailed. It is certain, for example, that the early population of Taiwanese regularly suffered heavy attrition by mortality. As late as 1906, at least 35 deaths were still occurring per thousand in the population. If this was the case after ten years of pacification, conscientious civil administration and preliminary sanitation measures by the Japanese, then the usual level of mortality before must have been even higher.

The Taiwanese on the island before 1895 were already a firmly established population, and no longer relied on immigrants to replenish their numbers. In age composition the population was a settled and not a transient one (see Fig. 3). If the decade or so preceding the first census had not presented unusually high risks of death, the age structure would have been almost the same in 1905 as it was in 1940. Even so, it was marked by large proportions of infants and young children, indicating steady and high fertility in the past. Though we have given migration credit for most of the population growth in Taiwan before 1895, there is every sign that fertility continued there at the same rate that was customary on the mainland.

Chinese culture from the earliest known times has been faced with mortality that was proverbially high. As a normal state of affairs, this imposes certain requirements if a population is to continue in existence. For example, barring large migration, enough births must regularly be produced to offset the risks of dying. Failing this, a population would also fail to survive. Prolonged high mortality thus helps to develop social institutions that encourge high fertility.

Sufficient numbers of births, however, are not forthcoming due to this necessity alone. Their supply is ensured in countries of high fertility through elaborate features of social organization. Custom and moral precept in such societies create firm sentiment in favor of the obligations and continuity of family relationships. They furnish powerful incentives to bring forth abundant offspring. There are strong and subtle pressures toward marriage of young men and women. Family life receives great emphasis, and becomes the center of numerous activities that give it additional weight. When a wide enough range of social functions is carried on in family units, individuals cannot readily participate in the society except as family members. Their contacts with the rest of the society may come to depend on ties of kinship, lacking provision for being conducted on other terms.

Familial institutions have always been one of the most prominent elements in Chinese society. The culture of China is dominated by a morality that systematically urges and abets the production of progeny. We have already seen the by-products of this situation among the Taiwanese. The organization of livelihood, the inheritance of occupation, the immobility of the rural population and the character of migration to cities all reflected the influence of family relationships in the decisions of individuals.

At the same time, events under Japanese rule undeniably altered many of the conditions of life in Taiwan. In fifty years of selective exposure to modern innovations, Taiwanese were showing the effects of this contact, though none of these effects—except the gains in longevity—could be called spectacular. It now remains to be seen whether these developments had created more than superficial social changes, and had begun to exert any influence on fertility.

The Course of Fertility in Taiwan

Due to its peculiar nature in Taiwan, the system of vital registration recorded the numbers of Taiwanese births with a high standard of accuracy. Births were registered by the same system as were deaths, which has been described in some detail in Chapter VI. It functioned as part of a more comprehensive scheme of control; this scheme in turn owed its effectiveness to the ingenious way that it was fitted into local solidarities and backed by police power. Since the system recorded deaths accurately and since the figures it helped to compile in census enumerations were practically complete, the tests illustrated in Chapter VI indicate that few live births went unregistered.

By this token the data for births are nearly as valid as were the figures for deaths. In other respects, however, they are less adequate. It is not enough for the study of fertility to know the numbers of births that occurred. The significant event is in reality parenthood rather than the birth itself—we do not search for the motives of a child in entering the world, but of its parents in bringing about the event. Accordingly, some information is needed about the circumstances of birth, and in particular about the characteristics of parents. Though Taiwan's Research Bureau issued copious data each year in its regular report on vital statistics, no direct information of this sort was published. Births were tabulated simply by the civil division in which they occurred. The few other characteristics that were shown did not include any usable information about parents.[3]

Japanese showed no interest in taking advantage of their excellent birth statistics in Taiwan. Their failure to do so all but precludes any detailed study of the nature of fertility in this society, for it has denied us the information that might reveal some of the motivations surrounding parenthood. Since many of the relevant details are lacking from published sources, we shall have to fall back on approximations to conduct the sorts of measurements that will have some meaning in comparison with other countries.

"Fertility" is usually defined less precisely than mortality. Records

TABLE 74
CRUDE BIRTH AND DEATH RATES OF TAIWANESE, 1906-1943, AND RATES OF NATURAL INCREASE*

Years	*Births per Thousand Persons*	*Deaths per Thousand Persons*	*Natural Increase per Thousand Persons*
1906–10	41.7	33.4	8.3
1911–15	42.9	28.6	14.3
1916–20	40.4	31.0	9.4
1921–25	42.8	25.0	17.8
1926–30	45.0	22.1	22.9
1931–35	46.0	21.2	24.8
1936–40	45.4	20.6	24.8
1941–43	42.1	18.5	23.6

* Figures here are unweighted averages of annual birth and death rates for each year. Before 1915, births and deaths have been adjusted slightly on the basis of the internal pattern of infant mortality in later years. Otherwise no allowance has been made for under-registration.

Source: *Statistical Summary*, Table 64.

3 The vital statistics did contain tables of births by occupation of parent, but the standards of classification were different from those used in the census (though the categories were the same), and did not receive much care in compilation. Similarly, tables were published purporting to show whether or not births were legitimate, but these cannot be relied upon to indicate the actual marital status of parents, because the Japanese did not recognize marriages that were not legally registered. Basic demographic data like the ages of mothers and actual marital status were never published.

On the credit side, the tables of births by place of occurrence were reliable, and were not noticeably affected by arbitrary allocations to other places or the migration of pregnant women just before childbirth, as in Japan. (See Taeuber, I. B., and Beal, E. G., Jr. [October 1946], pp. 17-18.) It should be noted that even this advantage did not hold for Japanese in Taiwan. Some of their births were recorded in Taiwan, and some allocated to the legal residence of their families in Japan, making it almost impossible to estimate fertility or infant mortality of Japanese in Taiwan.

of births are kept primarily as records of the persons being born, whereas for purposes of measurement we have seen above that they must be viewed in relation to some population of actual or potential parents.[4] When the ages of mothers have not been specified, for example, arbitrary procedures have to be adopted for deciding which women might have been parents. There is consequently more latitude in devising measures to express the level of fertility than of mortality. Each different convention that is adopted bears some different significance.

The simplest expression for fertility is the births of each calendar year per thousand total population, or crude birth rate. By including everybody in the denominator, it avoids most of the problems that arise with more complex measures.[5] Table 74 summarizes the trend of crude birth rates for Taiwanese. Crude rates are useful in showing the balance of the two in changes of population size, for they place births on the same footing as deaths. In contrast to their death rates, Taiwanese crude birth rates scarcely changed in almost forty years. In a sense, therefore, the rates of natural increase rose almost solely because of decline in mortality; but they would not have risen to their high level in Table 74 if crude birth rates had not remained nearly constant at between 40 and 50 per thousand.

These data show no tendency for fertility to fall along with death rates. Quite to the contrary, birth rates actually rose slightly over the period. Crude birth rates, however, have a well-known property of indicating trends that are spurious, due to changes in age composition of the population. Before attaching much significance to these minor movements of rates, one should first examine the evidence of more precise indices of fertility.

[4] Moreover, as events occurring to adults, births are more complex in their distribution than deaths. A birth can happen more than once to any one parent, as death cannot, and introduces at least one more possible dimension for measurement.

[5] Use of crude birth rates does not avoid all of these problems. (It also creates new ones, as indicated below in the text.) Usually part of the births of a given year are included in both terms of the rates.

More important, however, is another difficulty which all measures share equally. Birth itself is not so definite an event as death. In societies where infant mortality is high, it is next to impossible to determine exactly what is a "live" birth. In Taiwan we have seen this problem illustrated in the case of unregistered non-survivors—babies who were perhaps born alive but died in the first few hours or days of infancy. Some of these may have been listed as stillbirths in the statistics, but an unknown number were probably omitted completely. Hence any measure of fertility based on these figures is certainly in some degree an understatement. Aside from the adjustment of births made before 1915, we must accept the figures of "live" births as they were published, with only minor adjustments to bring them into line with the numbers of children counted in the census.

Trends in fertility can be better approximated in terms of child-bearing by potential mothers. In countries where this information is known, practically all women who become mothers do in fact have their births between ages 15 and 50. General fertility ratios, or total births per thousand women in this age interval, give a better idea of actual trends among women who might have become mothers. The first column of Table 75 shows a series of such ratios centered around

TABLE 75
GENERAL FERTILITY RATIOS FOR TAIWANESE, 1905-1940
Births per 1,000 Women 15-49, Based on Three Separate Estimates of Births

Year	*Births Registered During Census Year*	*Three-Year Average of Registered Births, Centered Around Census Year*	*Births Estimated From Infants Counted in Census*
1905	170*	170†	188‡
1915	179	176	188
1920	174	177	184
1930	199	200	204
1935	209	206	215
1940	203	201	206

* This is the value actually computed for 1906.
† Represents the unweighted average of ratios for 1906 to 1909.
‡ Births estimated by adding to infant survivors the deaths implied by the infant death rate in each calendar year.
Sources: Vital Statistics Reports for each year involved; tables of population by age and sex from each census, and special tables of infants by month of age.

census years. It is based on the births as registered, just as were the crude rates in Table 74. These ratios make the apparent rise of fertility seem just as prominent as when based on the evidence of crude birth rates. Neither index is conclusive, for there is reason to suspect omission in the early birth registration.

There is available still another resource, one that is not impaired by defective birth reporting in the early years. Through the combination of Chinese consciousness of age and careful Japanese census procedures, enumerations of infants at each census year were more complete in their coverage than birth registration.[6] Since the census was always taken on the first day of October, the Japanese scheme

[6] They have been invaluable, in fact, in testing the adequacy of birth registration for small civil divisions in later census years. This information was omitted in the tabulation of one census, that of 1925.

for allocating age (by calendar year of birth) gave an age interval for infants representing only three-fourths of a full year's births. Recognizing this shortcoming, census authorities tabulated full information on infants by month of age and published supplemental tables with all enumerated infants born since October 1 of the preceding year.[7] These tables make possible an estimate of births in each of the early census years that is nearly independent of the bias in the registration system. Given thorough enumeration, it should hence be consistent over time and not exhibit as increasing fertility what was in fact improvement in registration.

The last column of Table 75 gives general fertility ratios based on these special enumerations at each census. Here the infants have been used to estimate births occurring over the preceding year. For this estimation we have assumed that the births preceding the census date were affected by mortality conditions that prevailed during the calendar year of the census.[8]

These figures represent the trend of fertility in Taiwan more dependably than crude birth rates. Far from declining in the slightest, these ratios of all adult Taiwanese women evidently *increased* slightly. The fertility ratios based on census infants show that the rise before 1920 was probably a matter of improvement in registration, for infants were so carefully enumerated that they could not have been over-counted. On the other hand, the numbers of census infants counted at any one date may reflect an extraordinary crop of births in the preceding year. This was apparently the case in 1935. Taken separately, that year yielded the highest observation for fertility. Averaged with adjacent years it produces a value that is less extreme, and more appropriate to use in estimating the trend. (The same interpretation does not apply to the discrepancy between the single-year ratio and the 3-year ratio for 1915; here births were exceptionally low in 1916, possibly in reaction to an outbreak of malaria in 1915. To judge from the large number of deaths among potential mothers in that year, they must have been heavily affected by the disease.)

[7] As for validity, these show consistency of age reporting even by single months when tested against births by month of occurrence. The same tables continued to be published after 1930, when the age system above infancy was changed.

[8] Specifically, that the calendar-year infant death rate is a true mortality rate. The calculation is based on the life-table term l_1, converted to L_0 by the arbitrary weights $.28\,l_0 + .72\,l_1$ for males and $.29\,l_0 + .71\,l_1$ for females. If the life table radix is 1, then the ration $1/L_0$ applied to infants of each sex serves to estimate births over the preceding year. This figure is always conservative, for in years of under-registration infant mortality was not fully reported.

Insofar as any actual change can be detected from the ratios before 1930—and this was very slight—it was not downward. The situation after 1930 is less clear. There is little to be gained by augmenting the materials used so far with observations for single years, for yearly fertility ratios indicate fluctuation as well as trend. There were two high points, in 1935 and 1937, after which they fell slightly until 1943.

Since fertility had remained high enough up to this time to maintain an accelerating rate of growth in population, it is of special interest to see whether we have observed after 1935 merely a wavering in its upward course or the portent of actual decline. Unfortunately, the figures presented in Table 75 are the total of direct knowledge about the problem that is at present available outside of Taiwan. They cannot be verified, nor investigated in further detail, nor disproved on the basis of other data now at hand. They cannot even be examined for differences between civil divisions, for such data too are lacking after 1935.

The trends of the 1930's can be given closer scrutiny, however, by recourse to indirect procedures. Using supplemental data from Japan, it is possible to make a closer comparison of points within the census period by means of gross reproduction rates.[9] With the allowance that these make for varying age composition among the women in reproductive ages, fertility in 1940 appears to have been just slightly less than in 1935, and less *in both years* than in 1930.[10] General fertility ratios followed their peculiar course during the 1930's primarily because a large group of women were passing through their ages of greatest childbirth in the middle portion of the decade. The rise and fall of general fertility ratios after 1930 therefore indicated nothing but the unusual concentration of potential mothers: with-

[9] As employed here, the gross reproduction rate is no more than a procedure of age standardization for women. It is the sum of the age-specific fertility rates of women at all the reproductive ages 15-49, representing the average number of female births produced by one woman passed through all of these ages and exposed successively to all of these rates.

As we have remarked, births were not published in Taiwan by age of mother. Age-specific schedules of births have therefore been borrowed from Japan in 1930 as a way of estimating the distribution of births among women of different ages. Taking the age-specific rates associated with general fertility ratios that most closely fit those of Taiwan, we have used them to distribute a given number of total births among enumerated women by age. The total number of births that occurred is not altered by this procedure, but expected age differences in fertility are weighted by the number of women in each age. Cf. Taeuber, I. B., and Notestein, F. W. (1947), p. 15, where the original age-specific schedules are discussed.

[10] Actually, all three of these figures are based on 3-year averages of births centered around 1930, 1935, and 1940 respectively, with an allowance for under-registration.

out this fortuitous circumstance, the fertility ratios would have shown the same trend as the reproduction rates in Table 76.

TABLE 76
GROSS REPRODUCTION RATES FOR TAIWANESE, 1905-1940*

1905	2.93
1915	3.07
1920	3.00
1930	3.39
1935	3.31
1940	3.26

* Computed through the use of age schedules of fertility substituted from Japan in 1930. The number of births occurring in 1905, 1915 and 1920 was assumed to be the number of infants counted in each census plus those who had died since birth (according to infant death rates of the given calendar year). Rates for 1930, 1935, and 1940 are based on the average yearly number of registered births during 3-year periods centered on each census year, plus a slight allowance for under-registration.

These reproduction rates seem to be the closest approximation to the "true" fertility trend of Taiwanese women that is possible. It apparently increased between 1920 and 1930, though one must bear in mind that the procedure for estimating births in 1920 differed from that in later years.[11] On surer ground, fertility probably was declining very slightly from 1930 into the period of World War II. But if fertility did change at all, it changed very little, and at the end of Japanese rule in Taiwan was at practically the same level as at the beginning.

Taiwan and Selected Other Countries

A comparison with other countries gives a better idea of how high this level was. Because of the difficulties alluded to in measuring fertility, we shall again resort to gross reproduction rates as a standard form for this purpose.

Gross reproduction rates in Taiwan ranked among the highest recorded for any population in the world. Japan and Korea, for example, were the closest parallel cases. Both are Asian countries with large segments of rural population, who in the past had adjusted their livelihood and reproduction to conditions similar to those

[11] The difference was such that it might give false testimony about the trend. Since births were estimated from infants enumerated in the census, too low a value for infant mortality would give too low a figure for births. Moreover, the calendar year 1920 may have deviated from a "true" trend, for it was a year of unusual sickness in the population, which may have reduced the number of births.

TABLE 77
GROSS REPRODUCTION RATES
For Selected Countries

Korea*	
1935	3.38
Japan†	
Total Country	
1920	2.66
1930	2.40
1940	2.06
Hokkaido Province	
1920	3.32
1930	2.95
1940	2.35
Aomori Province	
1920	3.39
1930	3.05
1940	2.44
Chinese in Malaya‡	
1947	3.25-3.37
Rumania§	
1930-31	2.38
Palestine Moslems¶	
1935	3.57

* *Population Index* (1944), p. 239.
† Taeuber, I. B., and Notestein, F. W. (1947), p. 18.
‡ Smith, T. E. (1950), p. 73; based on two alternative estimates.
§ *Population Index* (1950), p. 175.
¶ *Ibid.*, p. 177.

confronting most Taiwanese. Korea stands somewhere between Japan and Taiwan in the agrarian condition of its people, but closer to Taiwan. Only there did reproduction rates exceed those of the Taiwanese. In Japan, during recent decades large groups of people had been drawn into a rapid process of industrial development, and had begun to pay overt attention to restricting the numbers of their children. There, to find reproduction rates for provinces as high as the averages of all Taiwanese, one must go to the "backward" frontier provinces of Hokkaido and Aomori, and go back in time to the years 1920 and 1925. Even in these areas, which were extreme in relation to the rest of Japan, gross reproduction rates became lower by 1930 than the ones we have found for all of Taiwan.[12]

[12] See Taeuber, I. B., and Notestein, F. W. (1947), p. 18.

Estimated reproduction rates for Chinese in Malaya are included in Table 77. They furnish a useful illustration of Chinese living outside of their own country. They are also outside the scope of the Japanese system of population statistics, and any possible bias that might be imputed to it. The range of the estimate brings it near to the level that we have found in Taiwan. This is a somewhat exceptional case, for almost half of the Chinese in Malaya in 1947 were living in towns and cities, and were engaged in non-agricultural pursuits. In their fertility they still resembled Taiwanese; their gross reproduction rates were higher than the agricultural Malaysians.[13]

Presumably fertility of this level is not actually uncommon in the world, but has existed without benefit of statistics to reveal the fact. One cannot find reproduction rates of this magnitude in recent years anywhere in Europe outside the Soviet Union. For comparable cases on a national scale it is necessary to go back to the turn of the century. In short, reproduction rates such as those of the Taiwanese have almost ceased to be characteristics of the nations that maintain adequate statistics.

The Spatial Pattern of Fertility in Taiwan

If the fertility of Taiwanese was so high and if it had scarcely changed over time, it becomes important to know whether it remained the same everywhere in the island. Familial traditions drawn from China being what they were, it would be surprising if differences had been widespread before Japanese occupation. Previous chapters have shown that only selected portions of the population came into direct contact with the new influences generated by Japanese administration. Consequently one should not expect that any large number of Taiwanese had been led to change their reproductive behavior as a result. The mode of selection and the extent of participation by Taiwanese in non-traditional activities, however, did touch some groups more than others. The question that remains to be decided is whether these factors were sufficient to induce any appreciable portions of the population to depart from their accustomed levels of fertility.

The same advantage of gross reproduction rates for international comparison also makes them useful for examining different portions of the same population—they make allowance for inequalities of age distribution in different groups of women. The only groups of

[13] See Smith, T. E. (1950), pp. 48-52; 73.

Taiwanese for which births can be matched to parents are those counted in each civil division at census dates. Migration was small, and so it happens that age differences between civil divisions were not large. Such elaborate indicators would not be needed were it not for the fact that differences in fertility were likewise small, and require sensitive tests to be discriminated at all (see Fig. 32).

These measures do reveal that average fertility was not identical as between the main sections of the island (see Table 78). By Prefecture, reproduction rates varied from high to low in somewhat the same spatial arrangement as mortality. Northern Taiwanese had lower fertility on the whole than those in the south. These differences, which were consistent from 1930 to 1935, appear to have been present for many years.[14]

A clue to the source of this variation is given by the fertility of Taiwanese in cities. Reproduction rates for cities in Table 78 were also consistent from 1930 to 1935—consistent both in relation to each other and in relation to the surrounding countryside. The differences were most extreme for cities as compared with the remainder. In a rural region, a city is a center of most activities that differ from those of its hinterland. Since urban boundaries are arbitrarily defined, it is easy to presume that the lower reproduction rates in some Prefectures had their roots in cities and spread out to the surrounding population. The presumption holds true only in part. Taipei and Chilung, for example, are bordered by an area that shared many of the activities distinguishing the city populations as more "urban" than the rest. But the other cities were less like their bordering Districts, even though they tended to differ still more from Districts of other Prefectures (see Fig. 32).

It is important to find that Taiwanese women in some cities tended to be less fertile than those in rural Districts, for our treatment of migration showed that the cities were centers of Japanese influence in the population. It appeared that this influence was not the same in all cities; hence there is no reason to suppose that its effect on fertility should be identical everywhere. But the differences within the group of nine cities in 1935 *exceeded* the variation between Prefectures. Gross reproduction rates for Taiwanese in Kaohsiung City—one of the most rapidly developing urban centers of the island —actually were very slightly higher than the average of those who

14 Provisional estimates of fertility in 1905 have some trace of the same pattern. They are less precise and less reliable than these, however, due to the difficulty in determining the levels of births and infant mortality in this early period.

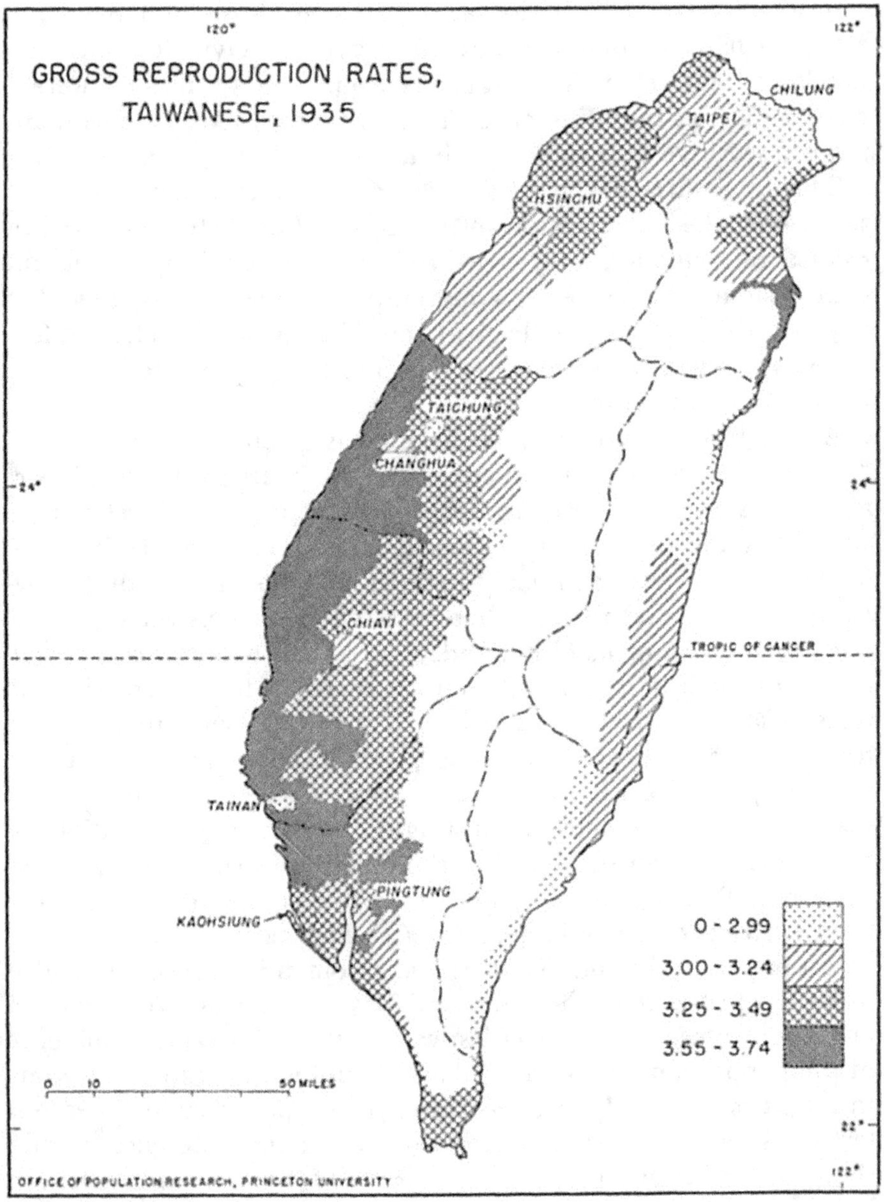

Fig. 32. Gross Reproduction Rates of Taiwanese, by Civil Division, 1935. Aborigine Territory is excluded.

TABLE 78

TAIWAN. GROSS REPRODUCTION RATES, 1930 AND 1935
Prefectures, Major Cities, and Prefectures Outside Cities

Prefecture	1930 Total Pref.	1930 Inside Cities	1930 Outside Cities	1935 Total Pref.	1935 Inside Cities	1935 Outside Cities	(City)
Taipei	3.12		3.24	2.99		3.10	
		2.78			2.69		(Taipei)
		2.76			2.76		(Chilung)
Hsinchu	3.34		3.35	3.23		3.24	
		3.13			3.05		(Hsinchu)
Taichung	3.56		3.57	3.39		3.42	
		3.17			2.93		(Taichung)
		—			3.16		(Changhua)
Tainan	3.59		3.66	3.44		3.51	
		3.04			2.90		(Tainan)
		3.19			3.06		(Chiayi)
Kaohsiung	3.39		3.39	3.39		3.36	
		3.40			3.40		(Kaohsiung)
		—			3.16		(P'ingtung)
Taitung	2.83			2.97			
Hualien	3.27			3.06			
Total Island	3.39			3.31			

Source: Based on census tables of Taiwanese population by age, registered births, and fertility schedules substituted from Japan, 1930.

lived outside in the same Prefecture. The range of variation between cities was also greater than between Prefectures. It nearly coincided with the range over all of the rural Districts, if the small settlements on the east coast are excluded.[15]

But we are really interested in variation among individuals or non-territorial groups of individuals. In an agrarian society it is probably more inefficient than elsewhere to use civil divisions as units of observation for this purpose. One of the principal features of agrarian social organization is that localities are as far as possible self-sufficient.

[15] It is difficult to compare these with fertility over the rest of the island. Registration of births was less complete, and fertility estimates were based on smaller numbers of cases. Since these reproduction rates are a complicated type of ratio, it is impractical to estimate the random error to be expected when cases become few. It seems best not to consider these observations as being equally reliable with the remainder.

When this is the case, grouped differences in activities tend to be distributed in much the same way within the various geographical units. The same should follow for the motives and interests that one might expect to find associated with substantial differences in fertility. If, for example, wives of rural gentry were more or less fertile than those of rural peasants (and there is no evidence on either side of this question), the fact that most gentry subsisted as landowners in rural villages and towns would in every case conceal the variation in the average of each civil division observed.

The case is identical with all other types of activities that are organized with the same local scope. Since we know that very few people migrated from one part of the island to another, and not many people changed their type of employment, such sources of variation apparently were contained within the boundaries of Districts. For this reason, it has not been possible to find any evidence of association between fertility and other recorded types of behavior of rural Taiwanese by Districts. It is not a fault of the statistics, but a characteristic of the society.

This diagnosis explains why fertility is not observed to have varied with other characteristics of Taiwanese over the various rural sections of the island, but it leaves two other questions unsettled. First, the strongest spatial pattern of fertility was the sectional one, viewed in prefectural units. This is surprising to find, especially since Taiwan is small in size and new in its settlement, and Taiwanese displayed little variation in demographic characteristics among Prefectures. One would not expect to find "regional" differences, which would most likely stem from long tradition and established usage. Yet this pattern was present, and lacks any apparent reason to explain it.[16]

Second, if the social structure of most rural localities was homogeneous because they were agrarian, that of cities ought not to be, since they were responsible for the greatest differences in economic and related activities over the island. Yet fertility of Taiwanese in the major cities in no instance fell outside the range established by

[16] Conceivably it could reflect traditional practices brought over from the mainland with the original migrants and preserved intact in local villages, though there is no evidence on this point. It appears not to have been related with the one outstanding difference by place of origin, however; in 1920 general fertility ratios of descendants of Fukien Chinese and Kwangtung Chinese were substantially the same. There remain the possible "factors" of climate and different types of agriculture, which did vary more or less with the sectional pattern of fertility. But knowing these is not of much help, for they supply no reason why fertility actually should have varied.

rural Districts, though each city tended to have somewhat lower rates than the whole of the Prefecture to which it belonged. The diagnosis above thus seems inadequate in two respects: it fails to account for the broad sectional differences in fertility that existed, and by implication it accounts for differences between city and countryside that did not exist.

Those differences that can be found in fertility do not appear to be coupled with other known features that are thought to affect the motives of reproduction. Reproduction rates showed no consistent patterns of association with the different kinds of livelihood prevailing in civil divisions, with the standing of the various places with respect to migration, or with the extent to which most localities had felt Japanese influence. Over the island as a whole, the case was the same where marriage is concerned—it is not possible to explain the variation that existed in fertility by saying that it reflected differences in the desire or opportunities of women to marry.

In Taipei City, however, it does appear that conditions preventing women from being married may have offered some interference with their childbearing. Many of its women avoided marriage and abstained from remarriage, and gross reproduction rates there were the lowest of all Districts or cities. As between the separate "wards" of the city, ratios of children to women (an alternative measurement of fertility) were closely related to the proportions of Taiwanese women who were married: those wards with more of their young adult women married had higher ratios, and the ratios where there were many unmarried women were lower. Taipei's low fertility might even be said to have depended on preventing potential mothers from marrying, for those who did marry exceeded the rural women of the same Prefecture in childbearing—the gross reproduction rate for *married* women in Taipei City was very slightly higher than that for the remainder of the Prefecture in 1935. Lower fertility, *where found,* was hence not a matter of fewer children among the married, but of absence of children among those who did not marry.

But though this conclusion seems to fit, since the Taiwanese were not yet subject to the better-known pressures for raising small families, it is not sufficient to establish a general rule for the rest of Taiwan or for Chinese people living elsewhere. In other parts of Taiwan lower birth rates were not often to be found. Other cities, for example, did not lose in distinctness from their respective Prefectures when the reproduction rates of their married women are compared. Basing these fertility rates on married instead of total women makes very little difference in the way they are distributed, and practically none in the observed trend of fertility, for the ages in which marriage patterns changed were not the ages in which women made their large contributions to fertility. Insofar as the factor of marriage did make a difference it seems to have cancelled out some of the variation that can be observed, but not enough of it to alter the relative standing of most civil divisions in their fertility.

Viewed in relation to other peoples who have come to restrict their fertility under modern conditions, however, the whole range of variation among Taiwanese by civil divisions seems trivial. The very lowest of "urban" gross reproduction rates, in Taipei City, corresponds to very high fertility in most other countries. In Japan, even in 1935 more than half of the provinces *outside* the principal cities had lower rates than this. There is no way to determine, then, whether or not the observed differences in Taiwan might have presaged further declines in the segments of Taiwanese that were exposed to outside influence. But two things are certain: such a decline had not proceeded very far, and its progress was extremely slow. It may have been nothing more than a continuation of differences that existed before the arrival of Japanese in Taiwan.

CHAPTER X

Conclusion

The results of Japanese rule in Taiwan are of little consequence to social science as an isolated series of events. They gain their strongest claim to importance by revealing some social and demographic implications of policies that are often urged and undertaken towards non-industrial peoples. Whether through sinister and selfish motives or through a benign desire for improvements "to fit the needs" of the recipients, such policies can equally well have the same effect. They all may be tempted to eschew any radical social changes and may run the risk of starting an uncontrollable growth of population—growth that is initially gratifying but cannot be maintained, and can be checked only through disaster.

In order to give these findings a wider application, we have therefore stressed those points of Taiwan's development which are of general significance, and have dwelt less on problems that are peculiar to this one example. We have not supplied a chronicle of events or a source book of information about Taiwan. Facts have been presented so as to illustrate the general problem: what are the consequences of introducing "backward" peoples to certain advantages of modern technology without its counterparts in social organization? We have shown, for example, that it is possible to "raise the levels of living" by measures having the least interference with indigenous custom, without affecting the formidable structure of familial institutions that the poorer peoples have relied upon in the past for survival. If policies either of betterment or of exploitation follow this course, they may reduce mortality but not fertility, and must eventually face the consequences of population growth where it is the last thing that is needed.

From both a demographic and a sociological point of view, the outstanding fact about the Taiwanese population has been its phenomenal increase in recent decades. After setting forth the dimensions of this growth in the first chapter, we have proceeded to search out some of the factors which were responsible. This inquiry has led through an examination of the social structure of the Taiwanese, of the types of innovations that were imposed upon it, and of the modes of response to these changes by the people of the island. By this time it should be possible to review some of the salient points and to see how they are pertinent to problems encountered elsewhere.

Taiwanese entered the twentieth century as an agrarian people, one that had just come under the rule of a colonial regime dedicated to instituting change. The Japanese who controlled the island were determined to make its economy more efficient, but also to concentrate rather than distribute the gains. Though their success in devising an orderly program of development was unique, and though the response of Taiwanese was likewise so, the objectives of the program and the type of reactions to it had a close resemblance to those in other areas. Japanese took their lessons in overseas administration from the record of European powers in the last century, particularly of Dutch policies in Indonesia. As a colonial dependency they governed Taiwan in a manner that was nothing short of exemplary by these standards—indeed, they excited the admiration of Old Colonial Hands who had a chance to witness their methods.

Their experience in Taiwan thus embodied the aspirations of most colonial rulers since the Industrial Revolution. With the benefit of past experience of others, and the advantage of their own firm determination, Japanese made strides that were sure and exceedingly quick. Their success represented the techniques and policies of others carried to a new degree of refinement.

In fact they succeeded too well, for their endeavor was out of date. The techniques of colonial rule that they shrewdly adapted and developed in Taiwan were capable of promoting individual survival in the population more effectively than before. Their methods also frustrated the types of social changes that might have induced Taiwanese to lower their fertility. Unabated growth at the rate attained by 1940 ultimately would have disrupted the goals of the Japanese themselves, for Taiwanese could not have continued to increase at this pace indefinitely—the world itself in a few centuries would not have been large enough to hold all of them.

Achievement of Japanese economic goals in Taiwan turned on their energy in building up investment in the island and their ingenuity in finding cheap ways to aid its agriculture. As we have seen, extended industrial development was an afterthought. The steps that they took to gain these ends improved the health of Taiwanese and reduced the hazards of dying—sometimes directly as with medicine and sanitation, sometimes as a by-product of ordinary administration.

As investment began to expand, they also took steps to concentrate it in a few hands. This was the more remarkable since capital was not poured in from outside. As we have seen, through heavy taxation, charges for capital services, conscription of labor, and manipulation of farm prices, the authorities and businessmen managed to defray the expenses of their program and to secure net proceeds for export to Japan. Taiwanese more than paid their own way in economic development.

The Japanese, who initiated most of the social changes in Taiwan after 1895, kept the greater part to themselves. When it came to their overt policies toward the population, practically all indications have pointed in this direction: they systematically avoided modifying the social structure except for separate and specific purposes. After discovering where and how to apply authority in rural villages, they approached most details of local government by indirection (e.g., through the *pao-chia* system), and husbanded their administrative resources for more urgent objectives. By confining their modern changes to a few major cities, Japanese obstructed the spread of these influences to the rural parts of the island. Even in the cities, barriers like favoritism in employment and segregation of the two groups prevented free intercourse between them. At every turn, the forces that might have drawn Taiwanese into more varied types of activities were consistently deflected from this result. Farming never ceased to be their main source of support, and the operation of individual farms was scarcely altered by the improvements around the fringes of agriculture.

The only aspect in the lives of Taiwanese subject to marked and unequivocal change was their mortality. The chances of surviving were steadily improved at all ages. Levels of living must have increased to some extent, denying poverty its former part in undermining health. Japanese also brought to Taiwan the knowledge and the drugs of modern Western medicine, with which they treated disease and forestalled its spread. The quality of their medical practice fell far short of usual standards in Western countries, and the expenditures on actual medical equipment were modest. But Japanese health authorities put these limited resources to use in a way that made spectacular progress against the risks of death. Their health effort, so niggardly with its facilities, succeeded largely because of the energy that was devoted to its administration.

In former times, the Taiwanese population had survived in spite of its high mortality. One of the conditions thus imposed on the society was the maintenance of high fertility. It contained a complex and pervasive set of injunctions to preserve the continuity of family lines, traditions of fondness and indulgence for children, pressures to marry, and incentives to rear large families. Family membership became a status through which an individual was linked to most other activities. The portions of the social structure where these ties were strongest were the portions that the Japanese left intact. Many were features that Japanese depended on for keeping order and making their administration effective.

Since nothing occurred to diminish the strength of these familial institutions, there is no reason why fertility should have declined. Mortality was lowered by simple measures applied on a mass scale. They could be carried out cheaply and through the social order as it existed—indeed, these were the two greatest virtues of the program. Consequently, fertility remained sufficient to offset the risks of death that had prevailed in the past. The result was a natural increase in population as rapid as any that had yet been recorded.

Starting out with this increase in the Taiwanese population, inquiry into other aspects of the society has necessarily come full circle, and returned to the factors that were most conspicuous in making the growth possible—steady high fertility and persistence of the family system that maintained it. Using the best measurements that are available, the findings of Chapter IX have shown that average fertility declined inconsiderably as time went on, if at all.

If we know less about variation of fertility among Taiwanese at any one time, it is partly because the data are limited, partly because there is less to know. The entire range of our measurements for civil divisions in Taiwan would fall within what is today regarded as very "high" fertility. Even in cities, where birth rates in other countries have tended to be the first to decline, Taiwanese showed almost no desire to reduce the size of their families: urban conditions either had very little effect on fertility, or affected the fertility of only a few people.

It would be welcome if studying the demographic and social events of the past were to yield predictions about the future. Such questions are continually put to demographers, who must exercise all their scruples if they are to avoid giving answers that will mislead. In the case of Taiwan, half a century of rapid and accelerating growth has unfortunately given little indication of what is in store for later years. To predict actual trends in population implies some prognostication of events in related spheres. These events in turn will be the outcome of decisions that are not yet made, political tensions that are not yet resolved, and perhaps even wars that are not yet fought.

The Japanese made many contributions to the ability of the Taiwanese population to support itself on an increasing scale. Although one hears a great deal today about Japanese oppression in Taiwan, little is said about the large physical plant that they constructed. But the fact is that they bequeathed almost all of this, albeit in somewhat run-down and damaged condition, to the future of Taiwan and whatever power holds control of the island. On the other hand, the greatest factor, and the one they did not leave behind (though they would have been happy to do so), was the fund of skills residing in the Japanese community. Without these, or appropriate substitutes and watchful care, the island's economy could never be made to yield as before.

The removal of the Japanese left a great deal that still could be accomplished by a more enlightened regime. The best part of this opportunity was lost by the Chinese from the mainland who replaced them. The war-time deterioration of physical equipment under the Japanese was as nothing compared to the wanton destruction and almost deliberate undermining of the economy in the early postwar years. More recently the Nationalist government, since Taiwan became its refuge from Communist expansion in China, has acquired a stake in the island's future that it did not have before. Through creditable effort and outside assistance, it has restored most of the former productive facilities and in many ways has improved upon them. But in order to feed the population and their own nationals, the present authorities have found it necessary to fall back upon the island's agricultural resources, and have kept as much of an agrarian emphasis in their methods as did the Japanese. Under them, for example, industrial management has apparently been still further concentrated under official control, and has not become more widespread among the Taiwanese. Insofar as this amounts to a population policy, it seems to favor a continuance of high fertility and, if unchanged, to offer very little promise of a decline in the rate of growth from this source.

If more concrete predictions are to be made, however, it is safer to begin by guessing what will *not* happen. For example, natural increase of 25 per thousand, or growth compounded at 2.5 per cent per annum, could not long continue in any but an empty land. From their present numbers, at that rate Taiwanese would reach fantastic proportions in a few generations. They cannot emigrate in large numbers, for Asia has no countries that will accept them. Hence it is inconceivable that they should actually continue to expand on this scale. Thus the best of care may not ensure against some resurgence of mortality, unless drastic changes are made in the social environment of family life. If they are able to remain long enough in control of Taiwan, the Nationalist authorities will have to face this problem sooner or later. Having squandered their first chance to take over Taiwan's economy as a going concern, they must face it on terms that become progessively less advantageous as time goes on.

The lessons that are most pertinent to this example, however, cannot be drawn from it alone, but emerge only from comparison with other parts of the world. The factors that led to population growth in Taiwan were by no means novel events. They have appeared several times in recent history, and have become a familiar and unhappy pattern of colonial areas. Rapid natural increase, wherever it has occurred, has been an accompaniment of measures that assist human survival, and of some innovations in modes of livelihood for human support. But it has not everywhere been synonymous with poverty, for some countries have maintained a rising scale of wealth while their people increased.

Those countries that prospered during this expansion of their populations have usually done so in a spectacular degree, because for them it has been part of a much wider process that ushered in profound and sweeping alterations in their forms of social and economic organization. While this process of "modernization" has contained some unique and adventitious factors from case to case, it is usually associated with a general industrial development, with a tendency for people's activities of all sorts to become more specialized and more widely interdependent, with a decline in the influence of rural life, and with some ascendancy of the more flexible and less intimate social contacts afforded by large cities. And, finally, this process is also characterized by a shifting away from self-sufficient family units as the center for most human behavior, and towards more frequent association with people *outside* the context of family relationships.

Hand in hand with these changes, familial institutions have gradually lost some ground as the basis for organizing or coordinating people's actions, and more emphasis has been placed on other types of association and other forms of societal control. Though the details may vary, it usually happens that people find their survival to depend less on maintaining the continuity of their family groups, that family continuity ceases to require abundant children (owing to lowered mortality), and that competing interests begin to intervene and dampen the desire for abundant children as an end in itself. As a result, the recent industrial world has experienced sharp drops in its fertility—sometimes to a point that arouses alarm about *under*-production of births.

Because high fertility can make its contribution to population growth merely by remaining constant, without being modified in any way, it cannot be long overlooked by programs which seek to establish modern industry in non-industrial areas. It is easy to forget, however, that the permanent shift towards lower fertility is not to be expected by itself. Where observed in the past, it has been part of the entire *process* of change, which will not develop very far if sealed off in privileged segments of a society.

Unfortunately, the social correlates of this process are not yet well understood; one cannot say that, if one or another aspect of Japan's administration in Taiwan had been altered, the outcome would have differed in some definite way. Stronger and less restrictive measures might be required to shake the stability of traditional institutions, even if more opportunities were provided for popular participation. On the other hand, it is also possible that a program of truly radical proportions might be sufficient to precipitate revolutionary upheavals and might threaten the established order on which the leaders of agrarian countries must depend for their authority. But one thing seems certain: if more comprehensive results are desired from such programs, they cannot be achieved *without* more thoroughgoing changes, of the sorts we have been discussing, in the social structure.

Since the familial attitudes supporting high levels of fertility appear eventually to be incompatible with an industrial system, in a sense lowered birth rates are probably automatic features of successful modernization. But this is not of much help to those who would use such knowledge as a guide to policy, for it takes time for the process to develop to this point—time during which the techniques of mortality control, which now can operate efficiently without requiring extensive reorientation of values and sentiments, are capable of doing their part to start rapid population increase.

Today it is doubtful whether any non-industrial nation, desirous of securing for itself the advantages of an industrial system of production, can afford to rely on this "automatic" decline in fertility, even if it is prepared to let the social changes run their course. The time is too short, the starting position too precarious, and the large empty areas of the world are no longer open to migration if fertility fails to fall. The increase of people would probably have to be suppressed, either by accident or by design, through a restoration of high mortality. Agrarian countries that wish to play safe in their plans for development are now left with little choice but to promote the idea of deliberative fertility control among their people.

Of course, this does not mean that they will actually want to go this far. The traditions of the past are harder to part with than its archaic modes of production, and there are strong views that oppose any calculated weakening of these traditions. Furthermore, many people in these countries feel that policies overtly designed to popularize the restriction of births are morally offensive. These two influences—conservatism and outright taboos—may persuade the leaders of agrarian countries to try some middle path, to treat industrialization as merely a set of technical measures that can be adopted without the type of organization required to make use of it.

A program of this selective nature may have a wide appeal as a way of achieving "economic progress with social stability." And there is no reason why it should not enjoy short-run success, for methods that are now known can scarcely fail, barring mismanagement, to raise production, improve health and bring agricultural prosperity. But this kind of progress is illusory, for it fosters stability of economic organization as well as of social institutions, and hinders the growth of an industrial system. The result may amount to the same thing as "colonial development," whether or not a "colonial" relationship exists.

It is hard to imagine that modern changes can be kept away from non-industrial regions forever just because some people are lukewarm to their social implications. The prospects for a further diffusion of industrial culture are continually being strengthened as more people become aware of its material advantages. But the time consumed in the process, and the social and demographic consequences of the delay, may prevent industrialization from accomplishing the things that are hopefully expected of it.

Bibliography

OFFICIAL JAPANESE SOURCES

(All are published under the name of the Census Bureau unless otherwise indicated)

Census of 1905 (First Provisional Household Census)

1. *Descriptive Account [of Procedures]*. Tokyo, Government-General of Taiwan, Bureau of Official Statistics, 1908. 305 pp.
2. *Descriptive Report [of Population]*. Tokyo, 1907. xiv, 558 pp.
3. *Detailed Tables, by Prefecture*. Tokyo, 1907. 1481 pp.
4. *Detailed Tables, Total Island*. Tokyo, 1907. 1361 pp.
5. *General Volume of Statistical Tables*. Tokyo, 1908. 467 pp.
6. *Glossary of Occupational Terms*. Tokyo, 1907. viii, 150 pp.
7. *Special Population Census of Formosa, 1905*. Report of the Committee of the Formosan Special Census Investigation. Tokyo, 1909. v, 210 pp. [English translation of *Descriptive Report* above, with tables omitted.]

Census of 1915 (Second Provisional Household Census of Taiwan)

8. *Descriptive [and General Statistical] Report*. Taihoku, 1918. xliii, 565 pp.; Appendix, 439 pp.
9. *Glossary of Occupational Terms*. Taihoku, 1917. 153 pp.
10. *Statistical Tables*. Taihoku, 1918. vi, 537 pp.

Census of 1920—First [Regular] Population Census (Third Provisional Household Census)

11. *Descriptive Report, with Appendix of Statistical Tables*. Taihoku, 1924. xvi, 475 pp.; Appendix, 487 pp.
12. *Detailed Tables*. Taihoku, 1923.
13. *Statistical Tables, by Prefecture*. Taihoku, 1924. xii, 971 pp.
14. *Summary Tables*. Taihoku, 1922. 962 pp.

Census of 1925

15. *Statistical Tables*. Taihoku, 1927. ii, 1174 pp.

Census of 1930

16. *Statistical Tables, by Prefecture*. 8 Vols. Taihoku, 1933.
    (a) Taihoku. xlv, 255 pp.; Appendix.
    (b) Shinchiku. xliv, 211 pp.; Appendix.
    (c) Taichu. xlvi, 235 pp.; Appendix.
    (d) Tainan. xlvi, 239 pp.; Appendix.

(e) Takao. xlv, 211 pp.; Appendix.
(f) Taito. xliv, 147 pp.; Appendix.
(g) Karenko. xliv, 155 pp.; Appendix.
(h) Boko. xlii, 137 pp.; Appendix.

17. *Statistical Tables, Total Island.* Taihoku, Government-General of Taiwan, Bureau of Official Statistics, 1934. 134, 528 pp.; Appendix.

Census of 1935

18. *Statistical Tables.* Taihoku, Government-General of Taiwan, Bureau of Official Statistics, 1937. 87, 767 pp.
19. *Population Register of Taiwan. Statistical Tables* [by minor civil divisions]. 39 Annual Volumes; only selected years available. Taihoku, Government-General of Taiwan, Bureau of Official Statistics.
20. Taiwan. Government. *The Progress of Taiwan (Formosa), for Ten Years, 1895-1904.* Taihoku, 1905. v, 79 pp.
21. Taiwan. Government-General. Research Bureau. *Life Tables of Taiwan, 1926-1930* (First Issue). Taipei, 1936. 160 pp.
22. Taiwan. Provincial Government. Department of Statistics. *Life Tables of Taiwan, 1936-1940* (Second Issue). Taipei, 1947. x, 176 pp.
23. *Taiwan Province: Statistical Summary of the Past 51 Years.* [Published by Chinese authorities, from Japanese materials.] Taipei, 1946.
24. *Taiwan. Vital Statistics of the Population.* 37 Annual Volumes, 1906-1942. Taihoku, Government-General of Taiwan, Bureau of Official Statistics.

OTHER

25. Bate, H. M. *Report from Formosa.* New York, E. P. Dutton and Sons, 1952. 206 pp.
26. Callis, Helmut G. *Foreign Capital in Southeast Asia.* Introduction by Carl F. Remer. New York, Institute of Pacific Relations, International Secretariat, 1942. iv, 120 pp.
27. Campbell, W. *Formosa Under the Dutch; Described from Contemporary Sources.* With Explanatory Notes and a Bibliography of the Island. London, Kegan Paul, Trench, Trubner & Co., Ltd. MDCCCCIII, xiv, 629 pp.
28. ———. *Sketches from Formosa.* London, Marshall Brothers, Ltd. [1915]. 394 pp.
29. Canada. Department of Mines and Technical Surveys, Geographical Branch. *Formosa: A Geographical Appreciation.* Foreign Geography Information Series No. 5. Ottawa, Canada, 1952. 59 pp., multilith.

30. Ch'en Cheng-hsiang. *Atlas of Land Utilization in Taiwan.* Taipei, National Taiwan University, 1950. 121 pp.

31. ———. *The Growth of Taipei.* [Accompanying Chinese title reads: The Geography of Taipei City.] Taipei, National Taiwan University, 1952. 39 pp.

32. ———. *Land Utilization in Taiwan.* Taipei, National Taiwan University, 1950. 346 pp. [In Chinese]

33. ———. "Land Utilization in Formosa," *Geographical Review* 41 (3): 438-456. July, 1951.

34. ——— and Tuan Chi-hsien. *Population of Taiwan.* Taipei, National Taiwan University, 1951. 142 pp.

35. Cohen, Jerome. *Japan's Economy in War and Reconstruction.* Minneapolis, University of Minnesota Press, 1949. xix, 545 pp.

36. Davidson, James W. *The Island of Formosa, Past and Present.* New York, Macmillan and Co., 1903. 646 pp.

37. Davis, Kingsley. *The Population of India and Pakistan.* Princeton, Princeton University Press, 1951. xvi, 263 pp.

38. Durand, John D. *The Labor Force in the United States, 1890-1960.* New York, Social Science Research Council, 1948. 284 pp.

39. Frank, Harry A. *Glimpses of Japan and Formosa.* New York, The Century Co., 1924. xi, 235 pp.

40. Grajdanzev, Andrew J. *Formosa Today: An Analysis of the Economic Development and Strategic Importance of Japan's Tropical Colony.* New York, Institute of Pacific Relations, International Secretariat, 1942. 193 pp.

41. Hsü Tze-wei. *Today's Taiwan.* Shanghai, 1946[?]. [In Chinese]

42. Hu Hsien-chin. *The Common Descent Group in China and its Functions.* New York, Viking Fund, 1948. 204 pp.

43. Institut International de Statistique. *Aperçu de la Démographie des Divers Pays du Monde, 1929-1936.* The Hague, 1939. 433 pp.

44. Kawada, Shiro. "The Tenant System of Formosa." Kyoto University, Memoirs of the Department of Economics, *Economic Review,* Vol. III, No. 2, pp. 86-146. Dec., 1928.

45. Kerr, George H. "Formosa—Colonial Laboratory," *Far Eastern Survey,* Vol. XI, No. 4. February 23, 1942.

46. ———. "Formosa: Island Frontier," *Far Eastern Survey,* Vol. 14, No. 7, pp. 80-85. April 11, 1945.

47. Knibbs, G. H. *The Mathematical Theory of Population.* Census of the Commonwealth of Australia [1911], Vol. I, Appendix A. Melbourne, 1917. xvi, 466 pp.

48. Lang, Olga. *Chinese Family and Society.* New Haven, Yale University Press, 1946. xv, 395 pp.

49. Levy, Marion J., Jr. *The Family Revolution in Modern China.* Cambridge, Harvard University Press, 1949. xvi, 390 pp.

50. ——— and Shih Kuo-heng. *The Rise of the Modern Chinese Business Class.* New York, Institute of Pacific Relations, International Secretariat, 1949. 64 pp. Mimeographed.

51. MacKay, George Leslie. *From Far Formosa: The Island, Its People and Missions.* New York, Fleming H. Revell Co., 1896. 346 pp.

52. Mendiola, N. B. "Rice Culture in Taiwan," *Philippine Journal of Agriculture,* Vol. 14, No. 2, pp. 41-81. First Quarter, 1949.

53. Mortara, Giorgio. *Methods of Using Census Statistics for the Calculation of Life Tables and Other Demographic Measures.* U.N. Population Studies No. 7. Lake Success, 1949. v, 60 pp.

54. Naito, Hideo, Ed. *Taiwan: A Unique Colonial Record.* 1937-38 Edition. Tokyo, Kokusai Nippon Kyokai, 1937. 350 pp.

55. Nasu, Shiroshi. *Aspects of Japanese Agriculture: A Preliminary Survey.* Institute of Pacific Relations, Institute Research Series. New York, Institute of Pacific Relations, International Secretariat, 1941. 168 pp.

56. Notestein, Frank W., et al. *The Future Population of Europe and the Soviet Union: Population Projections, 1940-1970.* Geneva, League of Nations, 1944. 315 pp.

57. Pickering, W. A. *Pioneering in Formosa.* London, Hurst and Blackett, Ltd., 1898. xvi, 283 pp.

58. Quo Sung-ken. "The Population Growth of Formosa," *Human Biology* 22 (4):293-301. December, 1950.

59. Ravenholt, Albert. "Formosa Today," *Foreign Affairs* 30:612-624. July, 1952.

60. Reubens, Edwin P. "Foreign Capital in Economic Development: A Case Study of Japan." Pp. 103-120 in: Milbank Memorial Fund, *Modernization Programs in Relation to Human Resources and Population Problems.* New York, 1950.

61. Ri, Togaku. "Statistical Survey on Mortality Rates and Causes of Death Among Japanese Residents of Taiwan," *Taiwan Medical Journal,* June, 1938, pp. 1042-1061.

62. Riggs, Fred W. *Formosa Under Chinese Nationalist Rule.* New York, The Macmillan Company, 1952. ix, 195 pp.

63. Schumpeter, E. B., Ed. *The Industrialization of Japan and Manchoukuo, 1930-1940. Population, Raw Materials and Industry.* New York, The Macmillan Company, 1940. xxviii, 944 pp.

64. Shen, T. H. "Food Production and Administration in Taiwan," *The Scientific Monthly* 74 (5):253-268. May, 1952.

65. Smith, T. E. *Population Growth in Malaya: An Analysis of Recent*

Trends. London, Royal Institute of International Affairs, 1952. viii, 126 pp.

66. Society for Publication of Taiwan Economic Yearbook. *Taiwan Economic Yearbook, 1941*. Tokyo, 1941. 780, 63 pp.; statistical appendix.

67. Taeuber, Irene B., and Notestein, Frank W. "The Changing Fertility of the Japanese," *Population Studies*, Vol. I, No. 1, pp. 2-28. June, 1947.

68. [Taeuber, Irene B.] "Colonial Demography: Formosa," *Population Index* (Current Item), Vol. 10, No. 3, pp. 147-157. July, 1944.

69. ———, and Beal, Edwin G., Jr. "Guide to the Official Demographic Statistics of Japan," *Population Index*, Supplement, Vol. 12, No. 4, pp. 2-36. October, 1946.

70. ———. "Migration and the Population Potential of Monsoon Asia." Pp. 7-29 in: Milbank Memorial Fund, *Postwar Problems of Migration*. New York, Milbank Memorial Fund, 1947.

71. ———. "Population Increase and Manpower Utilization in Imperial Japan." Pp. 121-141 in: Milbank Memorial Fund, *Modernization Programs in Relation to Human Resources and Population Problems*. New York, 1950.

72. Takekoshi, Yosaburo. *Japanese Rule in Formosa*. Translated by George Braithwaite. London, Longmans, Green, and Co., 1907. xv, 342 pp.

73. Tu Tsung-ming. "Statistical Studies on Opium Addiction in Formosa (Second Report)," *Journal of the Medical Association of Formosa* 34 (6-7):131-150, 91-114. June-July, 1935.

74. ———. "Statistical Studies on Opium Addiction in Formosa. Third Report: About the Mortality Rates and the Causes of Death among the Addicts," *ibid.* 37 (8-9):23-80. August-September, 1938.

75. United Nations. Population Division and Statistical Office. *The Labour Force: Problems of Census Definition and Enumeration*. Studies of Census Methods, No. 4. Lake Success, April, 1948. 50 pp.

76. ———. Statistical Office. *Population Census Handbook*. Provisional Edition. Lake Success, October, 1949. v, 264 pp.

77. U.S. Office of Naval Operations (OPNAV). Civil Affairs Handbook. *Taiwan (Formosa)*. OPNAV 50E-12. Washington, June, 1944. xv, 198 pp.

78. ———. Civil Affairs Handbook. *Taiwan (Formosa)—Economic Supplement*. OPNAV 50E-13. Washington, 1944. xiv, 127 pp.

79. ———. Civil Affairs Handbook. *Japanese Administrative Organization in Taiwan (Formosa)*. OPNAV 50E-14. Washington, 1944. viii, 71 pp.

80. ———. Civil Affairs Handbook. Washington, 1944. 7 Vols.
 a. Taihoku Province. OPNAV 13-27. xii, 209 pp.
 b. Shinchiku Province. OPNAV 13-25. x, 110 pp.
 c. Taichu Province. OPNAV 13-26. xiii, 235 pp.
 d. Tainan Province. OPNAV 13-28. x, 106 pp.
 e. Takao Province. OPNAV 13-22. ix, 136 pp.
 f. Karenko and Taito Provinces. OPNAV 13-24. x, 101 pp.
 g. The Pescadores Islands. OPNAV 13-21. viii, 39 pp.

81. U.S. War Department. *Technical Bulletin* (TB Med 30). "Medical and Sanitary Data on Formosa," April 8, 1944. 18 pp.

82. Wickizer, V. D., and Bennett, M. K. *The Rice Economy of Monsoon Asia.* Published in co-operation with the Institute of Pacific Relations, International Secretariat. Stanford, Stanford University, Food Research Institute, 1941. xiii, 358 pp.

83. Winfield, Gerald F. *China: The Land and the People.* New York, William Sloane Associates, Inc., 1948. vii, 437 pp.

84. Yanaihara, Tadao. *Taiwan Under Imperialism.* Tokyo, 1929. xii, 361 pp. [In Japanese]

CHINESE CHARACTERS CORRESPONDING TO CHINESE AND JAPANESE AUTHORS AND TITLES IN THE BIBLIOGRAPHY

明治38年臨時戶口調查:

1. 調查顛末
2. 記述報文
3. 集計原表:地方ノ部
4. 集計原表:全島ノ部
5. 結果表
6. 職業名字彙

大正四年第二次臺灣臨時戶口調查

8. 記述報文
9. 職業名字彙
10. 結果表

大正九年第一回臺灣國勢調查

11. 記述報文
12. 集計原表
13. 集計原表(州廳ノ部)
14. 要覽表

大正十四年國勢調查

15. 結果表

昭和五年國勢調查

16. 結果表(州廳編)

(a) 台北州
(b) 新竹州
(c) 台中州
(d) 台南州
(e) 高雄州
(f) 台東州
(g) 花蓮州
(h) 澎湖州

17. 結果表:全島編

昭和十年國勢調查

18. 結果表

19. 臺灣現住人口統計

20. 臺灣十年間之進步

21. 臺灣住民生命表(第一回)

22. 臺灣居民生命表(第二回)

23 臺灣省五十一年來統計提要

24. 臺灣人口動態統計(原表之部)

30. 陳正祥 臺灣土地利用圖集

31. ——— 臺灣北都市地理

32. ——— 臺灣土地利用

34. ———,段紀憲 臺灣之人口

41. 徐子為 今日的臺灣

66. 臺灣經濟年報刊行會編 臺灣經濟年報

84. 矢內原忠雄 帝國主義下の臺灣

CHINESE OR JAPANESE TERMS REFERRED TO IN THE TEXT (GIVEN WITH MANDARIN READINGS)

Changhua	彰化
Cheng Ch'eng-kung	鄭成功
Chiayi	嘉義
Chilung	基隆
District	郡
Hsinchu	新竹
Hualien	花蓮
Kaohsiung	高雄
Lao-wu	勞務
Minseki	民籍
Municipality	市
P'enghu	澎湖
P'ingtung	屏東
Prefecture	州
Taichung	臺中
Tainan	臺南
Taipei	臺北
Taitung	臺東
Yeh-chu	業主
Yi-yüan	役員

Index

GPSR Authorized Representative: Easy Access System Europe - Mustamäe tee 50, 10621 Tallinn, Estonia, gpsr.requests@easproject.com

www.ingramcontent.com/pod-product-compliance
Lightning Source LLC
LaVergne TN
LVHW052257200926
848481LV00002B/388

* 9 7 8 0 6 9 1 6 2 3 9 4 8 *